EDUCATING ABOUT RELIGIOUS DIVERSITY
AND INTERFAITH ENGAGEMENT

EDUCATING ABOUT RELIGIOUS DIVERSITY AND INTERFAITH ENGAGEMENT

A Handbook for Student Affairs

Edited by

Kathleen M. Goodman,

Mary Ellen Giess, and Eboo Patel

Forewords by Cindi Love and Kevin Kruger

STERLING, VIRGINIA

COPYRIGHT © 2019 BY STYLUS
PUBLISHING, LLC.

Published by Stylus Publishing, LLC.
22883 Quicksilver Drive
Sterling, Virginia 20166-2012

Library of Congress Cataloging-in-Publication Data

Names: Goodman, Kathleen M. (Kathleen Marie), 1965- editor. |
Giess, Mary Ellen, editor. | Patel, Eboo, 1975- editor.
Title: Educating about religious diversity and interfaith
engagement: a handbook for student affairs / Edited by Kathleen
M. Goodman, Mary Ellen Giess, and Eboo Patel ; Forewords by
Cindi Love and Kevin Kruger.
Description: First edition. | Sterling, Virginia : Stylus Publishing,
LLC., [2019] | Includes bibliographical references and index.
Identifiers: LCCN 2018022991 (print) | LCCN 2018038055
(ebook) | ISBN 9781620366103 (uPDF) | ISBN
9781620366110 (ePub, mobi) | ISBN 9781620366080 (cloth :
acid-free paper) | ISBN 9781620366097 (paperback : acid-free
paper) | ISBN 9781620366103 (library networkable e-edition) |
ISBN 9781620366110 (consumer e-edition)
Subjects: LCSH: Student affairs administrators--Training of--
United States. | Student affairs services--United States. | College
students--Religious life--United States. | Religious pluralism--
Study and teaching--United States. | Cultural pluralism--Study
and teaching--United States.
Classification: LCC LB2342.92 (ebook) | LCC LB2342.92
.E38 2019 (print) | DDC 370.117--dc23 LC record available at
https://lccn.loc.gov/2018022991
13-digit ISBN: 978-1-62036-608-0 (cloth)
13-digit ISBN: 978-1-62036-609-7 (paperback)
13-digit ISBN: 978-1-62036-610-3 (library networkable
e-edition)
13-digit ISBN: 978-1-62036-611-0 (consumer e-edition)

Printed in the United States of America

All first editions printed on acid-free paper
that meets the American National Standards Institute
Z39-48 Standard.

Bulk Purchases
Quantity discounts are available for use in workshops and
for staff development.
Call 1-800-232-0223

First Edition, 2019

This book is dedicated to entrepreneurial interfaith educators who have paved the way. Thank you for your important work.

CONTENTS

FOREWORD

Historically, student affairs theorists and practitioners have circumnavigated the complex intersections and edges of religious diversity and its individual and community-assigned identities. They have done so in the context of managing U.S. public and private secular higher educational institutions, which sanctioned risk avoidance of controversy or challenges regarding church and state. Until recently, the voices of those trained in holistic student development have been excluded or have opted out of the challenging conversations about religious identities and whether they can be or should be effectively separated by students or our institutions.

I am grateful for the inspiration and courage evident in the publication of *Educating About Religious Diversity and Interfaith Engagement: A Handbook for Student Affairs*. The editors help readers traverse the rapidly changing religious demographics and issues on university campuses, offering an opportunity to incorporate foundational scholarship in student learning and development through spiritual and religious lenses. They invite professionals into a renewed construction of campus life, one in which all identities are truly welcomed, acknowledged, respected, and open to understanding through dialogue. These campuses can create cultures of advocacy rather than avoidance and adversity.

In these environments, professionals can ask themselves and one another whether the suppression or oppression of religious identity helps or hurts holistic learning and development. Is it possible to honor our values of inclusion and equity when student success often demands assimilation or, at minimum, adaptation in an adverse environment? Engagement can be tough when a student is from any underrepresented group, particularly when the student is non-White, non-Christian, or nonbinary. The organizational DNA of U.S. higher education is infused with majority Christian traditions, symbols, language, and authority structures and systems; however, as Galston (1991) suggested,

> the health and stability of a modern democracy depends not only on the justice of its institutions (higher education), but also on the qualities and attitudes of its citizens: e.g. their sense of identity and how they view poten-

tially competing forms of national, regional, ethnic or religious identities; their ability to tolerate and work together with others who are different from themselves. (p. 220)

To accept this reality is to accept responsibility for amending what has been to what can be. Most intractable conflicts on campuses are born out of the othering of human beings, our persistent unwillingness to organize individual and community relationships around human dignity, and our inability to initiate and sustain meaningful dialogue.

We owe a debt of gratitude to the contributors to *Educating About Religious Diversity and Interfaith Engagement: A Handbook for Student Affairs* for providing some necessary tools for restructuring our campuses around human dignity and respect for religious diversity.

Cindi Love
Executive Director (2014–2017)
ACPA—College Student Educators International

Reference

Galston, W. A. (1991). *Liberal purposes: Goods, virtues, and duties in the liberal state.* Cambridge, England: Cambridge University Press.

FOREWORD

The Pew Research Center reported that worldwide participation in virtually all religions would increase over the next 30 to 40 years (Pew Forum, 2018). However, despite the increase in total participation, the overall percentage of those affiliating with a particular religion will decrease. Over that same period, as has been widely reported, the United States will not have a single racial or ethnic majority. Changes in birthrates and trends in Asian and Hispanic immigration will create a minority majority in our country. These demographic changes in religion, race, and ethnicity will certainly create opportunities for some to advocate hate, discrimination, and injustice. But these major shifts in our society also provide inspiring opportunities for U.S. colleges and universities to embrace all types of diversity in our communities. If we are to achieve our goal of creating inclusive communities for all, it is imperative for us to recognize religious and secular diversity as an important component of our social justice efforts and to use the core values embedded in all religions as a foundation to involve members of the college and university community in critical dialogue. It is essential for us to engage and educate our students as future citizens of the world about religious and secular diversity and issues on spirituality. I am optimistic that these efforts on our college campuses will play a larger role in creating changes in our society in general.

Higher education professionals have the unique opportunity to interact with students as they experience some of the defining moments of their lives. Those moments require us to address the whole identity of the person, which can include supporting the person's religious, secular, and spiritual identity, an area that has been somewhat overlooked in higher education over the past few decades. Although we have increased our emphasis on racial and gender identity over the past 20 years, higher education has not made a commensurate effort to create a deeper understanding of the important role college years play in students' religious, secular, and spiritual identity.

This volume commits us to this important work and provides practical ideas for student affairs professionals to engage in religious, spiritual, and secular issues with students. It will serve as an important resource for those who work in higher education but feel ill equipped to tackle issues on religious diversity and spiritual identity development.

If we are to have true progress on our campuses regarding social justice, intentionality is required. This principle clearly extends to religious diversity. Through case studies and examples of relevant research and practice, this volume is an important resource for creating programs that encourage interfaith dialogue and promote a greater understanding of the religious and secular diversity represented by our students.

As we look at our communities, the growing resistance to the changing makeup of our society, and the ensuing culture wars we are experiencing, we must be intentional about our work with students in embracing religious diversity. As higher education professionals, we must own our own obligations to educate ourselves and to support programs that will create a true appreciation for the religious, secular, and spiritual diversity among our students. Only then can we truly create the inclusive and socially just communities we strive to build.

Kevin Kruger
President
NASPA—Student Affairs Administrators in Higher Education

Reference

Pew Forum. (2018). *The age gap in religion around the world*. Retrieved from http://www.pewforum.org/2018/06/13/the-age-gap-in-religion-around-the-world/

ACKNOWLEDGMENTS

When we started on this project, we felt strongly that we were closing a critical gap in the literature and resources on engaging religious diversity in higher education by providing educators with a how-to guide for leading this important work.

As we have pursued this project, however, we have come to more deeply appreciate the variety of efforts that are already transpiring in this space, led by innovators who often proceeded with engaging religious diversity without much guidance or support. For those who have committed their time and energy to address religious diversity on college campuses across the country, for those who recognized the power and importance of religious pluralism for the strength of our democracy, this volume is dedicated to you.

We are also deeply indebted to our incredible contributors of individual chapters and the educators who shared their program models for publication. Special thanks to Interfaith Youth Core staff and alumni Jeremy Tibetts, Wendy Low, Prerna Abbi, Suraj Arshnapally, Christian Van Dyke, Keryn Wouden, Jem Jebbia, Philip Nahlik, Jenan Mohajir, and Elaine Krebs for sharing their personal experiences to strengthen our foundational knowledge chapters. This volume is greater because of the diversity of insights and experiences offered by our collaborators. Thank you, sincerely, to everyone who contributed.

Thank you also to our colleagues at Interfaith Youth Core and Miami University of Ohio for their ongoing support, intellectual partnership, and cheerleading as we carried forward this important effort.

Thank you, Cindi Love and John von Knorring, for believing in this project and providing us with the early commitment that gave birth to this effort.

Finally, we owe thanks to our family and friends for the inspiration, community, and abundance they provide in our lives.

INTRODUCTION

Kathleen M. Goodman, Mary Ellen Giess, and Eboo Patel

When I, Eboo Patel, was in my final year as an undergraduate at the University of Illinois, I was asked to be part of a group of student leaders to meet with the president of the university system. It was scheduled for 30 minutes, and frankly I expected bromides about the importance of science and technology in the twenty-first century, fields in which the university excelled.

Instead, the conversation turned toward diversity issues. I'll never forget when President Stukel made the statement,

> I want to be able to shake the hand of Illinois graduates and have a reasonable degree of confidence that over the course of their undergraduate careers, they have developed multicultural literacy, built multicultural friendships, and had opportunities for multicultural leadership.

That is *precisely* what happened to me during my undergraduate years at Illinois. I had grown up as a Brown kid in the western suburbs of Chicago wanting to be White, and my experience at Illinois had dramatically expanded my understanding of myself and my country. My first-year orientation group seemed to magically mirror the ethnic and racial diversity of the state, and our group leader seemed to find every opportunity to turn the conversation toward identity issues. Many of the programs my resident adviser ran focused on multicultural issues, and when I was hired to be a resident adviser, half of the training we received dealt with race, gender, ethnicity, and sexuality. In campus volunteer activities, gathering a diverse group of people to go do environmental cleanups and tutoring projects was always named as a high priority.

Reflecting on President Stukel's comment, I realized that this was all by design. The university as an institution had high aspirations in regard to diversity issues, and it had the power to (at least partially) affect the environment so that the students might achieve that aspiration.

Student affairs played a central role in campus diversity efforts, not just in regard to implementing programs but in prioritizing diversity to begin with.

Like lots of college students who find their paradigm shifting in college, I liberally shared my experiences and points of view with my parents. I admit that sometimes these conversations turned into lectures on my part. I would constantly take my dad to task about his lack of people of color consciousness. My dad was mostly good natured about all of this, but one afternoon I must have gotten under his skin, because he turned to me and said, "Eboo, the next time you want to come home and lecture me on diversity issues, you first tell me how you are going to solve religious conflict." He pointed to the front page of the newspaper sitting on our coffee table; more than half the stories were about religious violence somewhere in the world.

It occurred to me that for all the conversations I had in college about identity issues, barely any had anything to do with religion. Many of the people I knew had one belief system or another, but they mostly kept quiet about it. It was clearly not an invited topic of conversation. And those of us who were politically engaged on campus had a kind of ambient awareness that religious conflicts were raging across the world, but we learned and talked little about them. In fact, as I thought back on my resident adviser training, a good 20 hours was spent on identity issues. The amount of time spent on religion? Zero.

That simply won't do anymore. Not for our increasingly religiously diverse campuses, not for our increasingly religiously polarized country, not for our increasingly religiously violent world.

We coeditors are not the first people to recognize the need for this work. We are part of a lengthy line of educators and researchers, scholars and students who have long understood the importance of engaging religious diversity for our overall civic health. Through the past several decades, small groups of leaders throughout higher education have championed the importance of engaging religious diversity as essential to the civic mission of higher education. Like Eboo, many of us carry personal stories that drive our passion for building bridges across lines of religious and worldview difference. Others were the lucky few who experienced intentional educational experiences that fueled our commitment. All of us, however, recognize that for educating across lines of religious identity to realize its full potential, it must become a campuswide endeavor. It is not enough for a religious life office or a group of interested staff to drive this effort (as essential as those energies are); rather, it must become a campuswide priority, which means simply that more leaders on campus must be activated to engage in this work successfully.

Nevertheless, many (maybe even most) campus professionals profess considerable discomfort with the idea of engaging with religious and worldview identities. There are good reasons for this; land mines abound when we enter this area of identity where it seems that disagreement is around every corner. In fact, in our many years of working in the area of religious diversity in higher education, the topic that found the most agreement is that campus professionals profess a lack of skills and knowledge in how to do this work. Many student affairs practitioners and faculty in student affairs preparation programs agree that the work must be done, but they don't know how to begin, and they are nervous about tackling such a divisive topic. This book is a direct response to this concern.

If the goal is to elevate the priority of educating people about religious diversity and interfaith engagement in student affairs (both in and out of the classroom), then we need to create resources to guide that work. In this book, we provide foundational knowledge, concrete teaching ideas, sample activities, and case studies all designed for use by those who work in student affairs. We hope that in these pages, student affairs practitioners and faculty will find the tools they need to increase their comfort level and their ability to address this important topic in and out of the classroom.

This book fills a gap by moving beyond the literature that explains the need for incorporating spiritual, religious, and interfaith work into student affairs providing practical guidance for how to do this work. It also serves multiple audiences in student affairs by providing teaching ideas for practitioners who want to include a session or two about interfaith in their programs as well as ideas for student affairs faculty who may be teaching one session on this topic or a whole course. We chose to call this volume a handbook because we hope it is a resource that readers will turn to again and again, as new opportunities for religious diversity and interfaith engagement arise.

The book is divided into five parts. Part one provides some context that many need before diving into this work. Topics discussed in this section range from preparing to engage in interfaith topics to the most current research findings about religious diversity and interfaith engagement. A final chapter in this section asks readers to consider the framework used to approach this work—a social justice framework that aims to highlight issues of power and privilege or an interfaith cooperation framework that aims to create religious pluralism.

Part two provides concrete ideas for creating new courses focused on spirituality, religion, secularity, and interfaith engagement in student affairs, as well as ideas for incorporating these topics into existing courses that are typically offered in student affairs preparation programs. A final chapter suggests reflection activities that faculty in student preparation programs could adapt and use with master's-level students inside or outside the classroom.

Part three provides ideas for creating professional development opportunities for student affairs practitioners who want to learn more about becoming involved in this work. It also includes two chapters with concrete ideas for activities, events, and programs that can be used by student affairs educators.

Part four contains several case studies to encourage students, practitioners, and faculty to think about campus situations related to religious diversity. Case studies are an excellent educational tool to use in or out of the classroom, and the introductory chapter of this section provides guidance on how to use these tools.

Part five provides some basic information about a variety of religions and worldviews held by college students including basic information on how to support these students to create an inclusive campus. Our hope is that these chapters provide a modicum of religious literacy, which we have heard many individuals seek as they aim to better work with the religious diversity present on their campus.

We anticipate that many student affairs practitioners and faculty in student affairs preparation programs will use the practical advice and tools in this handbook to increase educational opportunities focused on religious diversity and interfaith engagement. We also hope that this is just the beginning of how-to resources and will be followed by a proliferation of additional conferences, articles, books, and professional development opportunities focused on educating people about religious diversity and interfaith engagement in student affairs.

Campuses have the opportunity to be laboratories and launching pads for a new kind of ethic and a new kind of leader. In the 1980s and 1990s, student affairs staffs led the way by advocating for multiculturalism. That movement changed higher education and the United States. It is time to include religious identity in that mix. This handbook is a contribution to that end.

PART ONE

CONTEXT

I

PREPARING FOR INTERFAITH ENGAGEMENT

Christy Moran Craft and Kathleen M. Goodman

In the most recently published version of *Professional Competency Areas for Student Affairs Educators* (ACPA–College Student Educators International & NASPA–Student Affairs Administrators in Higher Education, 2016), four of the competency areas described in the document (personal and ethical foundations, social justice and inclusion, student learning and development, and advising and supporting students) either directly or indirectly illustrate the need for student affairs professionals to develop the knowledge, skills, and dispositions required to effectively plan and facilitate dialogues, programs, and other forms of interfaith engagement. Unfortunately, if student affairs professionals were asked whether they feel confident in their ability to plan and to lead interfaith activities and programs, most would probably say that they do not. Such a response might be because of the deeply personal and controversial nature of issues related to religion and spirituality. Others might respond with concerns about their ability to effectively engage all voices. Although the concerns about facilitating interfaith initiatives are usually valid, student affairs administrators can nevertheless take proactive steps to prepare themselves for those experiences. In this chapter, we attempt to help prepare educators for work focused on interfaith engagement by addressing the following topics: understanding legal and ethical issues, embracing mind-sets for constructive interfaith engagement, using a developmental approach to interfaith engagement, and avoiding the pitfalls of privilege.

Understanding Legal and Ethical Issues

Many student affairs professionals have admitted uncertainty, and even fear, concerning the expression of religion and spirituality in higher education (Moran & Curtis, 2004). One continuous concern relates to legal provisions encompassing religious expression, particularly in secular higher education. In this chapter, we review legal freedoms along with ethical guidelines because of the interconnected nature of the two.

Legal Freedoms

Legal questions drive many concerns about the appropriateness of interfaith engagement in higher education. The phrase *separation of church and state* has been so frequently misunderstood that many educators mistakenly believe that any type of religious expression on a public university campus will, in effect, violate constitutional guidelines. That is just not true, so it is imperative for those involved in interfaith programming to have an accurate understanding of the legal freedoms that exist for such endeavors. Although the constitutional guidelines that follow are for public colleges and universities, those who work in private higher education institutions can also benefit from considering the value of similar guidelines in their interfaith initiatives.

The First Amendment to the U.S. Constitution contains two provisions related to religious expression by governmental agencies (including public colleges and universities). The free exercise clause provides the freedom for individuals to express their religion, whereas the establishment clause prohibits public institutions, as governmental entities, from endorsing religion, either of a particular type or in general (U.S. Const., amend I). Ultimately, everyone on a public university campus should be guaranteed freedom of religion as well as freedom from religion. Admittedly, that is often a hard balance to strike, which is the source of much of the confusion related to religious expression in public higher education.

Interfaith engagement initiatives present perfect opportunities for rich discussions about religious, spiritual, and secular worldviews. Through such experiences, students are free to openly and honestly share their religious, spiritual, or secular perspectives as well as to challenge the perspectives of others in view of the freedom of religious expression that is guaranteed by the U.S. Constitution. The Constitution demands neutrality, neither privileging nor denigrating any specific identity or perspective. Assuming that a diversity of religious, spiritual, and secular perspectives are invited to participate in interfaith initiatives generally, student affairs professionals need not worry about promoting one religion over another, promoting religion over nonreligion, or vice versa.

Ethical Guidelines

Ethical statements and principles in our profession are intended to serve as guidelines for our own behavior as professionals working with students in higher education, particularly when faced with ethical dilemmas in our work. To be sure, interfaith dialogues might present situations in which the planner or facilitator feels ethically conflicted and does not know how to move past those concerns. For instance, if a participant in the dialogue makes a comment that appears to be harmful to another student or group of students, should the facilitator intervene? A review of some ethical guidelines can provide some assistance to the facilitator when ethical dilemmas arise.

Because most of the interfaith programming that student affairs professionals plan and implement on campus involves students, it is important to review some ethical principles related to student development and learning. ACPA–College Student Educators International (2006), for instance, reminds us of the importance of treating students "with respect as persons who possess dignity, worth, and the ability to be self-directed" (p. 3) and to "demonstrate concern for the welfare of all students" (p. 5). Furthermore, the way we approach conflict among students can be guided in part by ethical principles in our profession. For example, ACPA encourages us to resolve conflict "without diminishing respect for, or appropriate obligations to, any party involved" (p. 4). Moreover, the statement suggests that we should talk to students when they express "issues, attitudes, and behaviors" (p. 3) that might have ethical implications.

Ultimately, those of us who are interested in creating opportunities for interfaith engagement on our campuses are advised to remember and to practice Kitchener's (1985) five ethical principles, which ultimately serve as the foundation for the ethical statements in our profession: benefit others, promote justice, respect autonomy, be faithful, and do no harm. While so doing, we should be mindful of the nature of our work with students, as Jane Fried (2003) summarized so well in the following:

> We are responsible for maintaining a safe, civil, and educationally support-
> ive environment on our campuses, but we are not necessarily responsible
> for controlling student life so completely that students do not have the
> opportunity to learn from their own mistakes, either personal errors or
> errors made by student organizations. (p. 107)

We ultimately strive to do what we do in the profession of student affairs for the purpose of learning and development, which requires productive educational spaces. The next section of this chapter focuses on some mind-sets needed to create such productive interfaith engagement.

Embracing Mind-Sets for Constructive Interfaith Engagement

Although a number of resources exist related to setting guidelines for interfaith dialogues (e.g., Interfaith Youth Core, 2003), very little has been published about the mind-sets necessary for constructive interfaith engagement. A *mind-set* is defined as "an attitude, disposition, or mood" (Mindset, 2002) or "the ideas and attitudes with which a person approaches a situation, especially those that are viewed as difficult to alter." Mind-sets that are useful for engaging in interfaith activities include a propensity to withhold accusations, an eagerness to confront assumptions, the aspiration to overlook offenses, the desire to reflect humility in interactions with others, and the willingness to embrace tolerable discomfort. Educators involved in planning and implementing interfaith activities and the students involved in such activities are encouraged to embrace these mind-sets.

Propensity to Withhold Accusations

Humans are prone to pass judgment on others, whether they realize it or not. This phenomenon is especially apparent when facing ideas or behaviors that differ from salient personal beliefs or when encountering a situation that stirs up pain from the past. In such challenging situations, personal individual judgments may emerge in the form of accusations of intolerance or persecution. In the context of interfaith engagement in higher education, because accusations will do more harm than good, student affairs educators should encourage participants to develop a propensity to withhold judgement and accusation.

Several types of accusations often arise in conversations on religious, spiritual, and secular identity.

Accusations of Intolerance

Often individuals who claim that their religious, spiritual, or secular perspective is the only true or correct perspective (implying that the others are not true) are accused of being intolerant, whereas those holding ecumenical perspectives are deemed open minded and tolerant. In discussing religious tolerance, Alan Levinovitz (2015) wrote, "You can think a religious belief is wrong without being intolerant. Tolerance is not synonymous with 'believing someone else is right'" (para. 4). In other words, when people profess their beliefs, it doesn't mean they are being intolerant of differing beliefs. Don't we all believe that the perspectives we hold about religion, spirituality, and secularism are the right ones? Of course we do; otherwise, we would not hold them.

Tolerance does not require agreement with others or even the recognition that others' beliefs are equally valid. Simply stated, people have the right to believe that others are wrong. How they act on that belief is what makes them tolerant or not. Tolerance implies the ability to coexist with others and to treat them respectfully, regardless of beliefs. We would be well served to consider what Tim Keller (2014), a Christian, suggested about various perspectives: "Every religion or non-religion, even those that appear more inclusive, make exclusive claims." Thus, accusations of intolerance that are based solely on someone else's exclusive claims are often unfounded and usually result in destructive rather than constructive dialogue.

Accusations of Persecution

Unfortunately, it is all too common that someone being directly or indirectly questioned on their beliefs may interpret that experience as persecution. In a journal entry on November 8, 1838, Ralph Waldo Emerson wrote, "Let me never fall into the vulgar mistake of dreaming that I am persecuted whenever I am contradicted" (Porte, 1984, p. 206). Similar to the sentiments about intolerance, the existence of a contradictory belief and even questioning others' beliefs does not imply or necessarily lead to behavior that is characterized as persecution. Language that implies persecution when there is no behavioral evidence to support that accusation can be destructive in interfaith engagement initiatives.

Accusations of Extremes

We often hear individuals described as too religious or overly religious, with no moral compass, or phobic. What makes someone too much of his or her particular identity? Why should certain individuals be thought to hold no moral values? Although some harmful forms of *phobia*, typically defined as hate and fear, related to particular forms of religious, spiritual, or secular beliefs do exist (e.g., Islamophobia), simply disagreeing with a belief system does not constitute a phobia (hate or fear) of that perspective.

Language is power and has the ability to be life-giving or harmful. Student affairs educators must help students embrace a mind-set of withholding accusations rather than being accusatory. Understanding common accusatory language is a first step in understanding common assumptions about religious identity. Rather than making accusations, individuals must strive to confront their own assumptions and the assumptions of others.

Eagerness to Confront Assumptions

An equally important mind-set necessary for constructive interfaith dialogue is eagerness to confront one's own and others' assumptions. Many of the challenges related to religion and spirituality on higher education campuses result from assumptions that individuals make about others' beliefs and practices. Sometimes these assumptions seem to have a valid basis; for example, when individuals draw from their own experience of an identity or tradition. Other times, however, these assumptions are less well founded. Regardless of the source of the assumption, true wisdom is found in following Saint Augustine's advice to never judge a philosophy by its abuse.

Rather than making assumptions about the values, beliefs, and behaviors of people based on their religious, spiritual, or secular perspectives, individuals need to directly ask others how they live their identity. To be sure, not everyone who identifies with a particular religion, form of spirituality, or secular worldview holds all the same beliefs. Some of the core beliefs might be the same, but some of the other beliefs might be vastly different. One of the best mind-sets to embrace is the desire to confront assumptions, including perceptions about the likely beliefs and the potential actions of individuals based on their identity. Engaging in assumptions is essentially stereotyping and will only prove detrimental in interfaith engagement. As Nash (2001) aptly stated, "Stereotyping (no matter how trivial) frequently breeds counter-stereotyping" (p. 33). To engage in constructive interfaith initiatives, one should ask about others' beliefs and practices rather than make assumptions.

Aspiration to Overlook Offenses

Perhaps one of the most challenging mind-sets to embrace for constructive interfaith engagement is choosing not to take offense when hearing statements that contradict one's own beliefs, values, and behaviors. Often, complaints about comments being offensive arise not when someone speaking is explicitly derogatory but rather when the listener is subjectively offended (French, 2002). Ultimately, although comments spoken by others during interfaith dialogues are out of the control of listeners, the reactions to those comments can be controlled. One can choose to take offense or choose to leave it. Constructive interfaith dialogues tend to result when all participants make conscious decisions not to take offense and, instead, overlook comments that initially spur some sense of cognitive or emotional dissonance.

How might we teach students and ourselves to disagree with a religious, spiritual, or secular belief or comment without taking personal offense to it? First, student affairs educators should encourage everyone involved to believe the best about the others who are participating in interfaith programs. Educators can cultivate a mentality that the other participants mean well and have good intentions.

Second, we can encourage all involved to be confident in their own religious, spiritual, or secular identity and the beliefs that align with it. This idea was aptly communicated in a quote often attributed to the well-known atheist Richard Dawkins (n.d.):

> If you are offended by reading views that disagree with yours, then yes, you will be offended. However, it is not gratuitously offensive. It simply puts forward an argument, and if your views are strong enough, as I believe they are, you will be able to defend your views. You will not say, "Oh, it's offensive. It's offensive." Moreover, sometimes you gain more confidence in your own religious, spiritual, or secular perspective as a result of interfaith engagement.

Ultimately, if participants in interfaith dialogues embrace a mind-set to overlook subjectively offensive comments, more people would be willing to be honest and vulnerable in the discussions. Easily offended people silence other people by making them feel as if they have to walk on eggshells. It is difficult to plan and to implement constructive interfaith experiences when participants frequently choose to take offense at beliefs that differ from their own.

Desire to Reflect Humility

The next mind-set we propose as necessary for constructive interfaith dialogue is the desire to reflect a humble attitude toward oneself and others. The mind-set of humility allows people to live with the reality that they are fallible human beings and also encourages forgiveness for others who are also fallible by nature. One practical way to embrace a humble mind-set is to practice what Nash (2001) calls the "golden rule" of moral conversation: "a willingness to find the truth in what we oppose and the error in what we espouse, before we presume to acknowledge the truth in what we espouse and the error in what we oppose" (p. 178).

Humility also requires forgiveness for those who stumble in their well-intentioned attempts to engage in constructive interfaith dialogues. Participants in such dialogues are bound to make mistakes in how and what they say. Choosing to forgive others for such mistakes will actually serve to facilitate more honest, constructive dialogue in the future. All individuals are continually learning and making mistakes. In the context of interfaith dialogues, it is important to extend grace and teach others to do the same.

Willingness to Embrace Tolerable Discomfort

Related to choosing not to take offense is the equally important mind-set of being willing to embrace "tolerable discomfort" (Tierney, 1993, p. 11). As Sardelli (2011) aptly stated, "Civil discourse is not a sanitized, noncontroversial interaction" (p. 368). To be sure, interfaith experiences with the goal of resulting in development and learning for the participants should result in a certain amount of cognitive or emotional discomfort for the participants. This should not be surprising because most of the foundational theories in the student affairs profession propose some form of crisis or disequilibrium as the mechanism for learning and development to occur. For that reason, during interfaith dialogues, it is important to remember and to encourage students to consider that discomfort can be developmental. Constructive interfaith dialogue requires all participants to be comfortable with being uncomfortable; trying to shield students from uncomfortable interactions, or allowing them to shield themselves from discomfort, does not align with the primary goals of student development and learning.

Using a Developmental Approach to Interfaith Engagement

Student development should guide interfaith efforts, just as it guides work in other functional or topical areas in student affairs. Existing theory related to diversity can and should be applied in this context; some students may need opportunities for intrafaith work before engaging in interfaith work, and students will have different capacities for making sense of interfaith activities. Each of these areas of development are discussed in greater detail here.

Diversity Theory

Religious diversity, which is at the heart of interfaith engagement, can be informed and guided by existing theories of diversity. The refined model of intercultural maturity (Perez, Shim, King, & Baxter Magolda, 2015) and the intercultural development continuum (Hammer, 2012) are theories about how individuals think about cultural differences. Each theory uses a broad definition of *cultural differences* that includes multiple aspects of culture, including race; nationality; gender; and most relevant to this topic, religion. Both theories are grounded extensively in empirical research.

According to the intercultural maturity model, "more complex cognitive and intrapersonal capacities yield more complex interpersonal capacities in that they enable individuals to interact across difference with eagerness to connect to others instead of feeling threatened by difference" (Perez et al., 2015, p. 761). It is easy to see how this theory relates to interfaith engagement, which can be threatening to some students who have not developed intercultural maturity, yet inviting and exhilarating to those who have a more developed sense of intercultural maturity. The refined model of intercultural maturity described five levels of maturity across cognitive, intrapersonal, and interpersonal domains, providing depth and specificity student affairs educators can use to design programming for students at differing developmental stages.

The intercultural development continuum involves changes in thinking from simple to complex, with the focus on how individuals relate to cultural differences (Hammer, 2012). The model portrays two levels of monocultural mind-sets in which individuals primarily view the world from their own cultural perspective. The first mind-set is denial in which individuals deny or avoid cultural differences, and the second mind-set is polarization in which individuals have a defensive us-versus-them attitude about cultural differences. Related to interfaith engagement, students in these stages avoid interfaith activities and conversations altogether or exhibit defensiveness based on oversimplified views of religious, spiritual, or secular perspectives different from their own.

In the intercultural development continuum model, an intermediary mind-set called *minimization* connects monocultural thinking to *intercultural thinking*, which is defined as being able to view the world through multiple perspectives. Individuals with a minimization mind-set are aware of cultural differences but prefer to focus on commonalities. In interfaith engagement, this might be exhibited by focusing on what different religious, spiritual, and secular worldviews have in common (even if those commonalities aren't quite accurate), such as a focus on love, connection to others, or belief in something greater than oneself. Two mind-sets, acceptance and adaptation, characterize intercultural thinking, which reflects complex ways of thinking about differences and an ability to adapt one's thinking and behavior when encountering cultural differences. A more thorough treatment of how to apply the intercultural development continuum model to interfaith engagement can be found in Goodman (2014).

Intrafaith First

Identity development theory can also be applied to creating programs for intrafaith engagement. Consider that many identity development theories related to race, sexual orientation, and gender stipulate that individuals go through a stage of withdrawal, during which they are mostly focused on their own identity rather than interacting with those of other identities. Applying this concept to interfaith engagement suggests that students may need focused time on intrafaith engagement, focused on understanding their own religious, spiritual, or secular beliefs. Many campuses have considerable religious organizations for those who identify with dominant religions (typically Christian religions on most U.S. campuses) that provide opportunities for deepening their understanding of their own beliefs and interacting with those of similar beliefs. However, fewer means of support exist on most campuses for those from minority religious traditions (including Muslim and Jewish students, as well as those who identify with Eastern religious traditions such as Hinduism, Buddhism, Sikhism, etc.), those who describe themselves as spiritual but not religious, and those who identify with secular worldviews such as humanism, atheism, skepticism, and so on. Student affairs educators concerned with helping students develop a capacity for interfaith engagement may need to also create opportunities for intrafaith engagement in situations where it is not currently available. Creating these types of opportunities at public institutions is not a legal concern as long as you do not focus on one particular religion.

In a study of college students' spiritual identities that focused on Christian, Jewish, Muslim, and atheist students, Small (2011) discovered that students displayed greater openness and comfort when discussing their beliefs in groups of individuals with similar religious, spiritual, or secular beliefs. She studied students' discourse in intrafaith and interfaith groups and concluded that to better manage dialogue with students of differing beliefs, students may also need opportunities for engagement in groups with those of similar beliefs. Although providing and promoting intrafaith opportunities may seem counterintuitive to the goals of interfaith engagement, they may be a necessary piece that is currently missing on many campuses.

Developmental Capacities

In addition to applying developmental theory as already discussed, we also suggest that student affairs educators provide opportunities for students with different developmental capacities for dealing with risk. Given that some challenge is necessary for growth, educators would do well to consider which types of opportunities are best suited for particular students' developmental stages. Lower risk encounters such as watching a movie or listening to a panel may be well suited for some; other students may need more challenging conversations that necessitate sharing deeply personal beliefs about divisive issues (high-risk experiences most students may not be ready for).

Student affairs educators who have developed a capacity for interfaith dialogue may sometimes forget that it was a journey to reach that developmental capacity. Rather than expecting students to be able to dive into interfaith dialogue and being frustrated when students are afraid to participate or become combative, one must create a developmental scaffold. Interfaith programming and initiatives on campus should provide opportunities for students of differing developmental capacities to participate where they are comfortable. Ideally, the variety of programming will help students develop their capacities and eventually engage in deep, authentic interfaith dialogue.

Avoiding the Pitfalls of Privilege

Chapter 3 of this book suggests that when it comes to religious engagement, a student affairs perspective of social justice focused on power and privilege should be tempered in favor of community and relationship building. We have a slightly different perspective, believing it is impossible to do the work of authentic religious engagement without explicitly addressing issues of power and privilege. Fried (2007), who pointed out that the reverse is also true, that it will be impossible to tackle privilege if we aren't engaged in trusting, authentic relationships, stated, "As we unravel the problem of Christian privilege on campus, we must look at data and relationships and hold them both in our awareness at the same time" (p. 5). Therefore, we believe it is important to address power and privilege without making it the primary focus of interfaith work.

Evidence suggests that students are already aware of religious privilege. In her study of Jewish, Christian, Muslim, and atheist students, Small (2011) engaged the students in several intrafaith and interfaith dialogues to conduct a discourse analysis. A clear finding was that students perceived a three-tiered structure of religious privilege in U.S. society that affected their day-to-day experiences on the college campus. They viewed Christian students as the top of the hierarchy, holding the most privilege. This understanding of privilege affirms the belief that Christian privilege is prevalent on U.S. college campuses (Fried, 2007; Seifert, 2007). The students' perception of a three-tiered structure also extends the concept of religious privilege by suggesting that individuals who are not Christian but are religious also have a modicum of privilege. The students placed other religious individuals (those with non-dominant ideologies) in the middle of the hierarchy, indicating that they accrued privilege simply because they were religious (Small, 2011). They positioned atheist students at the bottom of the hierarchy, suggesting that they had the least amount of privilege in U.S. society. This hierarchy was "sufficiently real in students' minds to be detrimental to their feelings of well-being and respect on campus" (Small, 2011, p. 115).

If student affairs educators choose to ignore this hierarchy as they create opportunities for interfaith engagement, what message does that send? If students perceive that student affairs educators are ignorant about the hierarchy or, worse yet, they are okay with its existence, it could lead to negative outcomes such as resentment or anger over those at the bottom of the hierarchy not being cared for, greater resistance to participating in inter-faith engagement, questions about one's identity and perhaps disruption of identity growth, and feeling that interfaith engagement lacks honesty and authenticity. To ignore the extant system of privilege is a privilege in and of itself, and it serves to reinforce the hierarchy. Somehow, student affairs educators must find ways to simultaneously address inherent privileges asso-ciated with certain religious perspectives, dismantle systems of privilege in such a way that the privileged students still feel valued and do not become marginalized, and ensure that interfaith engagement opportunities are truly inclusive and welcoming to individuals from all religious and nonreligious perspectives. This is no easy feat.

Again, Fried (2007) provides some helpful insight into this dilemma. She provides the reminder that in U.S. culture, we tend to think in binaries, that is, things are either this way or that way but not both. This dualistic thinking is so prevalent that individuals "who think in more complex ways are considered unable to make up their minds" (p. 1). Yet to confront reli-gious privilege, individuals must be able to transcend binary thinking. They must "develop a new frame of reference, a new belief system that somehow allows for difference and similarity to co-exist, that permits differences of opinion and values without implying disrespect or looking for the one right answer" (p. 6). This will require enhanced cognitive skills, active listening skills, and an expanded view of self in a complicated campus and global context (Fried, 2007).

Although there are no easy answers for how to develop these complex cognitive capacities, we have some recommendations for working toward addressing the challenges related to the existence of religious privilege. Educators must attend to their own biases and the way they accept and enact religious privilege by vigilantly questioning and reflecting on their own beliefs. When working with students, starting with the mind-sets described earlier can go a long way toward minimizing privilege without directly addressing it.

Language choice can also be important. In the past, individuals in stu-dent affairs have tended to use the word *spirituality* as if it were a universal concept, even though 20% of students do not identify as religious or spir-itual (Astin, Astin, & Lindholm, 2011). We recommend always using the phrases *religious, spiritual, and secular* or *existential worldview* to be clear and inclusive.

Creating and implementing programs and support for interfaith engage-ment can also tip the balance away from the religious privilege that exists on many campuses. Making sure that students of nondominant religions or secular worldviews have adequate opportunities for intrafaith development can also create a necessary balance to religious privilege. Creating an infrastructure to support religious diversity and interfaith engagement, such as an office or person in the organization with the same capacity as those who work on other issues of diversity like race, gender, or sexual orientation, could also combat religious privilege.

We also suggest directly addressing the topic of religious privilege in developmentally appropriate ways. When working with undergraduates, the topic of food may be a relatively easy starting place. For example, at Miami University, the dining halls add vegetarian options on Fridays during Lent. A conversation that puts this in context with the attentiveness to meeting dietary needs associated with other religious traditions, including keeping kosher, eating halal, and daily vegetarianism, can appeal to students' desire for equity and illustrate religious privilege in a nonthreatening way. When working with graduate students studying to become student affairs practitioners, the topic of religious privilege should be addressed more deeply, using existing resources (e.g., Fried, 2007; Seifert, 2007; Watt, Fairchild, & Goodman, 2009).

Conclusion

According to Robert Nash (2001), "Religious pluralism, if left unattended, is a phenomenon that in the future will threaten to divide students, faculty, and administrators in a way that makes all other campus divisions look tame by comparison" (p. 31). One way to attend to the diversity of religious, spiritual, and secular perspectives represented in higher education is to plan and provide opportunities for interfaith engagement. As student affairs educators consider how to create those opportunities, we suggest keeping in mind legal and ethical issues, developing mind-sets needed for constructive interfaith engagement, using student development theory in new ways to guide the work, and dealing with the challenges of privilege. We have provided some thoughts on each of those topics with the hope of boosting the confidence and knowledge of student affairs educators to help them prepare to do this work.

Because interfaith work can feel daunting, we feel compelled to share that writing this chapter was an interfaith endeavor between an atheist and an evangelical Christian who did not know each other previously. As we worked together, we had the opportunity to challenge each other and to reflect more deeply on our own perspectives. To make sure that the ideas in this chapter accurately represented both our perspectives, we adopted the mind-sets described in this chapter and embraced an authentic desire to understand each other better. We have gained new understandings and developed a true friendship that bridges our differences, and we hope that our experience will encourage you engage in your own interfaith experiences.

The remainder of this book is filled with ideas to guide the development of educational opportunities focused on interfaith engagement, including sample programs and activities, case studies to use in the curriculum and cocurriculum, professional development ideas for student affairs professionals, classroom ideas for faculty in student preparation programs, and knowledge to fill gaps in religious literacy. Whether you choose to read from the first page to the last, or jump from one topic to the next for information and inspiration, we believe this volume will provide you with practical ideas that have been missing in the student affairs profession.

References

ACPA–College Student Educators International. (2006). *Statement of ethical principles and standards.* Washington DC: Author.

ACPA–College Student Educators International & NASPA–Student Affairs Administrators in Higher Education. (2016). *Professional competency areas for student affairs educators.* Washington DC: Author.

Astin, A. W., Astin, H. S., & Lindholm, J. A. (2011). *Cultivating the spirit: How college can enhance students' inner lives.* San Francisco, CA: Jossey-Bass.

Dawkins, R. (n.d.). Richard Dawkins quotes. Retrieved from http://www.azquotes .com/quote/575587

French, D. (2002). *A season for justice: Defending the rights of the Christian home, church, and school.* Nashville, TN: Broadman & Holman.

Fried, J. (2003). Ethical standards and principles. In S. R. Komives, D. B. Woodard, Jr., & Associates (Eds.) *Student services: A handbook for the profession* (pp. 107–127). San Francisco. CA: Jossey-Bass.

Fried, J. (2007). Thinking skillfully and respecting difference: Understanding religious privilege on campus. *Journal of College & Character, 9*(1), 1–7.

Goodman, K. M. (2014). The future of spirituality in higher education: Becoming more inclusive. In P. A. Sasso & J. DeVitis (Eds.) *Today's college students: A reader* (pp. 257–266). New York, NY: Peter Lang.

Hammer, M. (2012). The intercultural development inventory: A new frontier in assessment and development of intercultural competence. In M. Vande Berg, R. M. Paige, & K. H. Lou (Eds.), *Student learning abroad* (pp. 115–136). Sterling, VA: Stylus.

Interfaith Youth Core. (2003). *Shared values facilitation guide.* Retrieved from https:// www.ifyc.org/resources/facilitators-tools-interfaith-conversations-shared-values

Keller, T. [@timkellernyc]. (2014, March 1). Every religion or non-religion, even those that appear more inclusive, make exclusive claims. Retrieved from https:// twitter.com/dailykeller/status/439931951005175808

Kitchener, K. (1985). Ethical principles and ethical decisions in student affairs. *New Directions for Student Services, 30*, 17–30.

Levinovitz, A. (2015, October 2). The problem with religious tolerance. *Chronicle of Higher Education*. Retrieved from http://chronicle.com/article/The-Problem-With-Religious/233593

Mindset. (2002). In *Dictionary.com*. Retrieved from http://www.dictionary.com/browse/mindset

Moran, C. D., & Curtis, G. D. (2004). Blending two worlds: Religio-spirituality in the professional lives of student affairs administrators. *NASPA Journal, 41*, 631–646.

Nash, R. J. (2001). *Religious pluralism in the academy: Opening the dialogue*. New York, NY: Peter Lang.

Perez, R. J., Shim, W., King, P. M., Baxter Magolda, M. B. (2015). Refining King and Baxter Magolda's model of intercultural maturity. *Journal of College Student Development, 56*(8), 759–776.

Porte, J. (1984). *Emerson in his journals*. Cambridge, MA: Harvard University Press.

Sardelli, K. (2011). Drafting a community-wide blueprint for civil discourse. In P. M. Magolda & M. B. Baxter Magolda (Eds.), *Contested issues in student affairs: Diverse perspectives and respectful dialogue* (pp. 365–370). Sterling, VA: Stylus.

Seifert, T. A. (2007). Understanding Christian privilege: Managing the tensions of spiritual plurality. *About Campus, 12*(2), 10–17.

Small, J. L. (2011). *Understanding college students' spiritual identities: Different faiths, varied worldviews*. New York, NY: Hampton Press.

Tierney, W. G. (1993). *Building communities of difference: Higher education in the twenty-first century*. Westport, CT: Bergin & Garvey.

U.S. Const., amend. I.

Watt, S., Fairchild, E., & Goodman, K. (Eds.). (2009). Religious privilege and student affairs practice: Intersections of difficult dialogues. *New Directions for Student Services, 125*.

2

STUDENTS' PERCEPTIONS OF AND ENGAGEMENT WITH WORLDVIEW DIVERSITY IN COLLEGE

Benjamin P. Correia-Harker, Jeremy T. Snipes,
Alyssa N. Rockenbach, and Matthew J. Mayhew

Religious and philosophical diversity is growing in the United States (Pew Research Center, 2015), and preparing college students to meaningfully interact across these lines of difference is critical to the success of our democratic society. Differences because of religious and philosophical identities have the potential to create deep divides in our local and national communities, but when navigated successfully, this diversity also has the power to fortify social ties and build a stronger democracy (Patel, 2016). Colleges and universities serve as microcosms of democratic communities by providing living laboratories for students to learn about other religious and philosophical groups and practice interacting across worldview differences. Whether guided by structured experiences or encountered in informal spaces, students are regularly interacting with others who make meaning of religion differently. The purpose of this book is to provide knowledge and tools to help student affairs practitioners engage with worldview diversity.

What do we know about college campuses as laboratories for learning related to religious diversity and interfaith cooperation? What aspects of the campus environment influence student interactions with religiously diverse others? How does the campus climate potentially shape student perceptions of and attitudes toward meaningful engagement with peers of different worldviews? In this chapter, we discuss major findings from two national surveys, the Campus Religious and Spiritual Climate Survey (CRSCS) and Interfaith Diversity

Experiences and Attitudes Longitudinal Survey (IDEALS) to identify common themes that can be used to inform promising interfaith practices on campus.

The CRSCS is a cross-sectional survey developed in 2008 to fill an existing gap of research focused on the campus climate for religious and spiritual diversity (Bryant, 2008). After an initial pilot, Interfaith Youth Core formed a partnership with Matthew J. and Alyssa N. Rockenbach, the original survey developers, to administer the CRSCS to a broader cross-section of campuses across the United States. Since then, the CRSCS has been administered at more than 60 campuses and to more than 16,000 students. The research team has taken what it learned from the CRSCS to create a longitudinal survey, known as IDEALS, to explore causal connections between environments and outcomes.

This chapter aims to immerse practitioners in broad findings from the CRSCS and IDEALS to provide insights that can transform practice related to worldview diversity and interfaith engagement. We begin with an overview of the CRSCS and then highlight three key outcomes that are important for students to develop during their collegiate career. We then discuss important environmental factors, indicating why they might be influential components of the campus climate and college experience as well as entertain ways professionals can use these factors for greater interfaith learning. In addition, we offer some recent trends emerging from the first administration of the IDEALS survey. Finally, we provide some reflection questions to help readers consider how these findings directly relate to their campus communities. We hope student affairs educators can use this information to create powerful environments that promote constructive engagement with religious diversity, which may in turn shape students' future actions in careers and societal leadership after college.

Understanding the Campus Climate for Religious and Spiritual Diversity

The CRSCS and IDEALS were designed to capture essential features of Astin's (1993) inputs-environments-outputs (I-E-O) model, which accounts for student characteristics on entering college, the educational experiences and environments they encounter during college, and the qualities students develop as a result of engaging in those educational experiences. An adaptation of Hurtado, Milem, Clayton-Pedersen, and Allen's (1999) model depicting elements of the campus climate for racial and ethnic diversity also serves as a theoretical grounding for the CRSCS and IDEALS. Recognizing potential parallels between contextual factors that affect climate for racial and ethnic diversity and those that influence religious diversity, Rockenbach and Mayhew

Figure 2.1. Campus Religious and Spiritual Climate Survey factors overlaid on Astin's (1993) model.

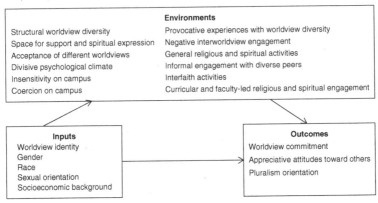

based several survey scales on three of the dimensions: structural diversity, psychological climate, and the behavioral dimension. Structural diversity pertains to the composition of a campus community, taking account of the degree to which a campus is homogeneous or heterogeneous in regard to religious diversity. Psychological climate refers to student perceptions of tension among, discrimination toward, and support for students of different religious and philosophical identities. The actions of individual students—how they engage worldview diversity on campus—represent the behavioral dimension of climate. These three dimensions when considered together paint a picture of perceived climate for students of diverse religious and philosophical backgrounds. Figure 2.1 depicts this multifaceted view of the campus religious and spiritual climate based on Astin (1993) and Hurtado and colleagues (1999).

Understanding the theoretical and empirical foundations of the CRSCS and IDEALS provides insight into the aspects of the campus religious and spiritual context researchers can explore and how they have examined environments and experiences in relation to interfaith outcomes. To effectively support student growth, campus educators must clearly comprehend how experiences on campus influence students' learning and development. When studies such as the CRSCS and IDEALS illuminate factors that relate to interfaith outcomes, campus staff and faculty can use that knowledge to build more inclusive and developmental-focused communities.

Outcomes of Interfaith Engagement

Three central outcomes incorporated into the CRSCS and IDEALS are strong indicators of students' future ability and willingness to meaningfully engage in interfaith work: self-authored worldview commitment, appreciative attitudes toward others, and pluralism orientation. Each is described in more detail in the following sections.

Self-Authored Worldview Commitment

College provides opportunities for students to interact with others who have belief systems and perspectives they have often not previously encountered. In that process, students are challenged to reconsider their assumptions about the world and to integrate new ways of knowing and being into their current belief system. This can be a disorienting experience for some students as they discern what these new insights mean in relation to the values and beliefs that were core to their upbringing. Thus, college is a place where students can examine and critically reflect on their beliefs, leading to a more complex and deeper commitment to a particular worldview. Self-authored worldview commitment measures the degree to which students reflect on and consider other perspectives in a process of committing to their own worldviews. Self-authored individuals have an informed, critical understanding of their worldviews and can describe themselves and interact with others in ways consistent with such an understanding (Mayhew & Bryant, 2013).

A common misconception of interfaith engagement is that it encourages the dilution of belief systems to a common base everyone can agree on. In reality, interfaith engagement should be a place where individuals can acknowledge deep disagreements because of diverse beliefs yet seek understanding and common action rather than agreement. Because of this process, students hone their worldviews, learn to clearly express their views to others, and thoughtfully consider other perspectives that challenge or support their current worldview. Ultimately, interfaith engagement should strengthen rather than weaken students' worldview commitment and motivate them to actively embrace a values system.

Appreciative Attitudes of Others

Sociologists Robert Putnam and David Campbell (2010) explored the potential of religion to be a dividing or unifying force in U.S. society. They describe a phenomenon called the My Friend Al Principle, which illuminates the importance of relationships to build bridges of understanding and appreciation of others. Individuals often have predisposed perceptions and biases toward specific worldviews. However, when individuals of different worldview identities form relationships through common experiences or activities, they then come to appreciate the other person, and by association start to develop a more positive regard for the other person's worldview as well as for others who subscribe to that worldview. In addition to Putnam and Campbell's research, other empirical work from the Pew Research Center (2014) supports this phenomenon, showing that individuals who have relationships with someone of a different religious identity also have more positive feelings toward others of that identity community.

Thus, appreciative attitudes can be an important indicator of meaningful engagement and relationships across lines of religious difference. For the CRSCS and IDEALS, appreciative attitudes reflect the positive regard or feelings individuals have toward those of another worldview identity. A number of appreciative attitudes scales were included in the CRSCS to ask about five specific groups: atheists, evangelical Christians, Jews, Latter-day Saints (LDS) or Mormons, and Muslims. IDEALS expands coverage to include attitudes toward 13 different social identity and worldview groups. Engaging in interfaith experiences should help students develop relationships with a variety of students of diverse religious and philosophical backgrounds, and as a result, cultivate more appreciative attitudes toward others, especially those with different ideological positions.

Pluralism Orientation

Diversity is often celebrated in higher education; however, Diana Eck (2001) has asserted that diversity is a neutral concept. As such, diversity can be used for positive or negative aims. Eck emphasized the pursuit of pluralism, which is the commitment to active and meaningful engagement with diverse others to work toward positive goals. Students who develop strong pluralistic orientations have the potential to strengthen a religiously diverse democratic society. The CRSCS and IDEALS measure pluralism orientation via a range of items that reveal students' respect for others' worldviews, recognition of common ground, and willingness to positively engage with others to address society's problems.

Theoretically, these three outcomes—self-authored worldview commitment, appreciative attitudes toward others, and pluralism orientation—are the fruits of interfaith experiences. Students who participate in activities that value religious diversity and bridge faith perspectives and communities should become more critically reflective on their own worldview identities, hold more favorable perspectives of others' worldviews, and develop a higher appreciation for engaging with diverse peers to address societal issues. But does this actually happen on college campuses? We now turn to results of several studies to illustrate key themes that surfaced from empirical research.

Environmental Factors That May Promote Student Development

Findings from the CRSCS research suggest that the following environmental factors positively influence interfaith outcomes: space for support and spiritual expression, provocative experiences with worldview diversity, negative interworldview engagement, informal engagement with diverse peers, and formal interfaith activities. These particular environmental aspects and experiences repeatedly emerged as influential factors that shape students' interfaith attitudes.

Space for Support and Spiritual Expression

The CRSCS research has consistently demonstrated that students' perceptions of space for support and spiritual expression on campus are associated with important developmental outcomes. The space for support and spiritual expression scale measures the extent to which students feel there are physical and social resources on campus to support their spiritual pursuits and expressions. It is a critical component of student perceptions of the campus' psychological climate. The scale consists of items such as the following:

- This campus accommodates my needs in regard to celebrating religious holidays and other important religious observances.
- There is a place (e.g., office, organization) on this campus where I can seek help with spiritual or religious struggles and questions.
- There is a place on this campus where I can express my personal worldview.

Space for support and spiritual expression is positively associated with self-authored worldview commitment (Mayhew, Rockenbach, & Bowman, 2016); pluralism orientation (Rockenbach, Mayhew, Morin, Crandall, & Selznick, 2015); and appreciative attitudes toward atheists, evangelical Christians, Jews, LDS or Mormons, and Muslims (Bowman, Rockenbach, Mayhew, Riggers-Piehl, & Hudson, 2017; Mayhew, Bowman, Rockenbach, Selznick, & Riggers-Piehl, 2018; Mayhew et al., 2017; Rockenbach, Bowman, Riggers-Piehl, Mayhew, & Crandall, 2017; Rockenbach, Mayhew, Bowman, Morin, & Riggers-Piehl, 2017). That is, students who perceive higher levels of support for their worldview identity on campus also generally report higher self-authored worldview commitment, appreciative attitudes toward others, and pluralism orientation.

The fact that a deeper self-authored worldview commitment is associated with stronger perceptions of space for support and spiritual expression on campus is encouraging. Campuses, particularly offices of religious and spiritual life, purposefully provide opportunities intended to foster students' exploration and commitment. Students' recognition of a supportive presence for their religious, spiritual, or philosophical identities may also provide a perceived safety to thoughtfully consider ideas that seem discordant with their worldview identities. Thus, the support provided for students' respective worldview identities not only directly helps them build stronger foundations in their traditions but also provides security to explore other belief systems, which in turn may foster more complex understandings of their traditions.

The strong relationship between space for support and spiritual expression and appreciative attitudes and pluralism might exist for a number of reasons. As Rockenbach and colleagues (2015) aptly noted, when students are respected and feel safe, they are more likely to be welcoming and accepting of others. Students who perceive the campus as accommodating and conscientious toward their worldviews may feel affirmed in those aspects of their identity. The affective disposition created from that feeling of support may make students more confident interacting with students who do not share their same worldview identity. Also, as students see other worldviews accommodated in similar ways as their own, they may follow the model the institution provides.

The implications of these findings for campus educators are clear. Practitioners should attend to accommodations and safe spaces on campus for a range of worldview expressions. To do this, educators should be aware of various accommodations needed for different worldview groups; this requires some degree of religious literacy and trusting relationships with students of diverse worldviews. Staff may want to conduct an audit or needs assessment to understand how students from different worldview groups feel supported regarding their religious and philosophical beliefs. Nationally, a larger proportion of Christian students report supportive spaces and resources on campus than their peers from other religious traditions or nonreligious students (Rockenbach, Mayhew, Kinarsky, & Interfaith Youth Core, 2014). This may not be too surprising to some given the strong Christian roots of many colleges and universities and the dominant Christian norms in U.S. society (Thelin, 2011). Administrators need to take note of ways they can institute reasonable accommodations for a greater diversity of religious and nonreligious traditions.

Campus staff and faculty should not only explore and implement broad changes to support students' worldview identities but also make small adaptations to help students recognize existing supports and resources. For example, campus educators should consider publicizing existing policies or modifying language. Many campuses have policies to accommodate students who must miss class because of religious holidays. Unfortunately, many students may not know these policies exist, or some faculty may not readily support such policies. Emphasizing these policies to students, staff, and faculty during their orientations or restating the policy prior to each semester may help to communicate the importance of providing religious accommodations on campus.

Another simple shift would be to alter language to be inclusive of a broader spectrum of identities, particularly the nonreligious. IDEALS research revealed that of first-year students entering college in fall 2015, 41% identified as religious and spiritual, 26% considered themselves spiritual but not religious, 11% indicated they were religious but not spiritual, and 22% characterized themselves as neither religious nor spiritual (Mayhew et al., 2016). A number of students do not resonate with religious or spiritual labels, yet these students still need support for understanding how they make meaning in the world. Students who do not identify as religious or spiritual might opt out of various opportunities to make meaning if the experiences are only framed in religious or spiritual ways. Using language that invites the nonreligious and nonspiritual into spaces where values and beliefs are discussed is critical for cross-worldview dialogue and for nonreligious students' own development. In making a series of small adjustments in their spheres of influence, campus educators can establish supportive spaces for students to explore and better understand their worldviews.

Provocative Experiences With Worldview Diversity

To understand the quality of encounters with others, the CRSCS includes a series of items to capture positive yet challenging experiences with students of diverse worldviews as well as harmful and unproductive exchanges. The positive experiences were measured with the provocative experiences with worldview diversity scale, which indicates the frequency with which students had meaningful and stimulating conversations or interactions with those of different worldviews. Some would consider these "aha" moments when students recognize a previously held assumption or develop new insight about their own or others' worldview identities. In contrast, negative interworldview engagement pertains to the tense or hostile exchanges students engage in with others of different worldviews. In these cases, students may foreclose on experiences, feeling the need to protect themselves or their worldview identities.

As one might predict, provocative experiences with worldview diversity are positively related with each of the outcomes of interest in this chapter; students who have more frequent provocative experiences also have higher pluralism orientation (Rockenbach et al., 2015), deeper self-authored worldview commitment (Mayhew, Rockenbach, & Bowman, 2016), and greater appreciative attitudes toward atheists, evangelical Christians, Jews, LDS or Mormons, and Muslims (Bowman et al., 2016; Mayhew et al., 2018; Mayhew et al., 2017; Rockenbach, Bowman, et al., 2017; Rockenbach, Mayhew, et al., 2017). Students who engage frequently in provocative experiences have opportunities to refine their worldview identities as they critically reflect on their own assumptions and seek to understand the experiences of others. From these moments of revelation, students may also develop more nuanced and appreciative understandings of other religious and philosophical traditions, thus resulting in stronger pluralism orientations.

In terms of negative interworldview engagement, students who have more hostile or tense interactions tend to have less favorable attitudes toward atheists, evangelical Christians, LDS or Mormons, and Muslims (Bowman et al., 2017; Mayhew et al., 2017; Rockenbach, Bowman, et al., 2017; Rockenbach, Mayhew, et al., 2017), as well as lower pluralism orientation (Rockenbach et al., 2015). Yet, those who have more experiences with negative interworldview engagement generally have higher worldview commitment (Mayhew, Rockenbach, & Bowman, 2016). The inverse relationship between negative interworldview engagement and appreciative attitudes toward others suggests that threatening interactions with someone of a different worldview result in less favorable attitudes regardless of the context in which the negative incident occurred. Negative interworldview engagement captured perceptions of interactions with others, but it did not focus on particular groups as did the appreciative attitude scales. So the mere exposure to harsh interworldview exchanges seems to reverberate beyond the feelings toward a particular group with which the negative encounter transpired. Instead of learning to value other perspectives, students who experience antagonistic interactions may instead begin to see *otherness* as harmful or potentially *less than*. This may then explain the inverse relationship between negative interworldview engagement and pluralism orientation; as students develop a mistrust of other groups, they may come to believe it less feasible for people to cooperate across lines of religious difference to improve the world.

The positive relationship between negative interworldview engagement and self-authored worldview commitment is counterintuitive at first glance. Students who work to cultivate a deeper commitment to their worldview identities have more frequent interactions with people of other worldviews. Inevitably, some of these encounters will be constructive (although provocative), whereas others will be more negative in quality. Although some experiences can be outright vitriolic, Mayhew, Rockenbach, and Bowman (2016) suggested that it might be more beneficial to interpret challenging experiences in terms of productive or unproductive rather than positive or negative. What a student perceives as a negative encounter in time may be seen retrospectively as a meaningful experience.

Similarly, provocative experiences with worldview diversity and negative interworldview engagement could be interpreted as two sides of the same coin. For instance, an assortment of students participating in an interfaith dialogue may leave with different interpretations of the experience. Some might report it as thought provoking and rewarding, and others consider it tense and hurtful. In addition to offering environments that allow students to explore controversial topics with vulnerability and honesty, attending to students' developmental readiness to engage in certain experiences may be critical for creating productive exchanges that foster growth rather than foreclosure. Campus educators should carefully consider what activities seem appropriate for various audiences depending on factors such as students' emotional maturity for interacting across difference or their cognitive ability to hold to contradictory views in tension with each other. Doing so can maximize encounters with otherness for productive growth toward interfaith outcomes.

When creating programs or interventions that bring religiously diverse students into conversation with each other, campus educators should strive to implement activities that do not merely put students in contact with one another but instead integrate intentional and productive exchanges. Educators need to build environments and experiences in which community members have opportunities and encouragement to share their diverse perspectives and grapple with the complex milieu of beliefs, practices, and values on campus. Ask Big Questions (see www.askbigquestions.org) is a strong programmatic example that situates thoughtful questions that can evoke mutually inspiring narratives, challenge students' assumptions, and highlight commonalities with others. Additionally, it is important to model respectful dialogue, readily validate feelings, provide follow-up reflections or conversations that allow students to make meaning of powerful interactions, and support students who may struggle to make sense of perceived negative experiences. If students have supportive student groups, staff and faculty mentors, or religious spiritual life offices, this caring network may be able to help students shift perceptions of negative experiences to opportunities for transformative learning.

Formal and Informal Interfaith Engagement Matters

Interfaith activities, which are cocurricular opportunities to engage across worldview identities, are another key environmental factor that can influence students' pluralistic growth. These activities can be formal or informal.

Examples of formal interfaith activities include attending an interfaith prayer vigil or memorial, participating in an on-campus interfaith dialogue, or working with students with other worldviews on a service project. Informal engagement with diverse peers, conversely, includes sharing a meal with someone from a different religious or nonreligious perspective, socializing with someone with a different worldview, or discussing religious or spiritual topics with other students outside class.

Formal and informal interfaith engagement are positively related to worldview commitment (Mayhew, Rockenbach, & Bowman, 2016), pluralism orientation (Rockenbach et al., 2015), and appreciative attitudes toward atheists, evangelical Christians, Jews, LDS or Mormons, and Muslims (Bowman et al., 2017; Mayhew et al., 2018; Mayhew et al., 2017; Rockenbach, Bowman, et al., 2017; Rockenbach, Mayhew, et al., 2017). In other words, the more often students participate in interfaith programs or engage in casual interfaith interactions with diverse friends, the more committed, appreciative, and pluralistic they tend to be. These findings bring to light the importance of identity exploration within the confines of religiously and philosophically diverse communities. It is likely that students engaging in interfaith activities are more likely to interrogate and develop deep commitments to their particular worldviews. Additionally, these findings affirm previous social science theory and research that suggests meaningful engagement with religious diversity bolsters individuals' positive attitudes toward others and their belief that people from different religious and philosophical traditions can work together to build a better society (Putnam & Campbell, 2010).

Even though formal interfaith activities seem to be influential experiences for students on the whole, just more than half of students have participated in interfaith cooperative action on a social issue, whereas fewer than one in five students has participated in interfaith dialogue (Rockenbach et al., 2014). With smaller portions of students choosing to participate in such interfaith programs, educators should consider ways to promote existing interfaith offerings and to creatively embed interfaith experiences into existing programs, spaces, and campus traditions. For example, educators might

- integrate various faith perspectives and practices into convocation or commencement;
- openly discuss worldview identity during orientation and residential programs alongside discussions of other identities such as race, gender, and sexual orientation; and
- incorporate reflection questions into community service opportunities that challenge students to connect their service work with personal values grounded in their worldview identities.

Bringing interfaith engagement opportunities to students, meeting them where they are, may help a broader range of students benefit from the educational fruits of interfaith cooperation.

In addition to formal interfaith activities, students report high levels of informal engagement with diverse peers. In fact, a large majority of students have conversations with peers of diverse worldviews regarding shared values or dine with someone with a different worldview (Rockenbach et al., 2014). This is particularly promising given that these casual interactions can result in strengthened relationships and are what we hope students will continue to practice as they enter their future careers and communities. In addition to creating a culture where students feel free to express and talk about their worldview identities, providing prompts that catalyze interfaith dialogue through dining hall table tents or campus bulletin boards can help students to become aware the interfaith encounters they have on a regular basis. For example, questions about what core values guide their actions and provide meaning in their lives as well as where those values are derived may spark conversation between peers about the commonalities and differences they have related to their worldviews.

Through mentorship, staff and faculty can also play integral roles in helping students realize how their and others' worldviews influence perceptions of society and daily actions. Parks (2000) emphasizes mentoring relationships as valuable occasions to stimulate student growth and learning by asking evocative questions and encouraging students to reframe their experiences. By explicitly calling out the benefits and providing reflective spaces where students can make meaning of and distill what they learn from informal exchanges, practitioners can help students become aware of and capitalize on the benefits of informal interfaith encounters.

Environmental Factors That May Inhibit Student Development

Whereas many of the factors outlined in the prior section are positive aspects of climate, other scales in the CRSCS captured negative aspects of religious and spiritual climate on campus. Two scales in particular emerged consistently in CRSCS studies as significantly related to key outcomes: insensitivity on campus and divisive psychological climate. Insensitivity on campus pertains to perceived mistreatment of self and others on campus based on religious or nonreligious identity. Students reported not only the frequency of witnessing insensitive acts and statements but also who mistreated them and others. In terms of divisive psychological climate, students reported the degree to which they saw conflict among different worldviews as well as whether those groups tended to avoid interaction.

Insensitivity on campus is negatively related to important outcomes such as pluralism orientation (Rockenbach et al., 2015) and appreciative attitudes toward atheists, evangelical Christians, Jews, LDS or Mormons, and Muslims (Bowman et al., 2016; Mayhew et al., 2018; Mayhew et al., 2017; Rockenbach, Bowman, et al., 2016; Rockenbach, Mayhew, et al., 2017). In other words, students who witness more mistreatment of certain groups tend to have lower levels of pluralism orientation and are less appreciative of others. However, divisive psychological climate positively predicted worldview commitment (Mayhew, Rockenbach, & Bowman, 2016), meaning that students who perceived more division among worldview groups on campus tended to have stronger commitments to their religious or worldview identities.

According to Patel (2016), when individuals encounter religiously diverse others, they can respond by avoiding interaction, denouncing the other, attacking the other, or building bridges with the other. Insensitivity and divisiveness on campus can be indicators of a community that avoids, denounces, or attacks those who are different. In such a climate, it is intimidating for students to build bridges of understanding. As students hear negative sentiments toward other religions or worldview perspectives, students might resist reaching out to others in fear of being scorned because of their worldviews. Left unattended, a campus climate marked by insensitivity and divisiveness could be harmful for students' interfaith development.

The positive connection between divisive psychological climate and worldview commitment is more challenging to interpret. At face value, the finding could mean that divisiveness on campus promotes retreating into one's own worldview community, which allows strong bonding with and reinforcement of individual worldview identities. However, the worldview commitment scale includes items that ask students not only about their depth of commitment to a worldview but also to what degree they have considered other worldviews before committing to their own. With this in mind, Mayhew, Rockenbach, & Bowman (2016) offer an alternative interpretation of this finding. They proposed that as students develop a more complex commitment to their worldview identities based on meaningful interactions with other worldviews, students' perspective on and awareness of the campus climate may shift. These students may be more attentive to attitudes and behaviors that promote division and marginalization of some worldview groups.

Campus educators must carefully attend to insensitive and divisive climates to minimize how such climates may hinder student development toward pluralistic ends. In doing so, educators should consider how they promote spaces to connect with others, yet teach and model positive skill sets to meaningfully engage across lines of difference. On campuses marked by divisiveness, students may need explicit messages and implicit signals indicating it is okay to openly discuss their worldview identities and interact with diverse others. Thus, campus staff and faculty may need to create intentional spaces that provide students with the opportunity to share values and stories of their worldview perspectives. Even more so, faculty and staff may need to model these behaviors by openly engaging in conversations about their worldview identities, inviting conversations about students' worldviews, and collaborating with staff, faculty, and students of other identities on community events or service. As campus educators do this work, they can provide positive examples of how to navigate these difficult conversations. This requires faculty and staff to become adept at navigating tense or hostile interactions and direct them toward positive ends for all students involved. Such facilitation is difficult and can be intimidating, so campus educators should seek out educational opportunities on cross-cultural facilitation to bolster their skill sets and efficacy to navigate interfaith dialogues. By emphasizing worldview as a meaningful aspect of identity to engage and by role modeling respectful exchanges across worldview identities, staff and faculty can have an impact on mitigating perceptions of negative climates and fostering supportive and positive climates and experiences.

Advancing Research on Interfaith Cooperation Using IDEALS

In 2015 the CRSCS research team launched a new project, IDEALS, which provides researchers with a way to clarify the causal direction of relationships and determine the effect interfaith practices and other campus climate factors have on student learning. The survey is longitudinal in design and tracks a cohort of students across 3 critical time points during their undergraduate experience. Participants completed the first survey before or in the first months of their collegiate career and again at the end of their first year. These students will be surveyed again in the spring semester of their fourth year in 2019. More than 20,000 students from 122 colleges and universities are participating in IDEALS.

Although findings from only the first survey administration are available at the time of writing this chapter, several trends are particularly valuable for campus educators to consider. Entering students, regardless of worldview, have high expectations of their colleges and universities regarding religious diversity and interfaith experiences. More than four in five students believe it is important for their institution to be welcoming for students of diverse religious and nonreligious perspectives (Mayhew, Rockenbach, Correia et al.,

2016). This is similar to their reported expectations for their institutions to provide a welcoming environment for people of different races, sexual orientations, and gender identities. Furthermore, nearly three-quarters of students expect opportunities to get to know students of other religious and nonreligious perspectives (Mayhew, Rockenbach, Correia et al., 2016). Campus educators should earnestly attempt to meet these expectations by implementing recommendations discussed in this chapter and the remainder of this book.

IDEALS data also reveal that incoming students seem to have a strong disposition toward pluralism and appear poised for interfaith cooperation; however, they have limited precollege interfaith experiences and may lack the necessary skill sets to help them meaningfully connect with others. When asked to what degree they believe different religious groups can work cooperatively to address the world's major problems or to what degree their worldview inspires them to address issues of common concern, students largely respond with high levels of agreement (Mayhew, Rockenbach, Correia et al., 2016). They also reported that they generally respect and admire people from other faiths. Educators can capitalize on these promising, pluralistic attitudes to encourage students to engage further in interfaith experiences during college.

However, faculty and staff should be aware of skill sets and perspectives that students still need to develop for productive interfaith encounters in college. Whereas a large majority of students agree that pluralistic engagement is important, only half of incoming students worked on service projects with others of different religious and nonreligious perspectives in their last year of high school, and even fewer students attended a religious service for another tradition or participated in an interfaith dialogue (Mayhew, Rockenbach, Correia et al., 2016). Additionally, students may have reported a general positive regard for other religious and nonreligious groups as a collective, but when asked about their attitudes toward specific religious and nonreligious groups, students reported only moderately positive attitudes. In sum, pluralistic engagement is generally embraced by entering college students, but they may struggle when they encounter pronounced ideological differences with specific identity groups.

Conclusion

Research based on CRSCS and IDEALS data has and continues to shed light on campus environmental factors that promote or constrain student interfaith learning. This review of the research illuminated findings that may help educators effectively promote students' interfaith capacity and appreciation of others. We offer the following questions for critical reflection.

Regarding support and accommodations:

- To what degree do students of diverse religious and philosophical traditions have appropriate access to resources that support their own worldview development? Which specific worldviews might need more support?
- How do campus educators shape the campus environment to be a space where students feel free to express and discuss their identities?
- In what ways are students taught productive forms of engagement with others? To what degree are these practices modeled by staff and faculty on campus?
- What structures or practices on campus support connections across worldview groups? What may hinder such connections and promote division?

Regarding experiences and interventions:

- What programs or interventions does the institution provide to encourage productive student interaction across different religious and philosophical groups?
  - How are these experiences provided to broad cross-sections of the student population?
  - In what ways could these experiences or interfaith practices be infused into current campus traditions?
- How does the institution provide a range of activities that provoke critical reflection for students about their own worldview identities and that spark genuine understanding of others' perspectives?
  - To what degree are these experiences structured to appropriately challenge students at different emotional or cognitive developmental stages?
- In what ways do educators structure and support more passive interventions (e.g., bulletin boards, interfaith spaces, residence hall lounges) that promote informal interactions and conversations?

Regarding elevating the priority:

- In what ways do educators express the value of interfaith work to other stakeholders on campus? How could they introduce stories or research that illustrate the importance of this work?

We encourage campus educators to take a moment to pause and reflect on these questions and note one or two key insights to inform change on campus.

In the end, improving the capacity for interfaith cooperation in this generation of emerging adults and strengthening our democratic society depends on several developmental aims that educators can cultivate in students during the college years. These aims include helping students deepen their awareness of and commitment to their worldview identities; fostering students' appreciative attitudes toward people with different worldviews, even those with whom they maintain ideological disagreement; and nurturing students' pluralistic orientations so that they come to value meaningful engagement with other worldviews.

References

Astin, A. W. (1993). *What matters in college? Four critical years revisited*. San Francisco, CA: Jossey-Bass.

Bowman, N. A., Rockenbach, A. N., Mayhew, M. J., Riggers-Piehl, T. A., & Hudson, T. D. (2017). College students' appreciative attitudes toward atheists. *Research in Higher Education, 58*(1), 98–118.

Bryant, A. N. (2008). Assessing contexts and practices for engaging students' spirituality. *Journal of College and Character, 10*(2), 1–5.

Eck, D. L. (2001). *A new religious America: How a "Christian country" has become the world's most religiously diverse nation*. New York, NY: HarperCollins.

Hurtado, S., Milem, J., Clayton-Pederson, A., & Allen, W. (1999). Enacting diverse learning environments: Improving the climate for racial/ethnic diversity in higher education. *ASHE-ERIC Higher Education Report, 26*(8).

Mayhew, M. J., Bowman, N. A., Rockenbach, A. N., Selznick, B., & Riggers-Piehl, T. (2018). Appreciative attitudes toward Jews among non-Jewish US college students. *Journal of College Student Development, 59*(1), 71–89.

Mayhew, M. J., & Bryant, A. N. (2013). Achievement or arrest? The influence of the collegiate religious and spiritual climate on students' worldview commitment. *Research in Higher Education, 54*, 63–84.

Mayhew, M. J., Rockenbach, A. N., & Bowman, N. A. (2016). The connection between interfaith engagement and self-authored worldview commitment. *Journal of College Student Development, 57*, 362–379.

Mayhew, M. J., Rockenbach, A. N., Bowman, N. A., Lo, M. A., Starcke, M., Riggers-Piehl, T., & Crandall, R. E. (2017). Expanding perspectives on evangelicalism: How non-evangelical students appreciate Evangelical Christianity. *Review of Religious Research, 58*, 207–230. doi:10.1007/s13644-017-0283-8.

Mayhew, M. J., Rockenbach, A. N., Correia, B. P., Crandall, R. E., Lo, M. A., & Associates. (2016). *Emerging interfaith trends: What college students are saying about religion in 2016*. Chicago, IL: Interfaith Youth Core.

Parks, S. D. (2000). *Big questions, worthy dreams: Mentoring young adults in their search for meaning, purpose, and faith.* San Francisco, CA: Jossey-Bass.

Patel, E. (2016). *Interfaith leadership: A primer.* Boston, MA: Beacon Press.

Pew Research Center. (2014). *How Americans feel about religious groups.* Retrieved from http://www.pewforum.org/2014/07/16/how-americans-feel-about-religious-groups/

Pew Research Center. (2015). *America's changing religious landscape.* Retrieved from http://www.pewforum.org/2015/05/12/americas-changing-religious-landscape/

Putnam, R. D., & Campbell, D. E. (2010). *American grace: How religion divides and unites us.* New York, NY: Simon & Schuster.

Rockenbach, A. N., Bowman, N. A., Riggers-Piehl, T., Mayhew, M. J., & Crandall, R. E. (2017). Respecting the LDS/Mormon minority on campus: College students' attitudes toward Latter-day Saints. *Journal for the Scientific Study of Religion, 56,* 798–819.

Rockenbach, A. N., Mayhew, M. J., Bowman, N. A., Morin, S. M., & Riggers-Piehl, T. (2017). An examination of non-Muslim college students' attitudes toward Muslims. *Journal of Higher Education, 88,* 479–504. doi:10.1080/00221546.2016.1272329.

Rockenbach, A. N., Mayhew, M. J., Kinarsky, A., & Interfaith Youth Core. (2014). *Engaging worldview: A snapshot of religious and spiritual climate. Part I: Dimensions of climate and student engagement.* Chicago, IL: Interfaith Youth Core.

Rockenbach, A. N., Mayhew, M. J., Morin, S., Crandall, R. E., & Selznick, B. (2015). Fostering the pluralism orientation of college students through interfaith co-curricular engagement. *The Review of Higher Education, 39*(1), 25–58.

Thelin, J. R. (2011). *A history of American higher education* (2nd ed.). Baltimore, MD: Johns Hopkins University Press.

3

SOCIAL JUSTICE AND INTERFAITH COOPERATION

Eboo Patel and Cassie Meyer

A colleague of ours at Interfaith Youth Core (IFYC) was on the phone with a student affairs professional who focuses on religious and worldview diversity and interfaith issues on his campus.[1] As part of his support for religious minority students, he was working with the university swimming pool to schedule a time each week when the pool would be reserved for women only so that observant Muslim women could use the pool without violating their commitments to modesty by wearing swimsuits around men. The athletics staff was generally supportive, but they had one caveat: If a transgender woman wanted to use the pool during the women-only swimming sessions, they were adamant that she must be allowed to.

The staff person was not sure what to say. He knew that many of the Muslim cisgender women he was working with would not be comfortable with a transgender woman sharing the pool with them because of their religious commitments. At the same time, he understood the athletics department's insistence on inclusion. He confessed candidly to our colleague that he simply hoped it would not be an issue, but if it did come up, perhaps the transgender student would be willing to forgo swimming during the times reserved only for women. By his reasoning, those were the only times the Muslim women would be able to use the pool, and transgender women could use the pool any time but those times.

But still, he wondered, was that a just conclusion? Whose rights should be prioritized? The rights of marginalized women who are a part of a religious minority and, in many cases, racial and ethnic minorities? Or the rights of the transgender woman, also marginalized, who may not feel safe using the pool when there are men around?

We suspect the questions raised by this story will resonate with student affairs professionals doing the difficult work of engaging students with diverse religious and secular worldviews while also attending to the many intersecting aspects of students' identities. From our work as partners with colleges and universities to foster interfaith cooperation on campus, we know that many student affairs professionals have long been working to build interfaith relationships in their programming and that religious and worldview identity, as in this story, can often complicate the work of building inclusive campus environments that also attend to students marginalized by dynamics of privilege and power.

In this chapter, we discuss some of the challenges posed by bringing religious and worldview identity into campus diversity work. To do this, we consider two influential models in student affairs. One is a social justice education approach, which often views religious identity as one identity among other identity categories and uses the frames of power, privilege, oppression, and social justice as a fundamental orientation. Our goal for this chapter is to continue the many one-on-one conversations we have had with campus leaders about the relationship between social justice and *interfaith cooperation*. To do this, we put social justice approaches to engaging religious and worldview diversity in discussion with an interfaith cooperation approach, the methodology that animates our work at IFYC. Interfaith cooperation, as we understand it, focuses on religious and worldview identity in particular among many other intersecting identities and as such prioritizes inclusion of all religious or secular perspectives willing to come to the table in a spirit of pluralism despite conflicting commitments. As we understand the social justice education model, it is concerned primarily with disruption of power structures and seeking justice; social justice is a process and the goal. The next model is concerned primarily with relationships, particularly relationships that can happen across lines of deep difference or disagreement; religious pluralism is the end goal.

In outlining these two models with attention to the challenges posed by religious and worldview diversity, we examine what adherents of both approaches can learn from each other. In doing so, we hope to prompt and contribute to an ongoing dialogue on the intersections, tensions, and possibilities for transformation when addressing religious and worldview diversity on campus. Before continuing, it is worth mentioning that our backgrounds and expertise are in interfaith work in higher education and the academic study of religion and not the study of higher education or student affairs administration. The engagement of diversity in higher education is a richly theorized area of practice, with a robust history and an active scholarly community we hope to do justice to in our conversation here. At the same time, our work at IFYC has put us in regular conversations with student affairs professionals who have challenged us with the questions this chapter seeks to explore. What follows is an attempt at a generous and empathetic reading of the perspectives we have encountered, while acknowledging there may be moments where our understanding may be limited because of our backgrounds or the nature of our work. In those instances, we look forward to correction and further conversation.

Two Approaches to Religious Identity in Higher Education

As we write this chapter, contestations about religious diversity and belonging in public life are reaching a fevered pitch. From President Donald Trump's executive orders focusing on Muslim immigrants to the United States to ongoing conversations about religious freedom and the legalization of same-sex marriage to the rise of hate crimes targeted at religious minorities (Southern Poverty Law Center, 2017), religion remains a vital element of our national conversation. College campuses have not been immune to controversies over religion: InterVarsity Christian Fellowship recently announced the "involuntary termination" (Merritt, 2016, p. 2) of all staff members who support same sex marriage; a student leader at University of California, Los Angeles, was temporarily denied a leadership position because of her Jewish identity (Nagourney, 2015); and a Christian professor at a Christian college was fired for her attempt to show solidarity with Muslims by wearing a hijab (Graham, 2016). Once primarily relegated to the personal sphere, religion has increasingly become a live facet of campus and civic life that can no longer be ignored (Jacobsen & Jacobsen, 2012).

We have written elsewhere that we understand there is a civic imperative for higher education to constructively and proactively engage religious diversity given its increase, continuing tensions on worldview identity, and higher education's impulse to support students for leadership in a diverse, global society (Patel & Meyer, 2011). Higher education has long been at the vanguard of supporting diversity with a larger goal of affecting how people from diverse identities interact, not just on campus but also in the world beyond. We hope higher education might play a role in transforming how society engages with religious diversity, moving from a model of distrust and suspicion to one of relationship and mutuality.

Although student affairs professionals have long been at the forefront of building interfaith coalitions and standing up for religious and worldview tolerance, we also encounter those who profess a lack of capacity to engage with religious and worldview identities on campus. Because of the complex character of religious and worldview identities and the varied ways students express or relate to those identities, many educators worry about how to engage with religion and worldviews without offending students or stoking an intractable doctrinal debate. Thus, they prefer not to engage religious and worldview identities if possible (Jacobsen & Jacobsen, 2012; Nash, 2001).

Further, we have found that educators who engage with religious and secular diversity proactively may do so through a framework of social justice, which they have found essential for their work engaging with other aspects of identity. Such an approach focuses on unearthing structures of privilege, power, and oppression and sees overturning those structures of injustice, on campus and beyond, as a fundamental goal of campus diversity work. From this perspective, engaging with diversity, including religious and spiritual diversity, in higher education should be a "complex process of recognizing, responding to, and negotiating the differences in power that diversity embodies in systems characterized by oppression" in pursuit of social justice (Stewart, 2012, p. 64).

This approach, however, is not without complications when it comes to working with students of diverse religious and worldview identities. If religious and worldview identities should be taken seriously in higher education, what happens when values connected to these identities come into conflict with the social justice commitments often prevalent in student affairs? How does a focus on power, privilege, and oppression translate to the complexity of religious identity? What happens when religious convictions lead to notions of justice that might not align with how many student affairs educators understand social justice? To respond to questions like this, we suggest that an interfaith cooperation approach, which focuses on religious pluralism rather than social justice, may be more useful and productive when it comes to matters of religious diversity.

We draw our understanding of religious pluralism from the work of Eck (2002), who argues that diversity is simply the fact of people with different identities interacting with one another. Diversity, in other words, is merely descriptive; it does not tell us how those individuals are interacting with one another. In Eck's view, pluralism is an achievement, building constructive relationships where they might not otherwise exist. Indeed, research from Putnam (2007) suggests that when diversity is not constructively addressed, communities suffer, leading individuals to "hunker down" (p. 149), stepping away from civic engagement and increasing suspicion of those who are different.

As Nash (2001) has argued, pluralism requires the right to dissent; although baseline civility and a commitment to engagement, relationship, and encounter is required, a particular political or ideological commitment to social justice is not. This is significant. We have campus partners who understand religious pluralism to be a result of or in full alignment with a vision for social justice, whereas we understand religious pluralism is about the robust and healthy functioning of a religiously diverse society, where those with progressive and conservative commitments are in active relationships and partnerships with one another, in spite of real disagreements.

In the remainder of this chapter, we continue to explore these two approaches for engaging religious diversity in higher education. We begin with considering why social justice is central to how many student affairs educators seek to engage diversity on campus. From there, we hope to articulate some of the challenges we have seen arise when engaging with religious and worldview diversity in a way that prioritizes social justice.

Religious Diversity and Social Justice

Growth of a Social Justice Approach

As Mueller and Broido (2012) argue, there has been a gradual shift from understanding diversity in higher education as being purely about demographics (i.e., ensuring there is racial, ethnic, gender, and socioeconomic diversity present in institutions) to one that asks about the quality of the education being received across all groups. This shift was prompted by the slow realization that diversification of a student body did not necessarily lead to educational success of marginalized or minority groups. Such attention to quality and access necessitates questions of what structures and realities might be inhibiting success for nondominant groups. Engaging diversity in higher education thus "is no longer only about increasing differences, responding to differences, and understanding and appreciating differences; it is also about interrupting systems that give privileges to some groups and confronting reluctance to dismantle those systems" (Mueller & Broido, 2012, pp. 90–91).

Thus, the very history of engaging with diversity in higher education has been one of a gradual awakening to the realities of inequality, lack of opportunity, and power structures that prevent many marginalized groups from experiencing the full possibility of their educational experience. A clear emphasis on seeking social justice in the form of overturning those structures of injustice is embedded in many current approaches to diversity (Landreman & MacDonald-Dennis, 2013). Although the primary result of these efforts may be to improve the educational experience of all students, it is fair to say that the goals of many educators extend beyond the campus educational experience to dismantling systems of oppression throughout society and, indeed, equipping students to do the same.

Based on this reading of the history of diversity and inclusion in higher education, engaging with diversity is not a value-neutral project; rather, for many student affairs educators, their work is oriented toward social justice, an end goal many educators name explicitly. As such, this work focuses on heightening students' and educators' critical consciences and disrupting the structures of inequality on campus as well as equipping students to continue this work beyond campus. Although this social justice–oriented work is, of course, only one element of the work student affairs educators do, it is worth noting the prevalence of this approach when discussing issues of diversity, identity, and inclusion. For example, these notions are built into the very ways that major student affairs organizations—ACPA–College Student Educators International and NASPA–Student Affairs Administrators in Higher Education (2016)—understand staff competencies in diversity.

Because of this connection between diversity and social justice in higher education, for many student affairs professionals and the student leaders they support, it is a natural move to see engaging with religious and worldview diversity on campus as part of the project of seeking social justice. Religious or worldview identity is, after all, another form of identity that is often deeply meaningful for students; confronting Christian privilege as well as seeking to empower marginalized or oppressed minority religious groups is necessary work on many college campuses. It follows that this work would fit well under existing social justice–oriented paradigms of identity engagement on campus.

Tensions Between Social Justice and Religious Pluralism

We have found, however, that engaging with religious and worldview diversity through a lens of social justice can seem to necessitate certain commitments that may be alienating for many religious students. In our experience, activities and programs focusing on social justice often have embedded, explicitly or implicitly, progressive political convictions. Put differently, an articulation of social justice that seeks to understand society and relationships in terms of power, privilege, and oppression often looks like a project that necessitates political commitments that may not be shared by many who hope to be included in interfaith work. Activities such as interfaith marches in favor of the Black Lives Matter movement, a training for resident advisers that teaches them about religious diversity by emphasizing Christian privilege, or interfaith advocacy for progressive political causes position interfaith engagement as complementary to progressive social action. Although this is often the case, as throughout history people have used interfaith engagement as a tool to further progressive social change, these types of activities may also marginalize many religious believers who might otherwise be interested in participating in interfaith activities.

Furthermore, for many deeply committed religious believers, the very notion of justice is shaped by how their race, ethnicity, or gender, for example, interacts with their religious identity. These observations will likely be intuitive for student affairs professionals who take seriously the idea of intersectionality. For example, Molly Harris, a Jewish student at McGill University in Montréal recounts being alienated and excluded from the progressive causes she cares most about such as feminist and lesbian, gay, bisexual, transgender, and queer issues and environmental activism because of her pro-Zionist commitments. In a diversity training session, she was told that although she may have experienced being oppressed for being a female, Jews are a privileged class in the United States and therefore any oppression she felt as a Jew was not legitimate (Harris, 2016). As a result, Molly felt she could not participate in many social justice issues she was drawn to because her experiences as a religious minority were not valued.

Molly is certainly not the only example of this. A Roman Catholic student, inspired by her traditions' articulation of Catholic social teaching on the core value of human dignity, might find herself aligned with several social justice causes on poverty and working to empower the marginalized while also insisting on pro-life values when it comes to abortion. A Muslim student might find himself committed to activism on Palestine while maintaining more conservative opinions on gender and sexuality. Engaging with religious identity raises the frequent possibility that the notion of justice itself will be contested.

We raise these questions because in an increasingly divided nation we feel acutely the need to create opportunities for building relationships across genuinely difficult religious, secular, political, and ideological divides. But we know this approach raises a challenge of competing priorities. For a student affairs professional committed to building social justice and religious pluralism, which should be prioritized? An uncompromising commitment to social justice that may alienate certain religious believers or downplaying certain commitments in an effort to engage with religious and secular students despite the deep theological and ideological disagreements that exist?

For those whose religious identity calls them to a politically conservative set of commitments, interfaith efforts that focus on social justice may lead them to feel these efforts are about including people of all diverse religious and philosophical identities *except for them*. When interfaith cooperation is assumed to be a progressive project, many religious believers may feel like they are not welcome, despite their desire to meet and engage with students of diverse backgrounds. In our work, despite the difficulties, we maintain that relationships across lines of religious and philosophical difference can be deeply transformative, so we understand it to be a genuine loss when the explicit premise or implied assumptions of an interfaith event might exclude people who want to participate because of their political or theological convictions on justice.

We do recognize, however, that many students and student affairs professionals may feel that their commitment to social justice is nonnegotiable. These commitments may be just as personally significant as the religious commitments we discussed earlier and are in fact often derived from deeply held values, including explicitly religious and secular beliefs. At the same time, we want to ask if there are benefits in terms of community and relationship building when such commitments to social justice are not required for dialogue so that more people may feel willing to come to the table. In the next section, we look more closely at our understanding of interfaith cooperation in light of these questions and present some of the critiques we have encountered from our partners in student affairs.

Interfaith Cooperation and Religious Pluralism

Interfaith cooperation begins with the assumption that when bringing together individuals of different religious and philosophical perspectives, real disagreements, tensions, and contestations of the meaning of justice will emerge. Interfaith cooperation also assumes there are genuine opportunities to build relationships based on mutual respect, shared values, and a commitment to common action. In our experience of interfaith cooperation, we expect there will be difficult and conflicting understandings of what justice looks like; we ask how individuals might still come together in equal dignity and mutual loyalty.

Because of our conviction that religious and worldview diversity poses unique challenges, we think authentic engagement requires interfaith cooperation to be more than just a dialogue of agreement among the most progressive members of every religion and worldview. The question is how to create spaces where authentic conversation, relationship, and common action can happen across religious and worldview lines, including the voices of all the people who are willing to come together with those who believe something very different from what they believe.

We believe that religious pluralism, which is the interaction of individuals with different religious identities and perspectives, can best be achieved through interfaith cooperation. Interfaith cooperation has three characteristics: respect for diverse religious and philosophical identities, mutually inspiring relationships across lines of difference, and common action for the common good (Patel, 2016).

Respect for diverse religious and philosophical identities means that individuals have a right to form their own religious or worldview identity and a right to express that identity. It also means those identities should be reasonably accommodated. This might mean everything from creating adequate facilities for the observance of various religious practices on campuses to ensuring that those from all religious and worldviews have the space to share their stories and have their voices heard. Respect for identity entails affirmation (e.g., supporting the right of others to have religious commitments one might personally disagree with) and accommodation (e.g., opportunities for Muslim women to swim in the campus swimming pool even when those affirmations and accommodations may cause others discomfort). To respect someone's identity does not require agreement but does require a community or society where everyone has the freedom to express that identity, regardless of the discomfort it may cause.

Mutually inspiring relationships across lines of difference require the existence of mutually inspiring relationships across lines of religious and worldview differences. By *relationship*, we mean positive, constructive, warm, caring, and cooperative engagement, which might take the form of informal conversations and activities as well as formal civic associations. On campus this means casual conversations among diverse students in the dining halls or residence halls about religious values and convictions, as well as formal partnerships among diverse groups like a regular meeting between Hillel and the Muslim Students Association. In these relationships, religious and worldview identity are not ignored nor are differences downplayed; instead, interfaith cooperation means engagement in full awareness that there are areas of commonality and divergence and a commitment to care for one another in recognition of both. In this scenario, when it comes time for students on campus to discuss Israel and Palestine, for instance, having strong relationships well in advance of contentious conversations makes it more likely that the relationships can withstand the sharp disagreements that may arise.

Finally, common action for the common good comes from our experience that something powerful and transformative happens when those of different religions can identify matters of broad shared concern and work together on those matters. Interfaith cooperation requires a move beyond just articulating the value of diverse identities and finding opportunities for relationship building. Rather than assuming that all are in general consensus on a certain vision of justice, interfaith cooperation requires the hard work of identifying shared values and defining a common good in spite of disagreements and diversity.

What the common good looks like will inevitably vary depending on the community defining it. In a community where conservative and progressive voices are working together, interfaith cooperation will be more likely to focus on, say, tutoring in a local school as opposed to activism on reproductive rights. For many driven by a commitment to social justice, this work of defining and working on a shared common good might feel like a compromise or neglect of critical and significant issues like addressing structural inequality or fighting to uncover privilege. At the same time, we think interfaith cooperation has the potential to build deep and meaningful relationships, which in a moment of deep division in our public discourse and life together, will allow the opportunity for reconnecting over a vision for a shared life. The power of this common work is supported by social science research, which suggests that when those of diverse backgrounds engage in common work together or share networks of engagement, social capital is built, distrust goes down, and civic society strengthens (Putnam, 2007; Varshney, 2002).

Understanding the Limitations of Interfaith Cooperation

Although we believe that interfaith cooperation offers a powerful approach for engaging with religious and worldview diversity, we want to underscore that it is not without difficulties, particularly for those coming to diversity work with progressive social justice commitments. One could reasonably claim that interfaith cooperation is trying to create a neutral playing field that does not really exist by insisting all should have an equal voice in dialogue and conversation. Even further, by not challenging inequalities, many would argue that interfaith cooperation simply serves to perpetuate unjust structures. Indeed, our focus on shared storytelling and the value of everyone's story in relationship building is counter to the approach of much antiracism work that centers on the stories of those whose voices have often been silenced.

Another critique from this perspective is that interfaith cooperation may at times look blindly apologetic. By focusing on appreciation of diverse traditions and identities rather than critiquing problematic rhetoric or injustices perpetuated by various traditions, it can appear that interfaith cooperation is simply glossing over the many problematic aspects in diverse religious traditions. By this argument, interfaith cooperation dangerously ignores the ways traditions can be patriarchal and oppressive, have been complicit in violence, and stifle disagreement.

These critiques are not without weight and should be taken seriously by anyone working to engage with religious and worldview diversity on campus.

The degree to which they should be emphasized will no doubt be dependent on the campus context and the interreligious dynamics at play. At the same time, we think the benefits gained from an interfaith cooperation approach deal productively with the unique challenges posed by religious diversity on campus and offer some important constructive and community-building tools that might be absent from other approaches. In the next section, we explore the potential for interfaith cooperation in more detail.

The Promise of Interfaith Cooperation for Engaging With Religious Diversity

This focus on pluralism may be unsatisfying for many in student affairs who have a deep commitment to social justice and who may be concerned that not prioritizing social justice will lead them to not only compromise their convictions but also find themselves complicit in the oppression and structures of inequality they seek to disrupt. This critique of pluralism resonates for us personally because of our theological and political leanings. At the same time, we think that not only are pluralism and the strategies of interfaith cooperation, at times necessitated by the unique challenge posed by religious and worldview diversity but also there are important positive reasons that those negotiating religious and worldview diversity on campus may find interfaith cooperation compelling.

Deepening Engagement

We have briefly touched on this already, but our hope in our work is that in a moment marked by deep partisan divides and what often feels like an entrenched unwillingness for those on opposing sides to interact with each other, interfaith cooperation can bring together those who otherwise might never share their stories. At an IFYC student training session several years ago, two students sat down together in dialogue: a liberal, transgender woman who identified as mainline Protestant Christian, and an evangelical conservative Christian who was the son of a Republican state lawmaker. We can imagine many spaces on campus, social media, or at local community events where these two might have encountered each other and simply seen each other as "other," an opponent to be battled on any number of issues. But the prompt we gave them—to talk about what in their religious or ethical perspective inspired them to work with and be in relationship with others—shifted the tenor of a conversation that might otherwise have felt intractable. Because interfaith cooperation starts with the assumption that relationships are possible, there are shared values across religions and worldviews, and there are real disagreements, the students found it possible to hear one another in a way they had not done previously. Instead of viewing each other with distrust and fear, they heard things in each other's stories that resonated with them. Furthermore, for the first time, they began to see a way to talk about their differences openly and honestly. Their relationship continued when they returned to campus, and they organized several interfaith projects and events together.

Hearing All Stories

The emphasis on respect for diverse identities in interfaith cooperation means that when acknowledging the realities of privilege and oppression, everyone's story and perspective should be heard. This work requires both sides to humanize the other, which in our current political and civic discourse seems an increasingly difficult task. It also allows individuals to share their deepest convictions with someone they disagree with. For someone committed to a progressive vision of social justice, this may mean there is a real opportunity to share a progressive vision of the world with someone who might not be open to that perspective. A commitment to interfaith cooperation insists that individuals can hope they will change their conversation partners' minds, as long as they adhere to agreed-on guidelines for civil discourse.

That being said, if we want others to be comfortable with our progressive social justice commitments, interfaith cooperation requires us to allow a conservative Christian's desire to convert others, for example, or disagreement on key political issues with a conservative Hindu. As Callahan said,

> I contend that it is perfectly appropriate in a pluralistic society for the various cultures within it to comment on and criticize each other—and where necessary attempt to change by persuasion each other's values when they seem harmful or mistaken . . . criticism and persuasion, yes; coercion, no. (quoted in Nash, 2001, p. 44)

At a time when our nation's divides seem so deep, we think creating space for this kind of encounter, critique, and relationship building is a profoundly countercultural activity that illustrates the transformative role higher education often seeks to play in the world.

Appreciating Diverse Traditions

Finally, the methodology of interfaith cooperation creates a focus on religious and worldview diversity that seeks to acknowledge what is constructive, good, inspiring, and beautiful in diverse traditions. In our work, we insist there is something to be gained from hearing and sharing positive, apprecia-tive stories and values from diverse traditions, even those that may be con-sidered privileged. Several years ago, when Patel spoke at a Christian college, the chaplain asked if she should remove the cross at the front of the room where Patel was speaking in case its presence was offensive or somehow hin-dered Patel's religious observance. This particular college had a long history of seeking to embody Christian values in its educational vision and had been one of the first schools in the Midwest to accept African American students in the 1800s. For Patel, that cross stood as a symbol of the radical work they had done in the past and the radical work they were doing now to think about interfaith cooperation by inviting a Muslim to speak in their chapel. Patel asked the chaplain to keep the cross front and center as a reminder for Patel to look to his Muslim faith and ask what in it inspires him to make the world a better place.

An emphasis on privilege and power in this situation may have resulted in removal of the cross and acknowledging all the ways Christianity has been harmful to religious minorities or focusing on the many microaggressions Muslims face in a predominantly Christian society. In contrast, keeping the cross in the chapel allowed a proclamation of the transformative work that a particular reading of Christian theology and ethics had played at that institu-tion. Thus, without negating the importance of these critiques, we want to ask what might be gained when we open up space for appreciation of diverse traditions.

Conclusion

We have attempted to show that religious and worldview identities can com-plicate a common approach to engaging with diversity in higher education that emphasizes social justice, power, and oppression. We suggest that an interfaith cooperation approach may be more effective for dealing with the complexities of religious and worldview diversity, and it has the potential to help create robust, healthy, diverse campus communities.

Our hope for interfaith cooperation is that it creates spaces for under-standing and connection that are often all too rare in our current politi-cal and civic climate. We want to foster more conversations like the one between the progressive transgender Christian woman and the conservative Republican evangelical, who, despite eating in the same dining hall, going to classes together, and walking the same paths across campus, have never had a real opportunity to get to know one another and ask what they might have in common. We imagine them building the kind of relationship that allows common ground and voicing disagreement, the kind that will shape the relationships they build in their professions and civic lives long after they have left campus. We see the work of interfaith cooperation as another step in the movement in higher education to create a more equitable and just world. The work ahead will be in finding the ways interfaith cooperation and a social justice framework can be employed to support students in navigating religious and worldview identities.

Note

1. Although the language is imperfect, we understand the interfaith movement to be inclusive of all those who come together despite different religious and secular commitments to relationship and common action. *Religious and worldview diversity* is meant to include people across the religious, ethical, and philosophical spectrum, including atheists, agnostics, humanists, those who identify as spiritual but not religious, those who identify with multiple traditions, and those who firmly identify with a single religious tradition. For a longer discussion, see Patel (2016).

References

ACPA–College Student Educators International & NASPA–Student Affairs Administrators in Higher Education. (2016). *ACPA/NASPA professional competencies rubric.* Retrieved from https://www.naspa.org/images/uploads/main/ACPA_NASPA_Professional_Competency_Rubrics_Full.pdf

Eck, D. (2002). *A new religious America: How a Christian country has become the world's most religiously diverse nation* (2nd ed.). San Francisco, CA: HarperCollins.

Graham, R. (2016, October 13). The professor wore a hijab in solidarity—then lost her job. *New York Times.* Retrieved from https://www.nytimes.com/2016/10/16/magazine/the-professor-wore-a-hijab-in-solidarity-then-lost-her-job.html

Harris, M. (2016, August 23). So you're a Jew and you're starting college? Prepare for anti-Zionism. *Washington Post.* Retrieved from https://www.washingtonpost.com/news/acts-of-faith/wp/2016/08/23/so-youre-a-jew-and-youre-starting-college-prepare-for-anti-zionism/

Jacobsen, D., & Jacobsen, R. H. (2012). *No longer invisible: Religion in university education.* New York: NY: Oxford University Press.

Landreman, L. M., & MacDonald-Dennis, C. (2013). The evolution of social justice education and facilitation. In Landreman, L. M. (Ed.), *The art of effective facilitation: Reflections from social justice educators* (pp. 3–22). Sterling, VA: Stylus.

Merritt, J. (2016, October 7). InterVarsity's move on gay marriage. *Atlantic.* Retrieved from https://www.theatlantic.com/politics/archive/2016/10/campus-ministry-a-culture-war-outpost/503426/

Mueller, J. A., & Broido, E. M. (2012). Historical context: Who we were is part of who we are. In J. Arminio, V. Torres, and R. L. Pope (Eds.), *Why aren't we there yet? Taking personal responsibility for creating an inclusive campus* (pp. 57–101). Sterling, VA: Stylus.

Nagourney, A. (2015, March 5). In U.C.L.A. debate over Jewish student, echoes on campus of old biases. *New York Times.* Retrieved from https://www.nytimes.com/2015/03/06/us/debate-on-a-jewish-student-at-ucla.html

Nash, R. (2001). *Religious pluralism in the academy: Opening the dialogue.* New York, NY: Peter Lang.

Patel, E. (2016). *Interfaith leadership: A primer.* Boston, MA: Beacon Press.

Patel, E., & Meyer, C. (2011). The civic relevance of interfaith cooperation for higher education. *Journal of College and Character, 12*(1), 1–9.

Putnam, R. D. (2007). *E pluribus unum:* Diversity and community in the twenty-first century. *Scandinavian Political Studies, 30,* 137–174.

Stewart, D. L. (2012). Promoting moral growth through pluralism and social justice education. *New Directions for Student Services,* 139, 63–72.

Southern Poverty Law Center. (2017). *Hate groups increase for second consecutive year as Trump electrifies radical right.* Retrieved from https://www.splcenter.org/news/2017/02/15/hate-groups-increase-second-consecutive-year-trump-electrifies-radical-right

Varshney, A (2002). *Ethnic conflict and civic life: Hindus and Muslims in India.* New Haven, CT: Yale University Press.

PART TWO

TEACHING IDEAS FOR
STUDENT AFFAIRS FACULTY

Kathleen M. Goodman

Part two of this book is written specifically for faculty in student affairs preparation programs who are looking for ways to address spirituality, religion, and secularity with their courses and programs. In chapter 4, three faculty members describe the courses they have developed specifically to address this topic. In chapter 5, two faculty members provide suggestions for how to incorporate spirituality, religious diversity, and interfaith engagement into courses that exist in many student affairs preparation programs: History of U.S. Higher Education, Higher Education Environments, College Student Development Theory, Diversity in Higher Education, and Student Affairs Practicum. Chapter 6 describes reflection exercises for use in or out of the classroom designed to help student affairs graduate students explore spirituality and professional purpose.

We recognize that every institution and student affairs program have their own unique context and culture. Therefore, it is unlikely that any of the courses, course additions, or programs described in this part of the book can be adopted without change. However, we have provided considerable details in each chapter hoping to give you enough information to inspire you to adopt some of these ideas for use in your program.

Faculty in student affairs preparation programs will find additional chapters of this book useful as well. Part four includes a series of case studies that could be used in the classroom or in professional development sessions. Part five includes chapters elucidating foundational knowledge of several religions and advice for working with students who identify with those religions.

4

DEVELOPING COURSES THAT ENGAGE SPIRITUALITY, RELIGION, AND SECULARITY IN STUDENT AFFAIRS PREPARATION PROGRAMS

Kathleen M. Goodman, Sherry K. Watt, and Tricia A. Seifert

For several decades, a considerable amount of literature has urged student affairs practitioners to attend to students' spiritual development (e.g., Astin, 2004; Astin, Astin, & Lindholm, 2011; Jablonski, 2001; Love & Talbot, 2000). Spirituality has been deemed a central component of students' holistic development (ACPA–College Student Educators International & NASPA–Student Affairs Administrators in Higher Education, 2004) and is associated with several academic outcomes, including leadership development, satisfaction with college, and academic performance (Astin et al., 2011). Yet in our experience, we find that few student affairs preparation programs provide the knowledge and skills necessary for new practitioners to attend to students' spiritual development.

Our goal in this chapter is to inspire educators to develop courses focused on spirituality, religion, and secularity in student affairs. We begin by sharing our stories of a course we experienced together in fall 2005 that shaped each of our approaches to teaching in this area. Sherry Watt taught a doctoral seminar on student affairs practice, focused specifically on spirituality in student affairs. Tricia Seifert and Kathy Goodman were students in the class. Our stories illustrate that although we took this course together, our motivations, reactions, and takeaways were quite different. The course inspired Tricia and Kathy to develop their own courses on *spirituality* (we use different language now, as discussed later), and Sherry has continued to teach the course in new ways. In the remainder of this chapter, we describe some approaches and content used in the courses we currently teach that we hope provides concrete inspiration and ideas for those seeking to develop their own courses.

Sherry's Story: Teaching in Liminal Spaces

In 2005, I was an assistant professor, African American, cisgender and female, heterosexual, and Christian. The doctoral seminar focused on pondering critical questions affecting higher education and student affairs practice. I viewed it as an opportunity to apply findings of my research, which focuses on participant reactions to difficult dialogues (issues such as racism, sexism, heterosexism) to issues in the field. What I loved about these seminars was the gift of the thinking space to wrestle with these questions along with the fresh minds of our developing scholars.

Prior to 2005, I had always chosen the seminar topic of exploring perceptions of race and racism on college campuses. There were few students of color in the course over the years, so I taught this course predominantly to White females and a small number of White males. Students received this theme with a wide range of emotional reactions. The mix of positive and negative feelings often resulted in consequences for me as the instructor. Some students were highly engaged in the conversation, which I found to be particularly gratifying as a person and intellectually rewarding as a scholar. Other students expressed frustration with being forced to face a controversial topic, and they took out their hostility on me by striking out in class, complaining to my colleagues, or expressing their dismay in course evaluations. I felt vulnerable as an African American untenured faculty member. I found simultaneously teaching and researching this topic personally exhausting. I decided that I needed a break from talking about race and racism in the seminar and decided that I would instead explore faith and spirituality on college campuses. Looking back, I do not know if I thought about whether this topic would be more or less controversial. I just knew I wanted an emotional break. However, I was not consciously aware that I was choosing to retreat into one of my privileged identities as a Christian.

You are probably not surprised to hear that the shift to focus on faith and spirituality did not leave behind the complexities of race and racism. Exploring this topic just shifted the lens from a central to a peripheral view on examining issues of race and racism and other social oppressions that manifest themselves on college campuses. For instance, we could not discuss religion without wrestling with the intersections of race with Christianity, Judaism, or Islam, or sexual orientation and fundamentalist Christian ideology. We could not leave behind our marginalized or privileged racial identities, our gender identities, our assigned sex, or the power dynamics inherent in student–faculty relationships. Indeed, we proactively examined the overriding ways Christianity and Christian privilege silences or limits space for explorations of other religions, secular, or nontheistic belief systems on college campuses.

Structured learning opportunities in this course revealed the roots of our belief systems and how religious privilege plays out on college campuses (Watt, Fairchild, & Goodman, 2009). It was serendipitous and fortunate that the students in that particular semester aligned with various forms of meaning-making. We had fertile ground to plant and grow. Along with the varying spiritual, religious, and secular perspectives of each class member, this group of students took their assignments and discussions in directions that explored the intersections of identities that expanded our views of the topic as well as our understanding of experiences and ideologies that were different from the belief systems of those in the class. We were able to honorably, though not perfectly, navigate a seemingly taboo topic in a public education system.

Today as a full professor, I share power in the classroom and create the space for controversy in a way that is still often met with resistance. I still question whether the costs to my personal psyche outweigh the benefits. Nine days out of 10, my answer is a resounding yes. These are disparate times in our country where, to my recollection, the divides among our philosophical, political, and social belief systems are revealing deep rifts in worldviews that have not been this pronounced since the 1950s and the Civil Rights Movement of the 1960s. This work is more important than ever.

Kathy's Story: The Struggle Is Real

I had never heard the phrase "The struggle is real," but if I had, I would have used it often during that first year of my doctoral program in 2005. I lived my first 39 years in the Northeast and moved to the University of Iowa to join the student affairs administration and research (SAAR) doctoral program in fall 2005. I had conducted an extensive exploration of possible doctoral programs and felt that SAAR was the ideal fit for me. Five days before classes started, my confidence in program fit was shaken when I went to the bookstore to purchase books for that first semester.

I was taking a required doctoral seminar from Sherry Watt. I had heard the course was focused on race, and I was excited to begin developing my understanding of racial diversity in student affairs. Therefore, I was truly puzzled that the books I was picking up had titles such as *Big Questions, Worthy Dreams* (Parks, 2000), *Exploring Spirituality and Culture in Adult Higher Education* (Tisdell, 2003), and *To Know as We Are Known: Education as a Spiritual Journey* (Palmer, 1993). I looked at the bookshelf nearby, thinking that the books for my course were misplaced. I opened up my course schedule to make sure I had the right course number. And finally, I simply stood, dumbfounded, for several minutes. Eventually, I bought the books, concluded that the course was about spirituality, and began to question whether coming to the University of Iowa was a good choice.

I know that sounds dramatic. I would have gone so far as to call it traumatic at the time. I did not want to take a course on spirituality, and I couldn't understand why it was being forced on me. I was an atheist, although I rarely thought about it and had never spoken about it to anyone other than my partner. I didn't have the language at the time, but I felt that *spirituality* was a word used in student affairs in an attempt to be universal, but it really was a mask for Christian privilege.

The rational part of me told me to be open, patient, and to learn from Sherry about her vision for the course. Unfortunately, the irrational part of me blurted out in the middle of the doctoral student orientation, "I don't understand why we *have* to take a course on spirituality. It is irrelevant to me." Although I don't remember much of the conversation that ensued, I remember Sherry's smile as she said that she hadn't thought the course would be controversial. She rubbed her hands together (think evil scientist) and stated, "This is going to be good." At that moment, I knew that Sherry would be open to multiple perspectives and that I would survive the class even if I didn't like it.

During the semester I had to be open about being an atheist and figure out what that meant to me. I also had the opportunity to lead one course session and pick the related readings, which allowed me to share atheist perspectives with my classmates.

Overall, the course was a personal and academic struggle for me. As I became more aware of my own atheism and learned about atheist students' experiences, I became more adamant that spirituality in student affairs was a Christian-centric concept, despite claims to the contrary. During every reading discussion in the course, I pointed out that the definitions and activities provided were not inclusive for non-Christian and nonbelieving students. My classmates were patient, but I sensed they were frustrated with me. I know I was frustrated with them for not getting it.

It became my personal mission in life to show the bias inherent in spirituality in student affairs by making presentations at conferences and writing articles such as *Beyond Spirituality: A New Framework for Educators* (Goodman & Teraguchi, 2008). The topic consumed me and my friend Tricia, who was also in the class. We definitely were not on the same page about spirituality in student affairs, but we both wanted to understand each other's perspective. We talked about the course at every possible moment, driving to conferences, during social gatherings, and while we were at our mutual assistantship site.

That course, the discomfort it caused, and the all-consuming conversations about it were a learning experience that became central to my work as an assistant professor of student affairs in higher education. I have moved from my argumentative stance about spirituality in student affairs, although I still advocate for inclusive language and approaches. Rather than thinking of spirituality as a college outcome, I conceptualize it as a means to an end. Spirituality provides a way (which I call pathway) for students to develop values, find meaning in life, and cultivate a life purpose. Religion and secularity and atheism are also pathways that students may use to find meaning, purpose, and values. My current research and scholarly writing focuses on these pathways. I have also developed a course about spirituality, religion, and secularity in student affairs (described later in this chapter), which has become my most meaningful and favorite teaching experience.

Tricia's Story: Evolving My Understanding

Unlike Kathy I was excited about the spirituality in student affairs class. Initially, I was disappointed that this seminar would not address issues of race, racism, and privilege in the United States, but I knew enough about religion, spirituality, faith, and belief to know they intersect in meaningful ways with race, ethnicity, and culture.

The class opened my eyes in ways that I didn't think possible. I came to realize that worldview (whether connected to a religious tradition, a deeply held personal spirituality, or a secular belief structure) is the dimension of diversity that has historically driven people to take up arms against their neighbors near and far and continues to do so today. The world has witnessed war because of differences in belief for millennia. If my desire was to examine dimensions of diversity, the growing diversity of U.S. college students' worldviews (Eagan et al., 2016) as shown in the spirituality in student affairs course provided a powerful learning opportunity.

Adams's (1997) chapter, "My Grandmother and the Snake," presented the intersectionality of race, culture, and spirituality in stark relief. In my class session, I chose to focus on indigenous students because of the transformative learning experience I had while learning about some of these spiritual and cultural practices. They contrasted profoundly with my own Protestant upbringing and caused me to think deeply about what I really knew about spirituality; indeed, I felt challenged by comparing my own upbringing with what I learned about indigenous spirituality.

I understood that one of the goals of the spirituality in student affairs course was to enhance our understanding of the role belief plays in undergraduate students' development. Of course this concern for the whole student is consistent with the field of student affairs' long-standing commitment to holistic student development (American Council on Education, 1937). I came away from the course thinking, "If I am to support students in achieving their academic goals as well as reflecting on and developing their worldview, I have to nurture my curiosity to learn about other religions, faiths, beliefs, and worldviews."

I intentionally use the phrase "evolve my understanding" to describe this learning process because cultural learning is a lifelong pursuit. One never arrives. Nowhere is this more evident than in comparing my understanding today to what formed the basis for one of my earliest articles, *Understanding Christian Privilege* (Seifert, 2007). Through my experience in the doctoral seminar, I was deeply influenced by the work of Clark, Brimhall-Vargas, Schlosser, and Alimo's (2002) use of Peggy McIntosh's White privilege framework to identify the ways Christian privilege exists in our culture and on college campuses. The fall semester's conclusion, conveniently at Christmas, now loomed large in my consciousness. Like a fish first feeling the water, I saw Christian privilege all around me. But cultural learning never ends, and my newfound sight provided blinders in another area, which I am thankful to my friend Kathy for helping me see. I came to realize that my focus on Christian privilege prevented me from seeing the *religious* privilege that pervades our culture. My relationship with Kathy helped me recognize how natural it was for educators to assume that one's worldview is connected to a religious faith tradition or a personal spirituality. It was as if I were seated at a dinner party, and my atheist friend did not have a place at the table (Nash, 2003).

I am grateful that Kathy was *good company* (a term I first encountered in Baxter Magolda, 2002) for me as my understanding of religious privilege evolved. Thinking about how educators can be good company as students wrestle with life's big questions (Who am I? What do I want to do? How do I want to be in my career and community?) is the foundation for much of the spirituality and higher education scholarship (Nash & Murray, 2009; Parks, 2000) and served as the building block for the Educators' Search for Purpose and Meaning course I taught at Montana State University in spring 2016.

Our Stories Influence the Courses We Teach

Our experiences in the spirituality class influenced our thoughts about spirituality, religion, and secularity, how those topics relate to race, and how we think about privilege. The courses we each teach now reflect those ideas, both in content and approach. In the following section, Sherry focuses on process as she explains how to use the authentic, action-oriented framing for environmental shifts (AAFES) method (Watt, 2015a) as an approach to teaching across differences such as religion, spirituality, and secularity. It is followed by Tricia's description of the course she teaches, Educators' Search for Purpose and Meaning, which is grounded in deep personal reflection. This section concludes with a description of Kathy's course, Spirituality, Religion, and Secularity in Student Affairs, which focuses on personal reflection on one's beliefs, the development of skills needed for interfaith engagement, and the incorporation of these topics into student affairs practice.

Sherry's Course: Setting Up the Environmental Conditions for Engaging in Controversial Dialogue

I believe it is important to create opportunities for people to practice interacting across controversial differences. Spirituality, religion, and secularity require discussions about how we view issues that are close to our hearts with perspectives that may be vastly different from those of our neighbors. I believe that exploring these controversies in a classroom setting increases the possibility for engaging difference productively, providing opportunities to strengthen the skills for engaging across difference. I believe that better skills for handling controversy can generate more just and inclusive outcomes when facing social problems on campus and in society. Courses on spirituality, religion, and secularity have this unique potential because of the integral nature of these ideologies in our daily lives. By *integral* I mean that these topics are the backdrop for who we are, how we view the world, how we were raised, what we are committed to, and what we value and believe.

I use the AAFES method (Watt, 2015a) to create the environmental conditions for engaging in meaningful controversial dialogue. The AAFES method is a process-oriented strategy that focuses on developing the skills of being in controversy. A process-oriented strategy means that this method focuses on how we exist together in controversial discussions and not on an outcome, a final result, or a decision. When focusing on process, the participants are invited to turn inward and explore their own identity, their relationship to the controversy, and how to communicate with others across their different perspectives and experiences. This method assumes that by attending to the process, productive and meaningful controversial dialogues will result in decision-making that leads to more just and inclusive practices. Next, I describe the AAFES method and how it can be employed when teaching courses on spirituality, religion, and secularity.

The AAFES method provides guideposts to create the environmental conditions that support the development of the skills needed for being amid controversies. The approach integrates ways of knowing that are part of intellect, emotion, and practice. The AAFES method process qualities include

> (a) being authentic by prioritizing self-exploration rather than solely analyzing the other, (b) being action-oriented by engaging in a thoughtful balance between dialogue and action, (c) reframing campus environments by embracing the realities of privilege, power and oppression (d) and creating welcoming spaces for inclusion and not just for surviving dehumanization. (Watt, 2015b, p. 138)

The authentic process quality includes thinking critically about one's own personal values and beliefs, nurturing the ideals and the practices of listening well to various perspectives, and being open to personal growth. Being authentic means that individuals examine their personal belief system, how it came to be, and how it fits within a social and political structure. The initial focus is on analyzing the self and not learning about others. A classroom instructor who intentionally aims to practice this process quality in the environment creates a space for community members to ponder the role spirituality, religion, and secularity plays not only in their own lives but also in society. This includes reflection and dialogue involving extensive examinations of the intersections of these ideas with power, privilege, and oppression. Creating an environment that values this exploration requires instructors to lead the group by example and is open to examining their own beliefs along with the students.

Being action oriented involves creating a learning space where explorations of spirituality, religion, and secularity are intentional reflections and examinations of how these issues translate to a real-world context. Action-oriented skills include leaving space for tolerating discomfort in the traditional classroom. This includes exploring not only thoughts but also emotional reactions to the content.

Framing for environmental shifts is a foundational characteristic of the AAFES approach. The teacher and the students question how spirituality, religion, and secularity may create structures for surviving dehumanization and name ways they see those structures playing out in society and on campus. For example, an instructor might create a case study that describes the use of space in a work setting and might explore the use of gathering space and how it differs for various religious and secular groups. The discussion might bring up the idea of what is needed in terms of space requirements for Muslim versus Christian students, for instance. The teacher intentionally poses questions that aim to increase opportunities for the students to consider how to transform an environment for inclusion. This might involve discussions in which the teacher and students practice deconstructing ideas such as the dominant culture influence, the ways to reimagine environments that prioritize serving the dominant group, and how to alter power structures.

It is my hope that the process-oriented approach described by the AAFES method can help to create learning environments whereby the teacher and the students can have meaningful dialogue about controversial and important topics in ways that matter. Students can then take these experiences and apply them to the opportunities they have leading group discussions about spirituality, religion, and secularity on college campuses as professionals.

Teaching courses on spirituality, religion, and secularity can be challenging because the topics are connected to students' belief systems that modulate how they interact with themselves, family, community, and society. When asking students to visit their belief system, examine the ways of knowing of others, and consider how it applies to professional practice, the teacher has to expect that controversial discussions will emerge in the classroom. Paying close attention to the process for creating the environmental conditions for authentic dialogue to deal with controversy can help the learning environment be more productive and the course content applications aimed at practice malleable enough so that students can implement their visions and design environments where multiple belief systems can respectfully coexist.

Tricia's Course: Educators' Search for Purpose and Meaning

I consciously chose not to use this course as a place to explore college students' diverse worldviews, even though this kind of exploration is an important undertaking. Instead, I wanted the course to focus on how educators can help students become comfortable asking, engaging, and wrestling with life's big questions. My goal was to help graduate students, many of whom are student affairs practitioners or future faculty members, see themselves as capable of being good company for students' journeys regardless of their religious, spiritual, or secular path. Despite the neoliberal and instrumental discourse that equates a college education with job training and workforce development, this graduate seminar invited students to consider college as a time when students "live the questions now" so that someday they "will be able to live into the answers" (Rilke, 1993[1903], p. 27). Taking into account that what is good for another is also good for oneself, the course centered on each individual student's personal engagement with big questions. To that end, reflection and keeping journals were included as critical skills and abilities for the course.

The course was crafted based on Parker Palmer's (2009) notion of community in a circle of trust. We spent the first weeks reading and discussing *A Hidden Wholeness: The Journey Toward an Undivided Life* (Palmer, 2009). Community was an important value of the course and was articulated in the syllabus with the following statement of disposition: Students in the course will appreciate community in developing an authentic educational practice. We adopted the ground rule that we were not in the class to fix people or solve their problems but to ask questions and listen so that each person could learn from the inner voice that is often silenced by someone else giving advice. It is important for student affairs practitioners to take the time to do their own inner work (Seifert & Holman-Harmon, 2009) because it is difficult to be good company for students if the practitioners have not taken the time to make the journey themselves.

I knew that part of any personal journey is holding the dynamic tension between solitude, what Nouwen (1986) calls the ability "to perceive and understand this world from a quiet inner center" (p. 38), and the fellowship one feels in communion with others. As the instructor, I carefully considered how to craft the course in a way that honored solitude and community. I acknowledged that the course had to be largely student-directed in that I could not know what readings or experiences would prompt students' personal journeys. In many ways, the course had a choose-your-own-adventure quality that was tethered by expectations for completing common assignments.

The course opened and concluded with an assignment that invited students to articulate their educator's statement of purpose by answering the question, What does it mean for me to educate? The objective of the assignment was to gauge the extent to which a semester of focused reflection on topics of purpose and meaning are manifested in students' understanding of themselves as educators. Along with the students' statements, they also named what part of the course (discussion, writing, reading, etc.) contributed to their answer. Although the statements did not always change substantively from the beginning to the end of the course, their articulation of their purpose of being an educator took on greater intentionality.

In addition to the two required texts, students chose six readings (articles, books, other media) and created abstracts of them for their classmates. I encouraged students to select from their metaphorical stacks about the educator's purpose, books they wished to read but never had the time for. Students' selections ranged widely from Frankl's (2006) *Man's Search for Meaning* to Brown's (2012) *Daring Greatly*. The abstracts were part book report, part personal meaning-making, and part practical application. The abstracts allowed others to learn the piece's central thesis, gain insight into their classmates' understanding of the thesis including points of agreement and critique, and consider how they might use this piece in their educational practice. Our collective abstracts, shared on the university's online portal, constituted a resource compendium for inspiration in future work.

Advancing the notion of personal journey, students were invited to adopt a focal practice for a portion of the course. We read a chapter from Boers's (2012) *Living Into Focus* in which *focal practices* are defined as commanding presence, providing continuity, and having the power to center us. Focal practices require energy and effort, they demand discipline and attention. Moreover, they connect past, present, and future moments so that we might recognize the continuity of our world. Finally, focal practices center us to reflect on what is truly needed and why. Focal practices have the capacity to lead us into a state of flow (Csikszentmihalyi, 1990). I shared my focal practice of baking bread from a sourdough starter, the yeast connecting me to thousands of bakers across space and time. In the hectic nature of our day-to-day activities, engaging in a focal practice appeared to be one of the hardest assignments in the class.

Walking 150 miles on the Camino de Santiago trail together brought the course concepts of community in a circle of trust, solitude and hospitality, and focal practice into stark relief. This was an optional part of the course that almost half of the students took advantage of. We walked our focal practice, one foot in front of the other, through eucalyptus forests and in the sweltering heat over the Little Pyrénées. Together we endured badly blistered feet but honored the commitment not to solve someone's problems or fix the person; instead, we asked individuals what they needed. Some days it was providing Band-Aids; other days, an Epsom salt foot soak; and on other days, it was shouldering someone's backpack, literally lightening their load. What I recall the most vividly, though, were moments of divine hospitality when I believe I offered good company on the journey. These were times of profound mentorship when I listened about the challenges faced with doctoral study or when I learned about someone's perspective on family.

On the trail, we were not teacher and students but *peregrinas* and *peregrinos*—pilgrims, travelers. Two weeks of walking solidified and exemplified what I had sought to accomplish during the semester, that is, engage personally in one's inner work to be good company on another's journey.

Kathy's Course: Spirituality, Religion, and Secularity in Student Affairs

As I began to design my course, I asked myself, what do I want students to gain from it? I knew that the course I was designing had to address spirituality, religion, and secularity on multiple levels—personal, interpersonal, and professional. In a former iteration of the course, I found the students reluctant to share their perspectives because they were afraid they might offend someone of different beliefs simply by sharing their own. Therefore, I had to think developmentally about the risks I was asking them to take. I designed the course for the following outcomes:

- Understand the many ways that spirituality, religion, and secularity manifest themselves in the lives of colleges students and educators.
- Reflect on and articulate the spiritual, religious, or secular influences on students' life values, purpose, and meaning.
- Cultivate knowledge and skills to engage in discussions with individuals of differing spiritual, religious, and secular perspectives.
- Develop a campus plan for integrating spiritual, religious, secular, and interfaith learning opportunities for students.

A Scaffolded Approach

During the first two weeks of class, I provided opportunities for the students to see interfaith engagement among other people, which required no risk from them. During the first week of class, we watched an episode of a documentary, *30 Days* (Spurlock, 2010), in which a Christian man moved in with a Muslim family for 30 days to learn about Islam. Although the video portrayal is somewhat contrived, I wanted the students to see that there were people willing to risk learning from one another even though they began with antagonistic feelings about the other's beliefs and perspectives.

During the second week of class, I invited my faculty colleagues to join me in a fishbowl activity in which we took part in an interfaith discussion in the center of the room while the students watched. This was my way of role modeling what the students perceived as risky. It happened that the faculty who participated represented a variety of worldviews, including Catholicism, Judaism, agnosticism, atheism, spiritual but not religious, and one who was uncertain of his beliefs. After the faculty modeled discussion, I asked the students to engage in a similar discussion in small groups and told them they could pass if they did not want to answer a question. One purpose of the activity was to provide an opportunity for students to think about what they believed and how to articulate it. A second purpose was for them to encounter differing perspectives. When we debriefed the small-group activity, I asked questions about the process rather than beliefs. I wanted them to explain how it felt to engage in the conversation, especially when differing opinions were shared.

As the semester progressed, the perceived riskiness of the activities increased. During the middle of the course, I set aside a portion of class time for an activity called Who Am I?, which I created based on Interfaith Youth Core's Speedfaithing activity (Interfaith Youth Core, n.d.). All students had 10 minutes to talk about their spiritual, religious, or secular beliefs, their journey to that belief, and their values related to their belief. After they spoke to the whole class, the floor was open for an additional 10 minutes for the rest of the class to ask them follow-up questions.

By the end of the course, the students were feeling good about the risks they had taken over the course of the semester and were interested in engaging in a whole-class dialogue. I provided the questions ahead of time so they could think about them a bit, but I asked them not to formulate responses. The point of the dialogue was to authentically discuss the big questions focused on the topic Why am I? as a follow-up to the semester-long focus on Who am I? The questions came directly from, or were adaptions of *Preparing Students for Life Beyond College* (Nash & Jang, 2015), which is an excellent source of questions about meaning and purpose in life. Of the hundred or so questions in the book, we focused on the following:

1. What is the purpose of your life?
2. If money were not an issue, what would you do with your life, now and for the rest of your life?
3. What gives meaning to your life?
4. If you knew you could not fail, what would you choose to do?
5. Why do people exist, and how does your answer to that question influence how you live?

Course Readings and Topics

Although this was not a course designed to teach students about every possible religious, spiritual, and secular worldview, I wanted to make sure students gained some knowledge about diverse worldviews. Therefore, we used *Understanding College Students' Spiritual Identities: Different Faiths, Varied Worldviews* (Small, 2011), which provided some insight into the experiences of Muslim, Jewish, Christian, and atheist students as well as ideas for supporting these various groups. I used several supplemental readings, many from Interfaith Youth Core as well as several articles written by scholars in our field.

Over the course of the semester we talked about why it is important to engage students on the topic of religious, spiritual, and secular identity, grounding the discussion in U.S. religious diversity, student affairs as a holistic field, and educational outcomes. We also discussed the many ways religious and Christian privilege present themselves in society at large and on campuses in general. The final third of the semester was focused on specific ways to incorporate this topic into student affairs practice. Several guest speakers helped bring these topics to life.

One day we were joined by the director of Miami's Center for Mindfulness and Contemplative Inquiry, who talked about the work the center does and walked us through a guided meditation. During another class session, we included the director of our student center who shared her knowledge of the legal issues that can affect the religious, spiritual, and secular work that is being done in student affairs. We also spent one class session with a staff member from Interfaith Youth Core who walked us through developing interfaith outcomes and using a religious pluralism rubric to guide and evaluate interfaith work. Bringing in these speakers was my way of demonstrating to students that this work is really happening on college campuses (although it is not always the most visible) and provided the opportunity for students to think through the many aspects of incorporating interfaith engagement into their own practice.

Assignments

The assignments supplemented the personal and professional aspects of the class. I included two dialogue assignments, one focused on connecting with an individual with a similar religious, spiritual, or secular perspective and one focused on connecting with someone with a different perspective. Students were asked to find a dialogue partner for each project and meet with them two or three times. They were asked to talk to the dialogue partner about their partner's beliefs, find out how those beliefs manifest themselves in their partner's life, get to know their partner, share their own perspectives in a reciprocal manner, and be open to understanding perspectives that are similar and different from their own. Students found this assignment to be a very meaningful experience that simultaneously helped them understand the perspectives of others while helping them clarify and articulate their own beliefs.

The final course assignment was to create a poster that represented a way to address religious diversity (spirituality, religion, and secular perspectives) on campus. Students created and illustrated a variety of programs including a living-learning community that connected religious, spiritual, and secular exploration to career choice, a leadership training program that incorporated interfaith engagement, and a movie and lecture series that highlighted multiple faith traditions. We held a poster session on the last day of class, which was attended by more than 50 colleagues from the division of student affairs and our student affairs preparation program.

My goal for making the assignment an interactive poster session rather than a typical paper was twofold. First, it was an opportunity to share ideas with our broader community in hope of inspiring more interfaith engagement opportunities on campus. Second, it was a chance for the students in the class to practice articulating why the topic of interfaith engagement is important to student affairs in general and their work as a practitioner in particular.

Conclusion

The three authors of this chapter, each influenced by experiences in our personal and academic lives, have come to believe that student affairs preparation programs must teach future practitioners to be deeply reflective and act authentically. We also believe that practitioners must be prepared to engage with the myriad religious, spiritual, and secular worldviews of our students. Our beliefs have driven us to create, teach, and develop courses that address these important topics. Our goal in sharing snippets of our journeys and descriptions of our courses and approaches is to inspire other faculty to develop their own courses focused on religious diversity and interfaith engagement. Social and political happenings all around us suggest that the time is right to add these courses to student affairs graduate programs. Our personal experiences tell us that students in our programs crave these courses and teaching them is a meaningful and fulfilling experience.

References

ACPA–College Student Educators International & NASPA–Student Affairs Administrators in Higher Education. (2004). *Learning reconsidered.* Washington DC: Author.

Adams, N. (1997). My grandmother and the snake. In A. Garrod & C. Larimore (Eds.), *First person, first peoples: Native American college graduates tell their life stories* (pp. 93–114). Ithaca, NY: Cornell University Press.

American Council on Education. (1937). *Student personnel point of view: A report of a conference on the philosophy and development of student personnel work in college and university.* Retrieved from http://www.myacpa.org/student-personnel-point-view-1937

Astin, A. W. (2004). Why spirituality deserves a central place in liberal education. *Liberal Education, 90*(2), 34–41.

Astin, A. W., Astin, H. S., & Lindholm, J. A. (2011). *Cultivating the spirit: How college can enhance students' inner lives.* San Francisco, CA: Jossey-Bass.

Baxter Magolda, M. B. (2002). Helping students make their way to adulthood. *About Campus. 6*(6), 2–9.

Boers, A. (2012). *Living into focus: Choosing what matters in an age of distractions.* Grand Rapids, MI: Baker Books.

Brown, B. (2012). *Daring greatly: How the courage to be vulnerable transforms the way we live, love, parent, and lead.* New York, NY: Penguin.

Clark, C., Brimhall-Vargas, M., Schlosser, L., & Alimo, C. (2002). It's not just "secret Santa" in December: Addressing educational and workplace climate issues linked to Christian privilege. *Multicultural Education, 10*, 52–57.

Csikszentmihalyi, M. (1990). *Flow: The psychology of optimal experience.* New York, NY: Harper & Row.

Eagan, M. K., Stolzenberg, E. B., Ramirez, J. J., Aragon, M. C., Suchard, M. R., & Rios Aguilar, C. (2016). *The American freshman: Fifty-year trends, 1966–2015.* Los Angeles, CA: Higher Education Research Institute.

Frankl, V. E. (2006). *Man's search for meaning.* Boston, MA: Beacon Press.

Goodman, K. M., & Teraguchi, D. H. (2008). Beyond spirituality: A new framework for educators. *Diversity & Democracy, 11*(1), 10–11.

Interfaith Youth Core. (n.d.) *How to hold a speedfaithing event.* Retrieved from https://www.ifyc.org/resources/how-hold-speedfaithing-event

Jablonski, M. A. (2001). The implications of student spirituality for student affairs practice. *New Directions for Student Services*, 95.

Love, P., & Talbot, D. (2000). Defining spiritual development: A missing consideration for student affairs. *NASPA Journal, 37*(1), 361–375.

Nash, R. J. (2003). Inviting atheists to the table: A modest proposal for higher education. *Religion and Education, 30*(1), 1–23.

Nash, R. J., & Jang, J. J. (2015). *Preparing students for life beyond college: A meaning-centered vision for holistic teaching and learning.* New York, NY: Routledge.

Nash, R. J., & Murray, M. C. (2009). *Helping college students find purpose: The campus guide to meaning-making.* San Francisco, CA: John Wiley & Sons.

Nouwen, H. J. M. (1986). *Reaching out: The three movements of the spiritual life.* New York, NY: Doubleday.

Palmer, P. J. (1993). *To know as we are known.* New York, NY: HarperCollins Publishers.

Palmer, P. J. (2009). *A hidden wholeness: The journey toward an undivided life.* San Francisco, CA: Wiley.

Parks, S. D. (2000). *Big questions, worthy dreams: Mentoring young adults in their search for meaning, purpose, and faith.* San Francisco, CA: Jossey-Bass.

Rilke, R. M. (1993). *Letters to a young poet.* (M. D. Herter Norton, Trans.). New York, NY: Norton. (Original work published 1903)

Seifert, T. A. (2007). Understanding Christian privilege: Managing the tensions of spiritual plurality *About Campus, 12*(2), 10–17.

Seifert, T. A., & Holman-Harmon, N. (2009). Practical implications for student affairs professionals' work in facilitating students' inner development. *New Directions for Student Services*, 125, 13–21.

Small, J. L. (2011). *Understanding college students' spiritual identities: Different faiths, varied worldviews.* New York, NY: Hampton Press.

Spurlock, M. (Producer). (2010). *30 days: The complete series* [DVD]. Available from https://www.amazon.com/30-Days-Complete-Morgan-Spurlock/dp/B0038P1CXI

Tisdell, E. J. (2003). *Exploring spirituality and culture in adult and higher education.* San Francisco, CA: Jossey-Bass.

Watt. S. K. (2015a). *Designing transformative multicultural initiatives: Theoretical foundations, practical applications, and facilitator considerations.* Sterling, VA: Stylus.

Watt, S. K. (2015b). Situating race in college students' search for purpose and meaning: Who am I? *Journal of College and Character, 16,* 135–142.

Watt, S., Fairchild, E., & Goodman, K. (Eds.). (2009). Religious privilege and student affairs practice: Intersections of difficult dialogues. *New Directions for Student Services, 125.*

5

ADDING SPIRITUALITY, RELIGIOUS DIVERSITY, AND INTERFAITH ENGAGEMENT TO STUDENT AFFAIRS COURSES

Jenny L. Small and James P. Barber

Graduate school curricula provide the baseline knowledge for professionals in the field of higher education and student affairs (HESA). Before beginning their careers, student affairs practitioners build their core competencies around a variety of relevant topics including, quite significantly, college student identity and diversity. ACPA–College Student Educators International (2018) offers an online syllabus clearinghouse as an open-access resource for faculty seeking to develop courses in HESA programs. Although 20 of the 29 clearinghouse syllabi that align with the courses discussed in this chapter mention religion, spirituality, or related topics, the type of inclusion ranges dramatically from a substantive element of a course, including readings, assignments, and discussions, to a mere mention of religion as one in a list of elements of student or campus diversity.

The lack of consistent inclusion of these topics in graduate preparation curricula has consequences for future professionals in student affairs. In a study examining the spirituality and professional practices of such professionals, Kiessling (2010) found that the participants' graduate school curricula were "not a predictor of holistic, spiritually-infused practice," (p. 4) because "graduate school preparation programs do not typically include concepts related to spirituality" (p. 5). As a result, new professionals at religiously affiliated campuses may find they are unprepared to work in an unfamiliar cultural environment (Renn & Jessup-Anger, 2008). Even when professionals desire to discuss concepts related to spirituality with students, they hesitate to do so given that guidelines for discussing spirituality-related matters with students are often "blurry" (Burchell, Lee, & Olson, 2010, p. 124). To combat this problem, "[higher] education graduate programs, staff trainings, and professional conferences should define and address spirituality in the workplace" (p. 124). Literacy in the various ways students make meaning during the college years is critical, given that "student affairs professionals need to be able to work with students along the paths (both individualized and communal) they use to find purpose and meaning in life" (Kocet & Stewart, 2011, p. 4). Indeed, "[practitioners] should have an understanding of how to have conversations about purpose in life with students" (Craft & Hochella, 2010, p. 6), and graduate school programs offer the time and space for future practitioners to develop such skills.

The faculty members in these graduate programs, however, do not necessarily know how to accomplish this important task (Rogers & Love, 2007). Although the addition of spiritual development and meaning-making to the curriculum has been considered in student affairs graduate preparation programs since the late 1990s, these additions have not been implemented in any regular or strategic manner (Stewart, 2015). In a small study of HESA faculty at a public state institution and two private religious institutions, Rogers and Love (2007) found that their programs did not consistently address teaching them how to respond to undergraduates' spiritual questions.

This gap between the needs of student affairs practitioners to adequately support the religiously diverse students on their campuses and the lack of relevant education in their graduate school curricula can and should be addressed. New coursework may not be required; rather, religious diversity and interfaith engagement can be integrated into existing courses in HESA preparation programs.

In this chapter, we advocate for including spirituality, religious diversity, and interfaith engagement in five courses that are regularly offered in these programs. We selected these five courses based on their natural affinity with elements of the topic area as well as the resulting gap when this material is not incorporated. For example, a student affairs practicum course that instructs future practitioners on how to support students experiencing various forms of transition during the college years but does not teach them how to support those encountering divergent religious views for the first time leaves those future practitioners at a serious professional disadvantage.

Course Recommendations

In this chapter we examine ways spirituality and religious diversity can be infused into the following courses in HESA preparation programs: (a) History of U.S. Higher Education, (b) Higher Education Environments, (c) College Student Development Theory, (d) Diversity in Higher Education, and (e) Student Affairs Practicum. These courses are commonly found in master's and doctoral programs and are requirements for many of the programs. In addition, these five courses represent areas of study recommended by the Council for the Advancement of Standards in Higher Education (2015).

We aim to increase religious literacy across all these courses by fostering a basic understanding of the beliefs and practices of diverse religious identities (see part four of this volume for related resources). For each course we use the same general outline to explore how faculty members may add spirituality, religious diversity, and interfaith engagement to existing curricula. We begin with our own suggested learning goals relevant to the course and issues of spirituality. Next, we offer several key readings to consider for inclusion in the course. Finally, we describe ways to intentionally engage students in the course on spirituality, faith, and religious diversity with diverse activities, and we include strategies for individual work, small-group, and large-group interaction.

Before we consider the details of these particular courses in the next section, it is important to keep in mind across the board that religion, spirituality, and faith are not often discussed in academic courses (or public life in general). We suggest scheduling the units about faith and spirituality toward the middle of the course to allow time for educators to establish rapport and build community in the class before diving into conversations and activities. Additionally, remind students well in advance that this topic is coming up, and acknowledge that it is sometimes difficult to talk about personal beliefs. Finally, encourage students to bring their full selves and identities to the discussion, even if it is uncomfortable at first. Instructors also need to consider how much of their own religious, nonreligious, faith, and spiritual identities or belief systems to share with the class.

We approach these five courses with an eye toward practicality. We understand that the faculty members leading these courses are busy and often have multiple roles in addition to teaching. This chapter offers suggestions for resources and activities that can be immediately implemented in existing courses as well as a discussion of working with colleagues for longer lasting, more substantial curricular changes in terms of religious, nonreligious, and spiritual diversity. Above all, we want educators to be able to use the ideas presented here to improve the student learning experience and better prepare graduate students for professional positions and leadership roles in higher education.

History of U.S. Higher Education

When integrating spirituality, religious diversity, and interfaith engagement into existing courses about the history of U.S. higher education, the overarching learning goal should focus on religious diversity of institutional types and of changing student demographics over time. Throughout the early history of higher education, institutional life could not be separated from religious observance. Some institutions eventually severed their religious affiliations, some transformed the nature of those ties, and some maintained their original religious affiliations (Marsden, 1994). This occurred alongside changing identities and values of students, such as whether they chose to attend religious services (Hastings & Hoge, 1981) and the types of religious groups they formed on campus (Marsden, 1994). After completion of the related units in a History of U.S. Higher Education course, we believe students should be able to identify the key historical influences on institutional religious affiliations; describe the changing nature of student religious, spiritual, and nonreligious identities and expression on college campuses; and offer insights into the reasons and implications for these evolutions.

A key reading for the first learning outcome, examining the history of religion on U.S. college campuses, is Marsden's (1994) *The Soul of the American University: From Protestant Establishment to Established Nonbelief.* This book is foundational for tracing the changing nature of campuses and the students who inhabited them over time. For a useful overview that brings the historical record up to the modern day but is shorter than assigning Marsden's entire book, we propose chapter 2 in Jacobsen and Jacobsen's (2012) *No Longer Invisible: Religion in University Education.* In addition, the rest of the book presents key current themes on religion on college campuses and could be used to reflect on history's impact on current circumstances.

To address the second learning outcome and examine the changing nature of students' religious, spiritual, and nonreligious identities and expression on college campuses, we suggest the following texts: Hastings and Hoge's (1981) report on the findings from their 1948 to 1979 longitudinal study on students' religious beliefs and behavior and the Higher Education Research Institute's analysis of 40 years of student demographics and opinions, from 1966 to 2006 (Pryor, Hurtado, Saenz, Santos, & Korn, 2007). These works can be used in comparison with two more recent reports that examine student worldview demographics and beliefs (Higher Education Research Institute, 2005; Mayhew et al., 2016). Although all these pieces draw conclusions, they also present considerable data (particularly in the case of Pryor et al., 2007), which students can use for their own analyses.

Various in-class activities and assignments can facilitate the third learning outcome, which is to enable students to offer insights into the reasons and implications for these historical evolutions. Faculty lectures can introduce other illuminating publications and focus on the thematic connections among changes in institutional types and student characteristics, such as the role of religious quotas in admissions practices (Synnott, 1979) and the rise in religious cocurricular organizations such as Hillel, Newman Centers, and Muslim Students Associations (Schmalzbauer, 2007). Faculty may also want to share information on how the realities of campus life changed after the significant historical events of September 11, 2001, particularly for Muslim students (e.g., Peek, 2011).

Small groups can be asked to trace the stories of different student groups over time, sharing their findings and insights with the rest of the class. A graded writing assignment can ask students to specifically analyze the dynamic relationship between students' worldview demographics and changing institutional affiliations or to analyze the impact of one of these evolutions on a broader element of the higher education environment.

Students can also be guided to examine how the experiences of individuals from a variety of religious backgrounds have changed over time by reflecting on their own personal identities and considering how students with those same identities may have fared at different institutional types during various historical periods. This could be facilitated by using a simple handout of a grid, with dates and institutional types making up the axes, and asking students to fill in boxes imagining a similar student's experiences in each setting. Students would then be asked to share their conclusions with a partner or with the entire class.

Finally, because history enables us to look constructively toward the future, students in this course should be encouraged to extrapolate from the material they have learned to consider implications for the continued impact of religious diversity on college campuses. This may take the form of an in-class reflection exercise in which students are asked to imagine the future of religious, spiritual, and nonreligious expressions of meaning-making on college campuses or an out-of-class writing assignment in which students map changing demographic realities onto evolving institutional types.

Higher Education Environments

The spaces and places where college students live and learn are key to postsecondary education, and courses focused on higher education environments are important curricular components of HESA preparation programs. Spirituality, religious diversity, and interfaith engagement are of particular interest in higher education environments because 19% of institutions are religiously affiliated, enrolling 9% of all college students (National Center for Education Statistics, 2014). Over the course of a career in higher education, even graduate students who consider themselves to be nonspiritual may find themselves working at a faith-based institution (and vice versa). We believe that students who successfully complete a graduate-level course in higher education environments should be able to understand the ways religious affiliation or history may have an impact on an educational environment, describe ways physical attributes of a campus environment (e.g., artwork, holiday displays, presence of a traditional Christian chapel) affect campus climate and student learning, and discuss the implications of working at faith-based and secular institutions.

Important readings for this unit include foundational works on college environments (Kuh & Whitt, 1988; Strange & Banning, 2015) to provide a framework for how faith and spirituality influence higher education contexts. Sources that explore the building blocks of campus cultures related to religion, faith, and spirituality are necessary to understand the components of a diverse yet inclusive environment (Dean & Grandpré, 2011; Mayhew, Bowman, & Rockenbach, 2014; Seggie & Sanford, 2010). In addition, research that examines how institutional variables affect spiritual development and student learning should be included (e.g., Bryant, Choi, & Yasuno, 2003; Weddle-West, Hagan, & Norwood, 2013).

Course assignments and activities can serve to reinforce the ideas presented in these readings. A detailed observation of a sacred space on campus using qualitative methods may reveal nuances of how students perceive and use the space. How do people interact in this space? Who is represented there? What symbols are present in the architecture or artwork? For whom or what is the space named?

Finally, case studies can be a powerful tool for students to grapple with different perspectives in a case. Two cases that may prompt discussion about faith and campus environments are from William & Mary in which the university president sought to remove a Christian cross from the historic chapel at the state institution (Jaschick, 2008) and Eastern Michigan University, also a state institution, that included footbaths for Muslim students in the construction of a new student union (Levin, 2007). Have students take on the roles of undergraduates, faculty, administrators, board members, and state legislators, for example, as they examine the nuances of each case. In addition, a field trip to an institution different from the one where the course is being taught can be informative. Meet with current students, faculty, and staff to discuss the similarities, differences, and impact of faith on the campus environment. More case study resources are available in part four of this book

College Student Development Theory

In teaching and learning about how people develop in college, faith and spiritual development should be a central area to consider. By nature, courses on student development theory are personal, focusing on the individual. We believe the primary learning goals in such courses should include an introduction to and appreciation of multiple perspectives on faith, spirituality, and religion. Learning goals should also be inclusive of nonreligious and nontheistic perspectives including atheism and agnosticism as well as beliefs outside the dominant monotheistic faiths. In addition, students who successfully complete a course on college student development theory should recognize faith and spirituality as one of the many ways people grow and change in the college context and be able to discuss the intersection of spirituality with other areas of development (e.g., cognitive, identity, moral).

In choosing readings that examine faith and spiritual development in college, it is important to pair foundational texts with later research. Fowler (1981) and Parks (2000) are pivotal works but often misrepresented as the only works on the topic. Much of the subsequent work related to faith and spiritual development is based on their writing, but critics (e.g., Stamm, 2006) have noted that their work is Christian-centric and not representative of the religious diversity present on U.S. college and university campuses today. Selected readings for college student development theory courses should represent perspectives that are often marginalized, including African American students (Stewart, 2002); gay, lesbian, and bisexual students (Gold & Stewart, 2011); Muslim students (Peek, 2005); nonreligious and atheist students (Liddell & Stedman, 2011); and Buddhist and Hindu students (Bryant, 2006). Small's (2009) concept of faith frames is inclusive and captures the concept of multiple perspectives on religious development and meaning-making, focusing on exploring development in Christian, Jewish, Muslim, and atheist or agnostic frames.

Class activities and assignments that challenge students to consider multiple perspectives in spiritual development are helpful in achieving the learning goals mentioned earlier. One approach is to have students work in small groups to review realistic profiles of undergraduates from various faith backgrounds. These profiles should be practical and customized to the campus. Include details in the profile that provide context about the students' family life, campus involvement, and career interests. Make this activity campus specific with prompts such as, What might this student's experience be like at our institution (including challenges and successes)? How might this student's spiritual development be fostered here?

Another, more personal, activity is Lockbox Reflection. Clydesdale (2007) described a common phenomenon among traditional-age college students in which they set their religious beliefs aside during the undergraduate years in a mental lockbox that is then reopened postcollege. For this reflection activity, students can write for 15 to 20 minutes about their own undergraduate development and whether they had a religious lockbox. This can take the form of a worksheet where students actually write inside a picture of a box that would prompt them to think about what beliefs and practices (if any) they put into a box when they came to college and whether they unlocked the box afterward. Questions for students to consider might include, For what reasons and from whom might you have protected these beliefs or practices? and Can you recall unlocking any locked beliefs or practices either during or after college? This should be a reflection that is shared only by choice to encourage honest disclosure.

Finally, an immersion activity could be an effective means to explore faith and spiritual development in a college student development theory course. Ask students to attend a meeting or service of a college faith or spiritual group different from their own identity. This can be very broad and not limited to only formal religious activities (e.g., Catholic Mass, secular student association meeting, meditation group). Students should bring insights back to the class in a format that can be easily shared with others, such as blogs, vlogs, or in structured class discussions.

Diversity in Higher Education

Many HESA preparation programs include a course focused on diversity in higher education (with course titles often including the language of diversity, equity, inclusion, and multiculturalism). The purpose of this type of course is to survey structural and cultural diversity present in U.S. higher education and how it affects institutional policy, curricula, and student learning. We advocate for religious diversity to be included in such courses alongside race, gender, sexuality, and other forms of human diversity. Students who are successful in a diversity in higher education course should be able to discuss the demographics of U.S. higher education relative to faith and religious beliefs (Eagan et al., 2015). They should be able to discuss diversity beyond race, gender, and sexuality, and recognize meaning-making as an important form of diversity.

Readings about the state of religious, nonreligious, and spiritual diversity in higher education must include resources that describe students' spiritual lives on college campuses in the twenty-first century (Higher Education Research Institute, 2005; Shushok & Perillo, 2015). Religious privilege should also be examined as part of the course readings, in particular, the ways privilege affects majority and minoritized groups of students (Goodman, Wilson, & Nicolazzo, 2015; Schlosser, 2003). In addition, readings should examine the changes in religious diversity over time in the broader U.S. context. *America's Changing Religious Landscape*, a report released by the Pew Research Center (2015), is an excellent resource in this vein, illustrating generational shifts using data from the 2014 U.S. Religious Landscape Study. The chapters in part five of this book are also an excellent resource.

Class assignments and activities to examine spiritual diversity in higher education should help students find concrete data about how students identify themselves in terms of belief systems and worldview descriptions. Worldview-majority students often underestimate the numbers of their peers who are from marginalized faith groups on campus, whereas those from worldview-minority backgrounds tend to more strongly perceive the absence of worldview diversity on college campuses (Interfaith Youth Core, 2014). Asking students to research the demographics of a particular subgroup on a campus of their choice can uncover detailed information about representation. The *Chronicle of Higher Education*'s "A Profile of Freshmen" (2017) data sets would be valuable resources for such an activity.

In addition, facilitating respectful discussions on the topic of religious privilege, power, and oppression would be meaningful in a course on diversity in higher education. Allen (n.d.) developed an activity called the Privilege Beads Exercise that is inclusive of religion, faith, and spirituality in the larger discussion of privilege and marginalization. In this exercise, a number of stations are arranged around the room to represent different forms of privilege (race, gender, sexual orientation, religion, etc.). Each station has a bowl filled with beads (a different color for each station) as well as a list of statements describing examples of privilege on that station's system of oppression and privilege. At each station, students should take one bead for each item on the list they can answer yes to. When students are finished with all the stations, they will have collected a set of beads that represents their individual set of privileges. During a facilitated debriefing discussion, students could be encouraged to craft their beads into an accessory (bracelet, necklace, keychain, etc.) to represent their privileged identities and serve as a reminder of the class activity and discussion. The Privilege Beads Exercise offers more privacy than activities that ask students to stand, sit, or position themselves in a line to acknowledge privileged identities; however, the exercise is still a very personal one and can elicit strong emotional responses from students and instructors during the activity and facilitated discussion.

Student Affairs Practicum

The Student Affairs Practicum course presents a somewhat different situation from the previous four we have presented in this chapter simply because much of the necessary curricular focus of this course is on the experiences students are having in their concurrent professional internship or assistantship position. Student Affairs Practicum allows the students to reflect on their work in those settings and learn best practices to enhance their skills. However, along with the professional competencies and career development topics they will inevitably discuss, we advocate for inclusion of religious diversity and interfaith engagement as important subject matter. Although campus professionals may be natural partners with interfaith work, "the field of student affairs has yet to reach its potential in positive engagement of religious and non-religious identities" (Patel & Giess, 2016, p. 9).

We suggest incorporating these topics into a session in the practicum course devoted to current issues on the college campus or to diverse undergraduate populations. At the conclusion of the relevant unit, participants in this class should be able to express their understanding of how students of diverse religious, nonreligious, and spiritual backgrounds may perceive the various functions of the professional office where students from the course are working as well as recall useful strategies for productively supporting interfaith engagement through that office's work.

Key readings for this unit are focused, practical, and immediately useful for students' parallel work environments. Depending on the students' positions where they are working, faculty may want to assign readings regarding legal issues on religious expression on campus (Moran, Roberts, Tobin, & Harvey, 2008; Waggoner & Russo, 2014), an overview of the statistical portrait and beliefs of religiously diverse college students (Higher Education Research Institute, 2005), basic understandings of students' varied ways of communicating through their faith frames (Small, 2009) and in interfaith settings (Mayhew et al., 2016), and the role of Christian and spiritual privileges on the college campus (Goodman et al., 2015; Schlosser, 2003). Specialized readings in various functional areas can be assigned to students working in those areas, including residence life (Rockenbach et al., 2014), multicultural affairs (Small, 2011), and spiritual life and multifaith offices (Johnson & Laurence, 2012). In addition, several chapters in *Intersections of Religious Privilege: Difficult Dialogues and Student Affairs Practice* (Watt, Fairchild, & Goodman, 2009) provide excellent instruction on working with Jewish, Muslim, and atheist college students as well as in navigating the intersections between worldviews and other elements of students' identities, such as race, culture, and sexuality. If there is sufficient time, we recommend having class participants read this entire text.

We understand there is minimal time available for discussing topics that go beyond students' practical professional development, so we suggest that in-class activities should go straight to the core of the matter, focusing on direct connections among religious diversity, interfaith engagement, and student affairs departments. Faculty should encourage students to consider the varying elements of worldview identity that may affect undergraduates' interactions in these departments and develop strategies for working with students in the most effective manner. It may also be useful to bring in outside materials to prompt conversation. For example, NASPA–Student Affairs Administrators in Higher Education offers several one-hour courses on practical topics related to religious diversity and the college student experience (keyword *religious* at NASPA Online Learning Community, 2016), which can be used for in-class viewing or in lieu of a reading assignment. Small groups could review portions of *A Guidebook of Promising Practices: Facilitating College Students' Spiritual Development* (Lindholm, Millora, Schwartz, & Spinosa, 2011) that cover campuswide efforts and various cocurricular programs and services for real-world application. Faculty members themselves may be interested in chapter 4, which covers curricular initiatives and teaching strategies. Finally, we recommend that students be introduced to the standards on campus religious, secular, and spiritual programs (Council for the Advancement of Standards in Higher Education, 2017), which have been revised to reflect the most current thinking on best practices in these areas.

Summary of Recommendations

Overall, the recommendations we have made for these five courses reflect our conviction that spirituality, religious diversity, and interfaith engagement are critical components of curricula for HESA programs. We believe that incorporating readings and activities will reinforce these necessary learning outcomes. We have striven to offer practical, accessible, and effective suggestions to enhance existing courses, with the understanding that faculty members will take this information and shape it to meet the specific needs of their graduate students. We also hope our colleagues around the country will consider other courses and even cocurricular settings where consideration of these topics would enhance student learning. All this being said, we understand these types of changes will not necessarily be easy to implement for a variety of reasons. In the next section, we address particular concerns of resistance or apprehensiveness arising from unfamiliarity of departmental colleagues.

Working With Faculty Colleagues on Curriculum Changes

In working to add spirituality to existing courses in student affairs preparation programs, it is essential to work with faculty colleagues to make a meaningful impact across the curriculum of a program. To do so, we recommend three approaches. First, become a vocal advocate for the inclusion of spirituality, religious diversity, and interfaith engagement in courses across the curriculum and explain the benefits of inclusion for your graduate students. There are likely supporters among your colleagues, but they may not know you value faith perspectives unless you share your ideas. It is also important for you to show support verbally in faculty meetings, curricula committees, and so on for why it is important to include spirituality for those colleagues who have questions about the purpose and greater connection to the higher education and student affairs profession.

Second, work individually with faculty colleagues to help them include resources, assignments, and other activities in their courses that are inclusive of faith and spirituality. In some instances, the barrier is very low to adding spirituality to existing courses. Having research articles, discussion topics, and course assignments (e.g., in this chapter) to offer colleagues can help with adding a new perspective to an established class.

Third, assess the student learning that happens in your courses relative to faith and spirituality. As with all other areas of the institution, data are necessary to illustrate the benefits to students, document student learning, and demonstrate application in the field after graduation. Collecting information from current graduate students about their learning in the classroom as well as from alumni about how issues of religion, spirituality, and faith are relevant in their work in higher education is essential to find out whether the additions to the curriculum are effective.

Conclusion

Faculty in student affairs preparation programs reside at a critical juncture in the careers of student affairs practitioners. They collaborate to provide the very foundations in knowledge, commitment, and even values for new professionals entering the field. The potential impact of faculty members adjusting their course content to be inclusive of spirituality, religious diversity, and interfaith engagement cannot be overstated. Jenny Small (2015) has written previously about the concept of *virtuous cycles* in student affairs. These cycles include "graduate preparation programs, new professionals impacting their home campuses, students passing through these more accepting institutions, and professional associations giving their support to the field," all combining to yield "a more inclusive field of student affairs, broadly speaking" (p. 169). When faculty members who embrace these topics have a positive impact on their graduate students, they empower the next generation of practitioners to have the same impact on their students, the undergraduates at their new places of employment. Those undergraduates may then grow to be more tolerant, accepting, and well versed in topics related to meaning-making, an outcome that can only benefit institutions of U.S. higher education.

References

A profile of freshmen at 4-year colleges, Fall 2016. (2017). Retrieved from https://www.chronicle.com/article/A-Profile-of-Freshmen-at/240775?cid=cp135

ACPA—College Student Educators International. (2018). *ACPA syllabus clearinghouse.* Retrieved from http://www.myacpa.org/syllabus-clearinghouse-0

Allen, B. J. (n.d.) *Privilege beads exercise.* Retrieved from http://differencematters.info/uploads/pdf/privilege-beads-exercise.pdf

Bryant, A. N. (2006). Exploring religious pluralism in higher education: Non-majority religious perspectives among entering first-year college students. *Religion & Education, 33*(1), 1–25.

Bryant, A. N., Choi, J. Y., & Yasuno, M. (2003). Understanding the religious and spiritual dimensions of students' lives in the first year of college. *Journal of College Student Development, 44,* 723–745.

Burchell, J. A., Lee, J. J., & Olson, S. M. (2010). University student affairs staff and their spiritual discussions with students. *Religion & Education, 37,* 114–128.

Clydesdale, T. (2007). *The first year out: Understanding American teens after high school.* Chicago, IL: University of Chicago Press.

Council for the Advancement of Standards in Higher Education. (2015). *CAS professional standards for higher education* (9th ed.). Washington, DC: Author.

Council for the Advancement of Standards in Higher Education. (2017). *Campus religious, secular, and spiritual programs.* Fort Collins, CO: Author.

Craft, C. M., & Hochella, R. (2010). Essential responsibilities of student affairs administrators: Identifying a purpose in life and helping students do the same. *Journal of College and Character, 11*(4), 1–8. doi:10.2202/1940-1639.1744

Dean, L. A., & Grandpré, E. A. (2011). Religious and spiritual diversity on campus. In M. Cuyjet, M. F. Howard-Hamilton, & D. L. Cooper (Eds.), *Multiculturalism on campus: Theory, models, and practices for understanding diversity and creating inclusion* (pp. 371–398). Sterling, VA: Stylus.

Eagan, K., Stolzenberg, E. B., Bates, A. K., Aragon, M. C., Suchard, M. R., & Rios-Aguilar, C. (2015). *The American freshman: National norms fall 2015.* Los Angeles, CA: Higher Education Research Institute.

Fowler, J. (1981). *Stages of faith: The psychology of human development and the quest for meaning.* New York, NY: HarperCollins.

Gold, S. P., & Stewart, D. L. (2011). Lesbian, gay and bisexual students coming out at the intersection of spirituality and sexual identity. *Journal of LGBT Issues in Counseling, 5,* 237–258.

Goodman, K. M., Wilson, K., & Nicolazzo, Z. (2015). Campus practice in support of spirituality, faith, religion, and life purpose: What has been accomplished and where do we go next? In J. L. Small (Ed.), *Making meaning: Embracing spirituality, faith, religion, and life purpose in student affairs* (pp. 118–140). Sterling, VA: Stylus.

Hastings, P. K., & Hoge, D. R. (1981). Religious trends among college students, 1948–79. *Social Forces, 60,* 517–531.

Higher Education Research Institute. (2005). *The spiritual life of college students: A national study of college students' search for meaning and purpose.* Los Angeles, CA: Author.

Interfaith Youth Core. (2014). *Engaging worldview: A snapshot of religious & spiritual campus climate.* Chicago, IL: Author.

Jacobsen, D., & Jacobsen, R. H. (2012). *No longer invisible: Religion in university education.* Oxford, England: Oxford University Press.

Jaschick, S. (2008, February 13). Presidential ouster at William & Mary. *Inside Higher Ed.* Retrieved from https://www.insidehighered.com/news/2008/02/13/nichol

Johnson, K., & Laurence, P. (2012). Multi-faith religious spaces on college and university campuses. *Religion & Education, 39,* 48–63.

Kiessling, M. K. (2010). Spirituality as a component of holistic student development: Perspectives and practices of student affairs professionals. *Journal of College and Character, 11*(3), 1–10. doi:10.2202/1940-1639.1721

Kocet, M. M., & Stewart, D. L. (2011). The role of student affairs in promoting religious and secular pluralism and interfaith cooperation. *Journal of College and Character, 12*(1), 1–10. Retrieved from https://doi.org/10.2202/1940-1639.1762

Kuh, G. D., & Whitt, E. J. (1988). The invisible tapestry: Culture in American colleges and universities. *ASHE-ERIC Higher Education Report, 17*(1).

Levin, T. (2007, August 7). Some U.S. universities install foot baths for Muslim students. *New York Times.* Retrieved from http://www.nytimes.com/2007/08/07/world/americas/07iht-muslims.4.7022566.html

Liddell, E. R. A., & Stedman, C. D. (2011). Nontheistic students on campus: Understanding and accommodating atheists, agnostics, humanists, and others. *Journal of College and Character, 12*(3), 1–7.

Lindholm, J. A., Millora, M. L., Schwartz, L. M., & Spinosa, H. S. (2011). *A guidebook of promising practices: Facilitating college students' spiritual development.* Los Angeles, CA: Regents of the University of California.

Marsden, G. M. (1994). *The soul of the American university: From Protestant establishment to established nonbelief.* New York, NY: Oxford University Press.

Mayhew, M. J., Bowman, N. A., & Rockenbach, A. B. (2014). Silencing whom? Linking campus climates for religious, spiritual, and worldview diversity to student worldviews. *Journal of Higher Education, 85,* 219–245.

Mayhew, M. J., Rockenbach, A. N., Correia, B. P., Crandall, R. E., Lo, M. A., & Associates. (2016). *Emerging interfaith trends: What college students are saying about religion in 2016.* Chicago, IL: Interfaith Youth Core.

Moran, C. D., Roberts, C. J., Tobin, J. A., & Harvey, L. M. (2008). Religious expression in residence halls at public colleges and universities: Freedoms and constraints. *Journal of College and University Student Housing, 35*(2), 48–61.

NASPA–Student Affairs Administrators in Higher Education. (2016). *NASPA online learning community.* Retrieved from https://olc.naspa.org/catalog?search=religious

National Center for Education Statistics. (2014). *Table 303.90: Fall enrollment and number of degree-granting postsecondary institutions, by control and religious affiliation of institution: Selected years, 1980 through 2014.* Retrieved from https://nces.ed.gov/programs/digest/d15/tables/dt15_303.90.asp?current=yes

Parks, S. D. (2000). *Big questions, worthy dreams: Mentoring young adults in their search for meaning, purpose and faith.* San Francisco, CA: Jossey-Bass.

Patel, E., & Giess, M. E. (2016). Engaging religious diversity on campus: The role of student affairs. *About Campus, 20*(6), 8–15.

Peek, L. (2005). Becoming Muslim: The development of a religious identity. *Sociology of Religion, 66,* 215–242.

Peek, L. (2011). *Behind the backlash: Muslim Americans after 9/11.* Philadelphia, PA: Temple University Press.

Pew Research Center. (2015). *America's changing religious landscape.* Retrieved from http://www.pewforum.org/files/2015/05/RLS-08-26-full-report.pdf

Pryor, J. H., Hurtado, S., Saenz, V. B., Santos, J. L., & Korn, W. S. (2007). *The American freshman: Forty year trends, 1966–2006.* Los Angeles: Higher Education Research Institute.

Renn, K. A., & Jessup-Anger, E. R. (2008). Preparing new professionals: Lessons for graduate preparation programs from the National Study of New Professionals in Student Affairs. *Journal of College Student Development, 49,* 319–335.

Rockenbach, A. B., Bachenheimer, A., Conley, A. H., Grays, S., Lynch, J., Staples, B. A., & Wood, A. (2014). Spiritual exchange in pluralistic contexts: Sharing narratives across worldview differences. *Journal of College and University Student Housing, 41,* 192–204.

Rogers, J. L., & Love, P. (2007). Exploring the role of spirituality in the preparation of student affairs professionals: Faculty constructions. *Journal of College Student Development, 48,* 90–104.

Schlosser, L. Z. (2003). Christian privilege: Breaking a sacred taboo. *Journal of Multicultural Counseling and Development, 31,* 44–51.

Schmalzbauer, J. (2007). *Campus ministry: A statistical portrait.* Retrieved from http://religion.ssrc.org/reforum/Schmalzbauer.pdf

Seggie, F. N., & Sanford, G. (2010). Perceptions of female Muslim students who veil: Campus religious climate. *Race, Ethnicity, and Education, 13*, 59–82.

Shushok, F., & Perillo, P. (2015). Personal exploration and national trends: The future for students of all faith backgrounds. In J. L. Small (Ed.) *Making meaning: Embracing spirituality, faith, religion, and life purpose in student affairs* (pp. 141–161). Sterling, VA: Stylus.

Small, J. L. (2009). Faith dialogues foster identity development. *About Campus, 13*(6), 12–18.

Small, J. L. (Ed.) (2015). *Making meaning: Embracing spirituality, faith, religion, and life purpose in student affairs.* Sterling, VA: Stylus.

Stamm, L. (2006). The dynamics of spirituality and the religious experience. In A. W. Chickering, J. C. Dalton, & L. Stamm (Eds.), *Encouraging authenticity & spirituality in higher education* (pp. 37–65). San Francisco, CA: Jossey-Bass.

Stewart, D. L. (2002). The role of faith in the development of an integrated identity: A qualitative study of Black students at a White college. *Journal of College Student Development, 43*, 579–596.

Stewart, D. L. (2015). The role of professional associations in advancing spirituality, faith, religion, and life purpose in student affairs. In J. L. Small (Ed.), *Making meaning: Embracing spirituality, faith, religion, and life purpose in student affairs* (pp. 82–96). Sterling, VA: Stylus.

Strange, C. C., & Banning, J. H. (2015). *Designing for learning: Creating campus environments for student success* (2nd ed.). San Francisco, CA: Jossey-Bass.

Synnott, M. G. (1979). The admission and assimilation of minority students at Harvard, Yale, and Princeton, 1900–1970. *History of Education Quarterly, 19*, 285–304.

Waggoner, M. D., & Russo, C. J. (2014). Making room at the inn: Implications of *Christian Legal Society v. Martinez* for public college and university housing professionals. *Journal of College and University Student Housing, 41*, 140–152.

Watt, S. K., Fairchild, E. E., & Goodman, K. M. (Eds.). (2009). Intersections of religious privilege: Difficult dialogues and student affairs practice. *New Directions for Student Services*, 125.

Weddle-West, K., Hagan, W. J., & Norwood, K. M. (2013). Impact of college environments on the spiritual development of African American students. *Journal of College Student Development, 54*, 299–314.

6

REFLECTIVE OPPORTUNITIES TO EXPLORE SPIRITUALITY AND PROFESSIONAL ENGAGEMENT

Mari Luna De La Rosa and Holly Holloway-Friesen

This chapter builds on the two preceding chapters by providing ideas for faculty in student affairs preparation programs. While chapter 4 provides models of student affairs courses focused on spirituality, religion, and secularity, chapter 5 provides suggestions for adding spirituality, religious diversity, and interfaith engagement to existing student affairs courses. This chapter focuses on two ways to work with student affairs graduate students through personal reflection activities, including some outside the classroom. The first part of this chapter describes a retreat developed at Azusa Pacific University (APU), which provides the opportunity for students to explore and link their spirituality and professional purpose. The second part of this chapter describes a journal activity with discussion questions (also developed at APU) that provides students with the opportunity to reflect on spirituality and religious diversity.

It is worth noting the unique Christian context of APU. We have particular opportunities at APU, given our religious affiliation, that faculty at other types of institutions may need to consider differently. Nevertheless, we hope these descriptions will inspire student affairs faculty to develop cocurricular and reflective opportunities suited to their own institutional and program context.

Spiritual Retreat for First-Year Student Affairs Graduate Students

The APU College Counseling and Student Development Program is situated in a unique learning context of Christian higher education and graduate professional preparation in student affairs. Each cohort consists of about 45 students. Our graduate program in college counseling and student development tends to draw ethnically and religiously diverse, mostly first-generation, college students, many of whom reside within an hour of this urban campus.

According to data provided by APU's institutional research department, the graduate student population in our program is ethnically diverse (35% White, 31% Latino and Latina, 11% multiethnic, 12% Asian and Asian American, and 8% African American and Black) and spiritually diverse (45% Protestant Christian, 41% Catholic, 10% atheist, 5% Buddhist). To help students integrate into the program socially and spiritually, a one-and-a-half-day spiritual retreat was established in the first year of enrollment in our graduate student affairs program. The spiritual retreat has proven to be quite effective in helping students reflect on their own religious and spiritual backgrounds, their personal and professional transitions, and purposes of being in graduate school. This personal reflection enables them to more successfully address issues of religious diversity and interfaith cooperation in their graduate school and professional trajectories. It also addresses experiences of marginality and fitting in, while fostering an understanding of diverse backgrounds in their cohort.

We have particular scheduling opportunities at APU that faculty at other types of institutions may need to consider differently. Our retreat is intentionally scheduled nine weeks into the fall term when students have finished their first two courses in the student affairs program, have worked a short time in their assistantships, and formed some friendships. In other words, they have had early experiences of being at our institution and becoming a student affairs professional. From our experience as faculty, questions arise among students about their transition into our program and graduate school in general; this retreat helps to answer their questions and alleviate their concerns while helping them adjust to their new roles.

Learning Outcomes

As a result of participating in the first-year graduate student retreat, students will

- describe their faith or spiritual belief system and their personal narrative of how they came to these beliefs;
- develop an understanding of their professional purpose, what has drawn them to this work, and what values guide them; and
- develop openness to and respect for a variety of faith and spiritual expressions in students they will serve, their cohort peers, faculty, administrators and student affairs professionals.

Retreat Day 1

Arrival and Ground Rules

The retreat commences with welcome remarks and an opening prayer, which is part of the practice of being at a private Christian campus such as APU. The prayer is performed in the Christian tradition and welcomes and appreciates all retreat participants. We then carry out an icebreaker that encourages the students to get to know names of cohort members they have not met yet. The icebreaker consists of finding someone who meets a particular category such as being a morning person; plays video games; camps out on Black Friday; likes black licorice; does yoga; likes Starbucks; does not use Facebook, Twitter, or Instagram; and so on. Categories were developed to be creative, safe, and low risk. The objective is to find someone who matches one of these categories then briefly introduce themselves. They repeat this exercise until they have met three to five people they had not interacted with before.

Students then reconvene for a welcome session that includes logistical information about the retreat and an overview of the activities planned. In this welcome session, the information provided puts the students at ease over what is expected of them. Toward this end, we created a theme for the program retreat, titled Voice, Engage, and Act (each is described later). The final task in the opening of the retreat is to set ground rules. Collectively, the students establish the ground rules for the retreat, and useful ones include being respectful of other's values and beliefs, using I statements and speaking from their own experience, being authentic, and having a willingness to be vulnerable.

First Reflection Exercise

The first session is a reflection exercise that involves two tasks. The first is to answer reflection questions about the article participants were given to read before the retreat. An article by Love and Talbot (1999) provides a framework for thinking about spirituality and discusses five propositions that can guide discussions, which acknowledge a wide range of belief systems. Students are asked to respond to the following questions in their reflection time: (a) Which of the propositions holds meaning for you? Why? How would you share your answer with someone else? (b) At this stage of your learning and development, how important is your faith or spirituality to working in student affairs and higher education? How would you share your answer with someone else? (c) How is your own faith or spirituality nurtured at APU? What are some ways you've felt uncomfortable about your faith or spirituality at APU? and (d) What can others in our program do to create a safe space for you to discuss issues related to faith and spirituality?

The second activity is intended to complement their reflection answers. Students receive a handout titled, "I am" at the top of the page. It includes blank lines for students to complete "I am" statements with words that describe who they see themselves to be. The papers will not be shown to anyone but will contribute to how students share their story and other sessions of the retreat. During this time, students are encouraged to walk around the grounds of the retreat center to find a quiet place to reflect. Students then return for dinner, which includes reflective conversation. Faculty and students dine together to get to know one another and discuss the afternoon's learning.

Exploring Voice

The second session of the retreat is directly connected to the theme of voice. Many times during the retreat students will hear the phrase *sharing your story,* which can involve a variety of factors such as growing up, family, college experiences, religious background, path to APU, and path to working in higher education. The purpose is for them to develop comfort and confidence in sharing their story and voice in a narrative way. Several faculty and student affairs professionals are invited to the retreat to share their story about their own personal faith journey, becoming a professional, and their responses to the reflection questions from the article. These faculty and professionals are mostly from the APU campus and help to model the importance of sharing one's story. We call the activity the Fireside Chat to create the picture of having meaningful conversations in front of a fire. The students are divided into small groups of six to eight for discussion, and the faculty and student affairs professionals are assigned to one of these groups.

The questions in the reflection activity from the prior session are used for these group discussions. About a half hour into the discussion, each group is given a sheet of newsprint for a recorder for each group to jot down two to three ideas or insights from their discussion.

To conclude the day, each group posts their newsprint sheets around the room. Each group tours the room, reading the answers from the other groups. A short debriefing takes place with the large group. Reflective questions include, What were some common ideas or insights? What were different ideas or insights? and Are there any general comments to share with the whole group?

Retreat Day 2

The day begins with breakfast and a fun icebreaker led by a second-year graduate intern. The goal of the activity is to help students get to know one another more deeply.

Spiritual Reflection Exercise

After breakfast, students are assigned a reflection exercise called Lectio Divina led by one of the faculty members who is an ordained minister in the Presbyterian denomination. Lectio Divina is an ancient spiritual practice, dating from the desert monastics of the early church. It is a slow, contemplative praying of the scriptures and other sacred texts, which enables participants to become a means of union with God.

The students are asked to listen while the faculty member reads out loud from a handout containing three pieces of text related to developing a life purpose. The first is a Bible verse, and the second is a paragraph on a philosophical perspective about the meaning of life and is not associated with a particular faith or religious ideology. Rather, this excerpt of prose challenges students to reflect on and develop the ability to identify and follow their own inner voice. The third and final option includes a poem. The types of reading sources highlight the inclusive nature of this exercise with the choice of biblical, Christian, or spiritual text. It offers the opportunity for spiritual reflection for those outside the Christian tradition. Students can choose the type of text they feel most comfortable with.

Students are asked to find a quiet place either outside on the retreat grounds or somewhere inside on their own and choose one of the passages that has the most meaning for them. They are to read it once, then again slowly and take notes on the words that catch their attention. Then they are asked to read the text they selected a third time and write down their thoughts on what the text is prompting for them. Before the exercise, some students and faculty take a solitary walk in the nature garden, sit on a shaded bench, or find a quiet spot for reflection somewhere on the retreat property.

Exploring Engage (Creating Community)

Following the individual time of reflection, students engage in a community-building session. Eight to 10 second-year students are invited to the retreat to share their story. The second-year students are asked to reflect on and prepare answers to questions specific to this institution and their spiritual and professional experiences during their time as students. The questions are about when they started APU to the present, how they describe their ability to share their story in a narrative way that describes their learning and development, how they would describe their path to APU and wanting to work in student affairs, how they would describe their religious or spiritual background, and what experiences stand out for them in their first year of the program that they consider important learning moments about themselves personally and professionally.

With one of the second-year students as a group facilitator, students then gather in small groups to engage in conversations about the second-year student's experiences and responses to the questions. Students can ask questions of the second-year student or compare and discuss their own experiences. There is a short debriefing of this session in a large group. General comments are shared with the large group and faculty.

Exploring Act

After lunch, students go through a session designed to build bridges of understanding with one another as a way to foster community development. This last session is connected to the theme of act so that students can take the stories they have heard and their own story to create ways to support their cohort as they continue in the program. The learning that is emphasized is how the students value the backgrounds and experiences of their fellow cohort members and how they create support and community in their cohort.

Students revisit their "I am" statements from the prior day. Next, they are given a handout titled "This is what I need from you." The handout contains several prompts to reflect on to help students articulate what they need from other people to feel secure and accepted. The prompts are,

> Spend time thinking about your life and identify a time/situation when you felt discriminated against because of who you are. You might have been treated differently because of your race, ethnicity, class background, gender, sexual orientation, religion, physical characteristics, abilities, etc. Write your story of this painful memory. On the other hand, spend time thinking about your life and identify a time/situation when you felt respected, honored and proud because of who you are. Write your story of this empowering memory.

Next, they respond to, What do you never again want others to say, think, or do toward your group? Finally, they respond to the statement: "What I need from my cohort is . . . ?"

The students can leave the room to complete the exercise. They return and select a partner they do not know to share their responses; they can use the "I am" statements from the previous day. The large group reconvenes, and those who wish can share their responses.

Students are then asked to write on sticky notes their responses to "This is what I need from you." After the students place these on a large white board, they are asked to read them and place them in common categories. The large-group debriefing for this session is on these common categories and creating action statements for the cohort on how to support each other.

This session is the most emotional of all the sessions and also where the students are the most vulnerable. The strategy is that from the prior sessions they have some comfort level in going deeper and more personal with their cohort. However, some students will be quieter than before, whereas some students will be brave and open about sharing their experiences. The facilitation for this last session requires communication that clarifies what this session is about: experiencing feelings of vulnerability and yet keeping in mind how to build community.

Photo Activity

All first-year students get their photo taken with a Polaroid camera. On the bottom white portion of the photo, students write a characteristic or strength they would like to possess when they walk across the stage on graduation day. Examples of some of their sentiments are confidence, spiritual growth, development of their own inner voice, becoming an advocate for others, and so on. The group of students form a large circle and tell the entire cohort the characteristic or strength they wrote down. While students are waiting to have their picture taken, they also complete the evaluation for the retreat. This activity has been a meaningful concluding event in building trust, vision, and spiritual purpose for students as they begin the process of entering the profession of student affairs.

Limitations

This is a time-consuming endeavor in the current format, and significant funds are required to secure an off-campus venue that provides lodging and meals. It can also be challenging to find an appropriate time for the retreat that matches students' readiness to have these conversations along with other schedule and work conflicts associated with the academic year. It would be possible to adapt this retreat to an effective half-day session using the exercises that have the most impact to foster personal and spiritual development.

Spiritual Reflective Journal and Discussion Exercise

To delve deeper into understanding students' own spiritual development and to gain a sensitivity and respect for difference, Holly Holloway-Friesen has students engage in a reflective activity she facilitates. The exercise has proven to be quite effective in helping students reflect on their own spiritual struggles and experiences of marginality as well as develop an understanding of diverse spiritual traditions. Although this activity is part of a research class, it could also be completed as a professional development activity, incorporated in orientation or other cohort meetings, or added to any class where it would be relevant.

Before the session, have students read the following to prepare for the reflection:

- "Perspectives and Experiences of Muslim Women Who Veil on College Campuses" (Cole & Ahmadi, 2003)
- "Examination of Muslim Students' Experiences" (Cole & Ahmadi, 2010)
- "Cultural Incongruity and Social Status Ambiguity: The Experiences of Evangelical Christian Student Leaders at Two Midwestern Public Universities" (Moran, Lang, & Oliver, 2007)
- "Engaging Religious Minority Students" (Ahmadi & Cole, 2014)
- "Singing in a Foreign Land: An Exploratory Study of Gospel Choir Participation Among African American Undergraduates at a Predominantly White Institution" (Strayhorn, 2011)

The spiritual reflective journal exercise is designed to allow students time to reflect on the readings in a personal way. Holloway-Friesen asks them to choose 1 of 3 scenarios (described next) to reflect on and write their journal responses. They have 20 to 25 minutes to think, reflect, and write in their journals. Because of the potential sensitivity of the exercise, once students have reflected and written their responses, they share their writing with 1 or 2 students they feel comfortable with during an additional 15 to 20 minutes. The small-group sharing session with peers is usually quite enlightening for students because they realize that others have had spiritual struggles as well or experienced feelings of marginality based on their spiritual identification like they have. Then participants reconvene as a large group, where about 4 students share their thoughts with the whole class, which takes another 10 to 12 minutes.

The benefits of this exercise are threefold. First, for students who identify with a faith perspective that is a minority viewpoint, it provides a safe venue to share this experience with students. Second, for students who come from a more mainstream religious perspective, it helps them connect with experiences of marginality in their own lives to build pathways toward empathy building and a common dialogue with those in the minority. Third, it helps students realize that there are experiences of marginality in most spiritual worldviews, even mainstream perspectives (i.e., persecution of religious minority and Christian student groups on various campuses).

Students choose from the following three scenarios to reflect on, write about in their journal, and share in a small group, then the large group. They are told to pick just one of the three scenarios. Additionally, the students are informed that what is shared in the activity must stay confidential and will not be allowed to leave the space. Furthermore, students are charged to speak with one another respectfully and lovingly.

Scenario 1: Reflection on Spiritual Struggle

1. Reflect on a time of spiritual struggle in your own life.
2. What changed in you as a result of that struggle?
3. How are you different today because of the struggle?
4. In what ways does that struggle shape the way you interact with students today?

Scenario 2: Reflection on Holding a Viewpoint That Is Different From the Dominant Religious Culture

Recall an experience in which you were not a part of the dominant religious culture in a particular institution. (The example you reflect on does not have to have occurred in the higher education context. It could have occurred in any location—a workplace, your church, your own family, a peer group situation, etc.). Write about that experience. Next choose one of the following questions to respond to:

- If you felt marginalized because of that difference, in what ways did your experience of being an outsider, because of your beliefs, shape your perspective about students or your practice with them?
- If you did not feel marginalized because of that difference, what was it about the experience that enabled you to *hold different beliefs without feeling like an outsider*? Are there lessons you can learn from that and apply to your work with students?

Scenario 3: Displaying Your Worldview

One of the reflection articles mentioned previously focuses on women's choice to veil (i.e. wearing a hijab, al-amira, shayla, khimar, chador, niqab, or burqa). The article suggested that some Muslim women chose not to veil on college campuses because of the way others would react, often because of a misunderstanding of the meaning of the veil. Can you identify a setting or experience when you chose (or currently choose) not to publicly reveal your worldview for fear that it will be misunderstood? Write about that, including how you feel about the following:

1. Your decision
2. The people who might misunderstand you
3. Yourself in that context

4. The extent to which your worldview is developed or hindered because of the context

Limitations

A limitation of this activity is that students will write in the journal only what they feel comfortable letting the faculty know about. One way to overcome this is making students' journals anonymous. However, Holloway-Friesen has found that knowing who the student responses were from helped her connect on a deeper level with her students and better advocate for them.

Conclusion

The two activities described in this chapter provide student affairs graduate students with the opportunity to deepen their understanding of their spiritual beliefs, to understand how their spiritual beliefs relate to their profession, and to understand others with differing beliefs. Furthermore, these activities can be completed outside the classroom, providing cocurricular opportunities for reflection. We believe these activities could be adapted to fit the context of other student affairs graduate preparation programs, and we hope they will motivate student affairs faculty to engage in worldview reflections with their students.

References

Ahmadi, S. & Cole, D. (2014). Engaging religious minority students. In S. J. Quaye & S. R. Harper (Eds.), *Student engagement in higher education: Theoretical perspectives and practical approaches for diverse populations.* 2nd ed. (pp. 171–186). New York, NY: Routledge.

Cole, D., & Ahmadi, S. (2003). Perspectives and experiences of Muslim women who veil on college campuses. *Journal of College Student Development, 44,* 47–66.

Cole, D., & Ahmadi, S. (2010). Examination of Muslim students' experiences. *Journal of Higher Education, 81,* 2, 121–139.

Love, P., & Talbot, D. (1999). Defining spiritual development: A missing consideration for student affairs. *NASPA Journal, 37*(1), 361-375.

Moran, C. D., Lang, D. J., & Oliver, J. (2007). Cultural incongruity and social status ambiguity: the experiences of evangelical Christian student leaders at two Midwestern public universities. *Journal of College Student Development, 48,* 23–38.

Strayhorn, T. L. (2011). Singing in a foreign land: An exploratory study of gospel choir participation among African American undergraduates at a predominantly White institution. *Journal of College Student Development, 52,* 137–153.

PART THREE

STRATEGIES AND ACTIVITIES FOR STUDENT AFFAIRS PRACTITIONERS

Kathleen M. Goodman

Part three of this book is written specifically for student affairs professionals who are looking for concrete ideas to address spirituality, religion, and secularity with students. Chapter 7 describes two types of training to prepare student affairs professionals to address religious diversity and interfaith engagement in their jobs, and chapters 8 and 9 present successful program models to engage students in curricular and cocurricular spaces.

We recognize that every institution and student affairs division have their own unique context and culture. Therefore, it is unlikely that any of the trainings, programs, or activities described in this part of the book can be adopted without change. However, we have provided considerable details in each chapter with the hope that there will be enough information to inspire you to adapt some of these ideas for use in your program.

Student affairs professionals will find additional sections of this book useful as well. Part four includes a series of case studies that could be used in many types of trainings and programs. (The introduction to part four [p. 159] is intended to help guide the use of these case studies; additionally, many of the educational opportunities described in parts two and three also provide examples of how case studies can be used in a variety of settings.) Part five includes chapters elucidating foundational knowledge of several major religions and worldviews and advice for working with students who identify with those religions.

7

TRAINING STUDENT
AFFAIRS PROFESSIONALS

Ariel Ennis and Tarah Trueblood

Campus professionals are often hesitant to address topics of religion, spirituality, secularity, and interfaith engagement because they feel they don't have the training. Although other chapters in part three address how faculty can incorporate these topics into student affairs preparation programs, such coursework does not solve the problem for working professionals who feel unprepared. As Patel and Meyer (2011) argue, religious literacy and interfaith encounters are powerful tools for preparing individuals for interfaith engagement. This chapter provides examples of two student affairs training programs that provide such religious literacy and interfaith encounters. The first model, titled Faith Zone Training, was developed at New York University (NYU) to provide training for student affairs practitioners, students, faculty, and other staff. The second model is an example of incorporating interfaith training into a professional development curriculum focused on several aspects of diversity.

Model 1: Faith Zone Training

As discussions about religious and spiritual identity become increasingly present in student affairs, universities around the world are beginning to dedicate resources toward helping students, staff, and faculty have these conversations in more open, honest, and thoughtful ways. At NYU, our response to this challenge is Faith Zone Training (Faith Zone), a three-hour workshop that promotes religious literacy and fosters the skills necessary to better understand spiritual and religious diversity. Faith Zone is one of the few diversity education initiatives at any university in the United States that directly addresses the challenges of working with a religiously diverse student population. It is the recipient of the 2014 NASPA–Student Affairs Administrators in Higher Education Spirituality and Religion in Higher Education Outstanding Spiritual Initiative Award, winner of NASPA's Silver Excellence Award, and subject of *Teaching Religious Literacy* (Ennis, 2017). Since its creation in 2012, the Faith Zone workshop has been conducted at numerous NYU sites in the United States and abroad as well as at other universities across the country. In all these settings, Faith Zone participants have demonstrated increased comfort discussing religious and spiritual issues and a more sophisticated understanding of religious literacy vis à vis their roles on campus.

At NYU we offer Faith Zone in one of two contexts: an open session that can be attended by any student, staff member, or faculty memeber throughout the university, or as a requested training session for groups of student leaders or administrative units that want to work collaboratively to improve their religious literacy. These sessions are facilitated by students, staff, and chaplains who have been trained in an extensive train-the-trainer module offered once a year. The curriculum we use for both versions of Faith Zone is the same, and we always focus on having participants demonstrate a specific set of the following four learning outcomes:

1. Define *religious literacy*
2. Explain three concrete areas where religious literacy affects their work or role at NYU
3. List and explain the resources available through our office (Global Spiritual Life) at NYU
4. List religious centers and student groups on campus and explain their relationships to Global Spiritual Life

These learning outcomes focus on understanding religious literacy and furthering knowledge of the resources available on campus through the Office of Global Spiritual Life. To accomplish these goals, all Faith Zone sessions contain six components.

Six Components of Faith Zone Training

First, sessions begin with an introduction to the goals of the program, which sets the intention and tone for the conversation. We provide a brief agenda to help direct the conversation throughout the session. Then we develop group guidelines similar to those one would find in any number of diversity workshops in student affairs, emphasizing ideas such as using *I* statements and maintaining confidentiality.

Second, participants are guided through exercises examining personal religious or spiritual beliefs and past encounters with religion and spirituality. These exercises encourage participants to reflect on the varying levels of influence religious or spiritual identity may have in different areas of their lives, including for participants who identify as atheist, agnostic, or have no particular religious or spiritual preference. Fostering this sense of religious and spiritual fluidity is critical to the session and opens participants to developing a more complex understanding of religious and spiritual identity.

Third, Faith Zone focuses on defining *religious literacy* and discussing its relevance to higher education. Religious literacy is the key framework for the entire workshop and provides the necessary context for understanding religiously diverse communities on campuses around the country. At NYU we begin by having the participants discuss terms and ideas they associate with *religion* and *spirituality* and analyze these ideas to uncover inherent biases or opinions that are relevant to the discussion. We want participants to realize that both terms come with a tremendous amount of complexity, and because of this we encourage participants to move toward an understanding of religious and spiritual identity through the prism of religious literacy. At NYU we define *religious literacy* as understanding the historic and contemporary interconnections of religion with cultural, political, and social life, and the ability to use this knowledge to promote allyship and engage in dialogue on issues of religious or spiritual concern. This definition allows us to stress a few critical points that are necessary when discussing religion in diverse contexts.

- First, relying heavily on the work by Moore (2010), we emphasize the external and internal diversity inherent in all religions and their consistent impact on culture and history. Most important, we want to emphasize that religion and spirituality do not develop in a vacuum, and understanding the relationship between religion and culture is a critical component of becoming religiously literate.
- Second, we introduce allyship as a primary characteristic of religious literacy to emphasize to our participants the importance of using this knowledge in practical contexts.
- Third, at no point in our definition of *religious literacy* do we state that an individual must be religious or spiritual to be religiously literate. We want to treat religious literacy as a skill that can be developed for everyone, regardless of religious or spiritual identity.

In aggregate, these ideas come together to provide a framework for thinking about religious diversity and allow participants to begin thinking about practical ideas that can have a direct impact on their campus.

Fourth, Faith Zone highlights relevant demographic data showing which religious groups are represented at NYU and how this relates to citywide and global religious populations. This provides participants with a context to explain why they are more familiar with specific groups than others and how they can begin to formulate a plan to increase their level of knowledge about other communities. After moving through these data, we then highlight various studies that show the prevalence of religious and spiritual concern in higher education (e.g., Astin, Astin, & Lindholm, 2011). This stresses how important conversations of religious diversity are to our current students.

Fifth, participants watch a video of interviews with chaplains from the NYU community discussing the unique needs of their specific communities and naming ways that staff, administrators, and students can be supportive of those needs. This video presents chaplains from our Buddhist, Catholic, Hindu, Humanist, interfaith, Jewish, Muslim, and Protestant communities, and we are always adding new portions to the video to accommodate new chaplains and communities on campus. The key here is not to use this video as an introduction to all world religions; rather, it is about introducing participants to the various types of student concerns that can arise on campus and helping them to begin thinking about ways to deal with these issues.

The sixth and final element of the Faith Zone training involves the creation of personal action plans to ensure that participants can apply what they learned from the training to their everyday lives. This personal action plan is built on the work of Lindholm, Millora, Schwarts, and Spinosa (2011) and asks the following four questions:

1. How is religious literacy important in my role on campus?
2. In what areas have I yet to consider religious and spiritual needs within my sphere of influence?
3. Who from my network, on campus and beyond, might be helpful in this area?
4. Is there anything covered today that is immediately useful?

Participants complete these personal action plans in small groups and then share suggestions and ideas with the larger group.

After reviewing personal actions plans, we present participants with 10 tips for religious literacy to help prime them for future issues and engagement. These tips include advice on familiarizing themselves with resources on campus, creating safe spaces for students, focusing on building relationships, and considering how to plan more inclusive events.

These tips are the final stage of the workshop and encourage participants to begin formulating practical ideas they can bring back to their work on campus. They are designed to cover theoretical and practical issues and prepare participants to deal with a wide variety of religious and spiritual concerns.

Assessment of Faith Zone

After a Faith Zone training session has taken place, we are still left with one critical question: How can we prove that participants are actually learning what we want them to learn during a Faith Zone workshop? At NYU we collaborate with the Office of Research and Assessment to evaluate Faith Zone through pre- and posttests and evaluation sessions as well as include demographic questions to ensure diverse participation in the sessions. All this information is used to continuously improve Faith Zone sessions and to further develop tools for increasing religious literacy.

Thus far, Faith Zone has consistently displayed three outcomes (all data begins with the academic year of September 2014). First, Faith Zone participants consistently report having a positive experience in the workshop and feeling better prepared to address questions of religious diversity when they leave. Although self-reported survey data can only tell us so much about whether we have met our learning outcomes, it is nevertheless critical to know that participants are consistently pleased and that they consider the knowledge they gained to be valuable.

Second, participants have displayed increases in their ability to define *religious literacy* and to apply the concept to concrete areas related to their work. Participants are asked before and after each session to define *religious literacy* and list three ways it affects their work, giving us a baseline to evaluate learning growth through the session. A complete explanation of this rubric with examples falls outside the scope of this chapter but can be found in Ennis (2017).

Third, awareness of local campus resources improved dramatically over the course of the the workshops. Participants' ability to list centers and programs increased an average of 52.8% per session, an enormous increase and incredibly important for our office, which is a new NYU office. More fundamentally, however, increasing awareness of local resources is a critical component of any workshop because it enables participants to feel comfortable asking their network for help when questions invariably arise.

In the four years that Faith Zone has been a key pedagogical tool of the Office of Global Spiritual Life at NYU, we have seen demonstrable learning across different groups and an increase in the popularity of these workshops. This reflects the increasing importance of religion and spirituality in higher education and the need to dedicate more time and resources toward this topic at universities across the country.

Model 2: Cultural Competency in Worldview Identity Workshop

In 2011 Tarah Trueblood was hired as the first director of the Interfaith Center at the University of North Florida (UNF). Her first priority was to include worldview identity and religious pluralism in any existing professional development framework for diversity, equity, and inclusion. Because UNF had not yet established such a framework, she recruited a handful of colleagues from various offices in the Division of Student Affairs[1] and together created, piloted, developed, and cofacilitated an 18-hour professional development curriculum called Cultural Competency Pursuit (CCP). Designed to achieve basic competency levels for equity, diversity, and inclusion (later revised to social justice and inclusion) for student affairs professionals as established by NASPA and ACPA–College Student Educators International, the CCP curriculum includes 8 interactive workshops: introduction to equity, diversity, and inclusion; a capstone at the end of the curriculum; and 6 core competency workshops, including Worldview Identity, an introduction to religious and nonreligious identities and worldview pluralism, developed in collaboration with Rachael McNeal (Interfaith Center) and Naomi Karp Tillman (Intercultural Center for Peace). The other core competency workshops are Dis/ability Awareness; Military Veteran Identity; Gender Inclusion; Race and Ethnicity; and Safe Space in Lesbian, Gay, Bisexual, Transgender, and Queer Identities.

Overview of the CCP

CCP 101 is the introductory workshop and prerequisite for all other workshops in the curriculum. CCP 101 introduces participants to concepts, themes, and pedagogical approaches used throughout the curriculum. For example, participants are introduced to Equitable Space Guidelines which are used in all eight workshops and are designed to empower people from different backgrounds to engage in equitable and civil discourse across difference. Workshop participants are keenly aware of the current highly divisive cultural climate, and they often remark that without taking time to agree on discussion guidelines it is difficult to have respectful disagreement.

Participants are also introduced to research on implicit bias and how such biases affect our daily attitudes, perceptions, and actions without conscious awareness. Self-reflection exercises are introduced to help bring conscious awareness to one's own biases and to the complexity of one's own identity. Common terms, concepts, and theories used throughout the curriculum are introduced. Learning outcomes for the overall curriculum are provided as well as the focus of those outcomes in three areas: awareness, knowledge, and skills that lead to concrete actions for creating a campus environment that is more equitable, diverse, and inclusive.

Most of the six core competency workshops are linked to short online tests that gauge implicit bias. In advance of these workshops, we sent an e-mail message containing a link to the test to participants to let them know that a prerequisite to the workshop includes the completion of one of Harvard University's implicit bias tests (to see the test, go to www.implicit.harvard .edu/implicit/selectatest.html, follow registration or guest access, agree to the preliminary information, and then select Religion IAT).

Capstone in Equity, Diversity, and Inclusion is taken after completion of all seven of the other CCP workshops and is designed to assist participants in synthesizing the learning that has taken place during the curriculum. Pre- and postcurriculum self-assessment surveys as well as postworkshop satisfaction surveys provide the CCP team and workshop facilitators with feedback for continuous improvement and a measure of the curriculum's impact on the division as a whole.

The entire CCP curriculum is offered each semester and once during the summer. Adopted by the Student Affairs Professional Development Committee, it is credentialed through UNF's Center for Professional Development and Training. In 2015–2016, the second year that curriculum was offered, Black students began protesting on college campuses across the country after police shootings of unarmed Black men. Following these protests, UNF's vice president of the Division of Student and International Affairs made the CCP curriculum mandatory for all department heads and highly recommended it for all other staff members. By the end of fall of 2016, the entire curriculum will have been offered 4 times to more than 250 participants, and 4 cohorts will have completed the entire 18-hour curriculum. CCP graduates receive a certificate of completion from the vice president and a bright CCP decal.

In August 2016 the UNF President's Commission on Diversity and Inclusion adopted a two-year strategic plan to scale the curriculum for the entire university including students, faculty, administrators, and staff outside student affairs. The dean of UNF's business school committed all incoming business students to complete a student-centered version of the CCP curriculum.

Foundations of a Worldview Identity Workshop

When the CCP curriculum was implemented, training in worldview identity was appropriately anchored in UNF's overall framework for professional development in equity, diversity, and inclusion. The Worldview Identity

Workshop lasts two hours. As with other workshops in the CCP curriculum, the Worldview Identity Workshop is oriented around outcomes in awareness, knowledge, and practical skills. Our learning goals state that participants of the workshop will

- increase their awareness that humans have complex worldview identities and that everyone has biases about worldviews;
- become more knowledgeable about worldview identity, how worldview intolerance is experienced on campus, the difference between worldview diversity and worldview pluralism, and some of the benefits of interfaith dialogue and cooperation in higher education; and
- start developing skills for creating a campus environment that is more equitable, diverse, and inclusive for members of the campus community of all worldviews.

One of the foundations of this workshop is an understanding of how and why the term *worldview* is used, which is to include the breadth of religious, spiritual, and other values-based ideological frameworks present on campuses today. We found it helpful to show that UNF's student worldview demographics align closely with the demographics for young adults across the entire country, particularly trends on increasingly religiously unaffiliated millennials (Pew Research Center, 2015). We use the word *worldview* to include all identities rooted in a system of values such as mutual respect, human dignity, hospitality, and care for the environment.

The Immigration Act of 1965 not only diversified the U.S. ethnic and racial makeup but also expanded the religious diversity in the country, making it the most religiously diverse country of all time (Eck, 2001). Now you may meet someone who identifies as a Catholic Hindu or a spiritual but not religious Christian. College is often the first place people encounter visible worldview differences (Patel, 2007). In addition to nurturing maturation of a worldview for themselves, students must be equipped to successfully interact across lines of worldview difference in our diverse democracy and the global community (Larson & Shady, 2013). By providing this framing to participants, they are able to arrive at an understanding of the urgency for developing competencies in worldview diversity. To help deliver on learning outcomes, the workshop is cofacilitated by staff members with different worldviews, who model worldview diversity and mutual respect. On the day of the workshop, facilitators introduce themselves and disclose their personal worldviews. This disclosure begins the process of normalizing conversation on religious, spiritual, and other values-based worldviews and demonstrates equity among them.

Another important foundation for this workshop is the creation of a safe environment for dialogue across difference. After all, most of us have learned early in life that religion is one of a handful of conversation topics to be avoided (in addition to race, politics, and sex). The Equitable Space Guidelines developed for the CCP curriculum encourage respectful disagreement and discourages debating and proselytizing. By the time participants take the Worldview Identity Workshop, they have already started integrating these guidelines for use in discourse across difference and often in everyday life.

We find it helpful to include a disclaimer at the beginning of the workshop to make it clear that we will not be providing an overview of all the various worldviews because of the number of different ones represented on campus and because most are highly nuanced and continuously evolving. It is simply not possible to be an expert on them all.

However, we can be an expert on our own worldview and draw from our own experience in modeling engagement across difference. Speaking from our own personal experience is new to many educators, particularly faculty members. As noted by hooks (1994), "Students should not be expected to share their experiences if we as teachers are unwilling to do the same" (p. 15). The Equitable Space Guideline that calls for the use of I statements goes a long way in helping facilitators and participants get comfortable talking about their own worldview and giving weight to personal experience. Also, I statements allow people to speak about their own worldview without having to represent or speak on behalf of everyone sharing it. These statements also minimize the risk of generalizing other worldviews. Rather, we simply speak of other worldviews from the perspective of our own experience of them, keeping in mind the other guidelines.

Another foundation for the workshop is a clear understanding that engagement with religious, spiritual, and other values-based worldviews does not violate the establishment clause of the First Amendment. That amendment prohibits the establishment of any form of government-sanctioned religion or nonreligious worldview. The First Amendment also prohibits the government (including public universities, which are an extension of the government) from interfering with the practice of one's chosen worldview (U.S. Const., amend. I). Therefore, exploring one's own worldview identity through interaction with people with other worldviews is perfectly permissible. We have also found that rather than dismissing one's own worldview as a result of exposure to other worldviews, engagement across difference increases understanding for everyone and usually serves to strengthen and cause one's own worldview to mature.

To achieve the learning outcomes established for this workshop, participants are exposed to a variety of pedagogical tools. For example, participants are provided with written definitions of terms that are unique to worldview identity. These terms also provide a common language for dialogue. Other methods include modules for individual self-reflection and interactive activities. For one of the first exercises, we often ask participants to reflect on the following: What has been your personal experience with religion, faith, or worldview? Has it been positive? Negative? Meaningful? Indifferent? Absent?

An interactive activity we often use is a sticky note–word association exercise designed to bring awareness to worldview implicit biases. This exercise involves participants in writing words on sticky notes that they associate with each of five or six different religious and nonreligious worldviews present on campus. A page from a flip chart for each of the five or six worldviews is posted around the room before the workshop. Participants are invited to walk around the room and anonymously post their word associations on the page bearing the name of the corresponding worldview. Facilitators then review aloud some of the more common word associations from each chart adding some that have been missed. This activity brings to life many of the implicit biases, stereotypes, and prejudices imbedded in culture and highlights the fact that bias is a shared experience among people of all worldviews.

Following the facilitator's review of the posted word associations, participants are invited to reflect on how it felt to participate in the exercise. They may be given prompts or stem questions to answer such as, During this activity, I noticed . . . , I felt . . . , I wondered . . . , I can offer . . . . After reflecting individually, the participants may be invited to share aloud any insights.

As with the other CCP core competency workshops, facilitators for the Worldview Identity Workshop help participants understand how implicit bias predicts behavior in the real world. For example, facilitators may provide a visual aid that shows the connections among implicit bias (attitudes or stereotypes that affect our understanding), intolerance (an unwillingness to accept views, beliefs, or behaviors that differ from one's own), prejudice (a preconceived opinion that is not based on reason or actual experience), discrimination (the unjust or prejudicial treatment of a person because of their worldview), and oppression (the systematic, social, or institutional mistreatment or exploitation of people because of their worldview).

Multimedia presentations provide diversity in terms of learning styles. At UNF we typically select one short video on a salient issue.[2] Frequently we use a clip that helps participants understand that worldviews are inherently nuanced, internally diverse, and embedded in culture. A postvideo reflective discussion can help participants harvest learning.

Each of the core workshops in the CCP curriculum concludes with an exercise called Start-Stop-Continue. On a sheet of paper, participants are instructed to draw three columns and to label them Start, Stop, and Continue. In each column, participants are asked to write down action steps, things they can personally start doing, stop doing, or continue doing to create a campus environment that is more equitable, diverse, and inclusive of people from diverse worldviews. Time permitting, participants may share with the rest of the group a commitment they added to their sheet. Start-Stop-Continue worksheets from all five core competency workshops are excellent workshop takeaways. They can be used to assist in preparing a participant's capstone project, a mandatory part of the curriculum that is due within two weeks after the capstone workshop.

The Worldview Identity Workshop concludes with participants completing a satisfaction survey designed for all courses offered through UNF's Center for Professional Development and Training. This survey differs from the separate pre- and postcurriculum self-assessments that track a participant's progress and the effectiveness of the entire curriculum in advancing competencies in equity, diversity, and inclusion as established by NASPA and ACPA in that it is an excellent source of immediate feedback for continuous improvement.

Gauging Impact

Participants in the Worldview Identity Workshop had comments such as, "I didn't realize how important it is to actually have these conversations," "Religious people can have meaningful dialogue with atheists," and "I appreciated the dissection of stereotypes because it helped me understand that religious intolerance is a shared experience among people of all worldviews."

Data are still being collected on the pre- and postcurriculum self-assessments of the CCP. However, during capstone discussions, participants reported a false sense of competency before completing the curriculum, thinking they already possessed a sufficient grasp on equity, diversity, and inclusion only to realize after completing the curriculum that they had many gaps. Capstone participants also noted that competency in equity, diversity, and inclusion is much more important to success in their current job than they had realized.

Additional Resources

In the summer of 2016, Trueblood served on a national curriculum committee of 12 experienced professionals assembled by Interfaith Youth Core (IFYC), a Chicago-based nonprofit founded by its president, Eboo Patel. The committee's purpose was to advise IFYC on overarching goals of a national worldview engagement curriculum and to create an outline for such a curriculum. IFYC's vision for this curriculum is to make it widely available for use by campus professionals to train other campus professionals to address worldviews in their work on campus. The resulting BRIDGE (Building Regular Interfaith Dialogue through Generous Engagement) Curriculum: An Introduction to Worldview Engagement was piloted at several universities across the country in winter and spring 2017. The UNF piloted the curriculum by incorporating it into the CCP Worldview Identity Workshop. Like other workshops in the CCP curriculum, the pilot was facilitated by two CCP team members. It received outstanding feedback from the facilitators and participants alike. The BRIDGE Curriculum is available for free on IFYC's website (www.ifyc.org/bridge) for use on campuses across the country and includes multiple modules that focus on a variety of issues related to worldview engagement.

Conclusion

Given the dearth of attention on religious diversity and interfaith engagement in student affairs preparation programs, it seems likely that many student affairs professionals could benefit from training in these areas. In this chapter we provide two examples of how institutions are implementing training on a rather broad scale. Faith Zone Training at NYU, an example of a standalone training, provides a model that campuses could adapt relatively easily based on their own context (public or private, large or small, religiously heterogeneous or homogeneous, etc.). The Worldview Identity Workshop provides a model of a more extensive program that unites a wide range of diversity and inclusion training into a single, cohesive effort. This could be adapted by institutions to create comprehensive programming focused on the social justice and inclusion competency of ACPA and NASPA. We hope readers of this chapter find ideas and inspiration in these models that they can use to create training opportunities at their institution to help student affairs professionals develop their religious literacy and comfort with religious encounters to create more inclusive campuses for religious diversity and interfaith engagement.

Notes

1. Deiderie Allard and Morgan Murray (housing and residential life), Kaitlin Legg and Jake Moore (LGBT Resource Center), Sheila Spivey (Women's Center),

Russell Dubberly (Disability Resource Center), and Ray Wikstrom (Military Veterans Resource Center).

2. Examples include Interfaith Youth Core's introductory video, www .youtube.com/user/InterfaithYouthCore; Eboo Patel on globalization and liberal education today, www.youtube.com/watch?v=kWe3a62h_h4; and Harvard University's misunderstandings of religion, www.youtube.com/watch?v=U-YQXRrNo70

References

Astin, A. W., Astin, H. S., & Lindholm, J. A. (2011). *Cultivating the spirit: How college can enhance students' inner lives.* San Francisco, CA: Jossey-Bass.

Eck, D. L. (2001). *A new religious America: How a "Christian country" has become the world's most religiously diverse nation.* New York, NY: HarperOne.

Ennis, A. (2017). *Teaching religious literacy: A guide to religious and spiritual diversity in higher education.* New York, NY: Routledge.

hooks, b. (1994). *Teaching to transgress: Education as the practice of freedom.* New York, NY: Routledge.

Larson, M., & Shady, S. (2013). Cultivating student learning across faith lines. Retrieved from https://www.aacu.org/publications-research/periodicals/cultivating-student-learning-across-faith-lines

Lindholm, J. A., Millora, M. L., Schwartz, L. M., & Spinosa, H. S. (2011). *A guidebook of promising practices: Facilitating college students' spiritual development.* Los Angeles: Regents of the University of California.

Moore, D. L. (2010). *Guidelines for teaching about religion in K–12 public schools in the United States.* Retrieved from https://rlp.hds.harvard.edu/publications/guidelines-teaching-about-religion-k-12-public-schools-united-states

Patel, E. (2007). *Acts of faith: The story of an American Muslim, the struggle for the soul of a generation.* Boston, MA: Beacon Press.

Patel, E., & Meyer, C. (2011). The civic relevance of interfaith cooperation for colleges and universities. *Journal of College & Character, 12*(1), 1–9.

Pew Research Center. (2015). *Millennials increasingly are driving growth of "nones."* Retrieved from http://www.pewresearch.org/fact-tank/2015/05/12/millennials-increasingly-are-driving-growth-of-nones/

U.S. Const., amend. I.

8

EDUCATIONAL ACTIVITIES FOR STUDENT AFFAIRS PRACTITIONERS

Kathleen M. Goodman

This chapter is a compilation of programs, activities, structures, and training sessions related to religious diversity and interfaith engagement. The educators from across the country who provided these activities represent a wide range of institutions, including public and private, religious and secular. Some of these institutions have staff dedicated to religious life, and others do not. Our goal in offering these activities is to provide ideas for student affairs practitioners to adapt them to work in any context or functional area, such as residence life, diversity offices, orientation, leadership programs. We hope you will use these ideas like a recipe, whether you follow them step-by-step or make changes to suit your particular tastes and contexts.

The submissions are divided into the following categories: religious literacy, dialogue and personal exploration, training, advocacy, and campus collaborations. Many of the submissions could fit into several categories, but each has been listed only once. We invite you to peruse all the ideas that were submitted and implement one or more of them on your campus.

Religious Literacy

Interfaith Staycation: An Alternative Spring Break

The Center for Spirituality, Dialogue, and Service (CSDS) at Northeastern University hosted a 4-day alternative spring break titled Interfaith Staycation, which brought 35 students together to explore sacred sites in the greater Boston area. A small steering committee of students from different faith traditions and staff planned the trip by contacting local places of worship and practice. We rented a bus to travel to farther locations but used public transportation or walked to the majority of sites.

The group visited nine sites in total: Gurdwara Sikh Sangat, the Jain Center of Greater Boston, Shivalaya Temple, Wat Nawamin Thai Buddhist Temple, Our Lady of Perpetual Help Catholic Church, Islamic Society of Boston Cultural Center, First Church of Roxbury, Beit Midrash at Hebrew College, and the International Society for Krishna Consciousness. At each site, students heard from a member of the community about practices and beliefs after observing and participating in a ritual, worship, or practice if they felt comfortable. Representatives at each site answered questions from the students.

Each day, the group shared a meal provided by one of the sacred sites or by the CSDS. The meals all corresponded to one or more of the sites visited on that date. For example, we attended a Kirtan, which is a worship service involving hymns and passages from the Sikh holy scripture, the Guru Granth Sahib, usually led by musicians who play and sing at the Gurudwara (a Sikh temple, literally meaning gateway to the Guru), and participated in Langar, the tradition of serving a meal to the community. Our group did intentional reflection at the beginning and end of each day, considering what we had learned, questions we still had, and how our learning made us reflect more deeply on our own spirituality.

The purpose of the staycation sacred spaces tour was to build interfaith literacy through experiential learning. The authenticity of observing and participating in practices of communities beyond campus gave participants a unique opportunity to connect what they learn on campus with communities beyond. Students received a certificate of religious literacy training at the end of the program. Because of the deep relationships built through shared experience and reflection, many of the students who had never attended a CSDS program visited the CSDS for the rest of the semester and even started a sacred spaces committee that visited a different sacred site every week. Students acted as hosts when others visited their places of worship or practice.

(Submitted by Karin Firoza, Center for Spirituality, Dialogue, and Service, Northeastern University, and Jem Jebbia, Department of Religious Studies, Stanford University)

Contemplative Series: A Study and Practice of Mindfulness Through Interfaith Exploration

At Benedictine University we have 10 Benedictine hallmarks we invite our students to contemplate and live: love of Christ and neighbor, prayer, stability, conversation, obedience, discipline, humility, stewardship, hospitality, and community. Each of these hallmarks is encompassed in the Benedictine phrase *ora et labora* (pray and work). We strive for our students to be mindful of the needed balance between their work life and their spiritual life.

Our contemplative series gives our students space to find their own balance through meditation and exploration. By introducing prayer and meditative practices from different faiths, our students find ways to contemplate and relax as well as gain a greater understanding of diverse faiths.

Description

Each contemplative series event begins with the introduction of two faith leaders from different faith backgrounds. For example, we may introduce a priest and an imam or a monk and a shaman to lead forms of faith meditation and prayer from their faiths.

We begin by inviting one of the faith leaders to talk about contemplative practices in his or her tradition (5–10 minutes). The individual then guides us through a contemplative exercise (10–15 minutes). We continue by inviting the second faith leader to talk about the contemplative practices in his or her tradition and guide us through a contemplative exercise as well. In conclusion, we invite the participants to ask questions or share insights following the experience with the faith leaders (10–15 minutes).

It is important to emphasize that students need not leave behind their own faith and worldview commitments to engage in this kind of learning. At Benedictine University, we begin each contemplative series session by reminding all present of the Assisi model of Pope St. John Paul I: "We may be in prayer together, but not praying together." We invite others to learn from other faith traditions but never sacrifice something from their own faith tradition.

Possible Adaptations

This program adapts easily to fit the needs of the community. Many faith traditions have methods of meditation and prayer. The more diverse the pairings, the more interesting the experience. Benedictine University has had sessions on Catholicism, Buddhism, Sikhism, Islam, Native American spirituality, and Hinduism.

This program could also be adapted to highlight a single form of meditation, which could be a part of a series or a one-time practice to introduce the discussion of a faith.

Materials

- Quiet space
- Trusted community faith leader from the tradition represented in meditation

- Candles (optional)
- Pillows (optional)

Learning Goals
- Gain perspective on the highly personal activity of meditation or prayer through a faith lens apart from one's own faith
- Relate new perspectives to one's own faith tradition and meditation style
- Understand the broader context of other faiths and their expression

Potential Learning Outcomes and Assessment
If offered as part of an ongoing series that included more background on each faith, participants could be asked to write and share reflections on what they learned about similarities and differences in meditation practices of different faiths. They could also integrate their ideas on how meditation practices are related to the tenets of each faith.

Ground Rules
- Cell phones are either turned off or silenced.
- It is important to remind the community present that the community faith leader is only speaking from his or her own personal experience and not on behalf of an entire group.

Limitations
This exercise works best with a smaller group of students (no more than 30). An intimate space and group creates a more meaningful and peaceful atmosphere.

(Submitted by Carrie Roberts, director of campus
ministry, and Megan Benham, coordinator, Global and
Intercultural Program, Benedictine University)

Everything You've Always Wanted to Know About Islam But Were Afraid to Ask

As Islamophobia increased across the United States in the wake of several high-profile events, students expressed their own concerns about national rhetoric and their ability to respond to it. Some non-Muslim students wanted to stand in solidarity with their Muslim peers but felt they did not have enough information about Muslim traditions and culture to counter the claims they heard in the media. Other non-Muslim students had questions about whether media reports were true or not but felt too embarrassed to ask. This program was designed to bring non-Muslim students together in an open and welcoming space to ask questions without fear of judgment.

Description
Our Muslim chaplain convened a series of teas or small-group conversations in collaboration with residence life. Our college has regular weekly teas in each residence hall as part of student life programming. By collaborating with residence life, our Muslim chaplain was not only able to meet students where they were in a comfortable and welcoming space but also use scheduled programming space to increase attendance and lessen stigma for attending. No one had to worry about being judged for attending as it was part of regular residence hall life.

At each tea, the chaplain handed out index cards to students and had them write one question on each card they had regarding Islam. The index cards were then put in a box so no one could see who wrote what question, and the cards were drawn at random. The Muslim chaplain answered each question from her own perspective and those of wider traditions. Students were then invited to discuss the question and answers in light of their own spiritual and secular traditions and culture.

The goal was to broaden the conversation from a question-and-answer session on one tradition to an exploration of similar issues across multiple religious and nonreligious traditions. By having the Muslim chaplain facilitate the dialogue, Muslim students were not put on the spot to explain their beliefs or defend their worldview. In addition, as a Muslim scholar familiar with multiple traditions in Islam, our chaplain was able to provide a broader view of Islam and debunk the idea of a monolithic Islamic worldview. Our chaplain was able to speak from her own personal experience and the wider traditions in Islam.

Possible Adaptations
This format could be used to talk about any religious or nonreligious tradition—Judaism, Buddhism, evangelical Christianity, Hinduism, secularism, paganism—the possibilities are endless. You could develop a series to discuss each religious and nonreligious tradition represented on your campus.

Total Time
Each conversation was 60 minutes. In the first 5 minutes, students wrote down and submitted their questions. In the next 10 minutes, the chaplain offered a very brief overview of the tradition and contemporary concerns that arose in the wider culture. The next 40 minutes were dedicated to discussing the questions. Not all questions were answered. The final 5 minutes

was spent closing the conversation and providing resources to learn more, including times when non-Muslim students could join Muslim students on campus in weekly activities.

Materials

Index cards and pens are the only necessary materials. We also provided tea and light snacks to create a warm and inviting atmosphere.

Limitations

The question-and-answer format runs the risk of universalizing particular traditions and forcing one person to defend the beliefs or worldview of a global tradition. The conversation must be framed to acknowledge these concerns, and the moderator should explain briefly why the conversation was intentionally structured this way. One way around these limitations would be to have a panel of Muslims respond instead of just the Muslim chaplain and to include non-Muslim allies.

(Submitted by Tiffany Steinwert, Office of Religious and Spiritual Life, Wellesley College)

Dialogue and Personal Exploration

Catholic Muslim Dialogue: Invitation for All

Benedictine University Campus Ministry sponsors a biweekly Catholic Muslim dialogue for students of the Catholic and Islamic faith to come together to talk about issues the students choose. In late fall of 2015 public hateful rhetoric was aimed toward Muslims in the national discourse. Our campus chose to demonstrate effective dialogue in response to the disrespectful debates in the media. We found this public forum to be an engaging way to share with a broader audience the importance of building community through diversity.

Description

Members of a dialogue group that meet biweekly created a public event titled Catholic Muslim Dialogue: Invitation to All. It was designed to be a public representation of healthy dialogue for the entire campus community. The students who created and served as the center of the event had already created an atmosphere of understanding and respect when talking with each other.

A table with chairs for each member of the dialogue group was placed on the first floor of our main learning hall. The main hall is an atrium with heavy foot traffic above and around the table. Along the hall near the table were 50 chairs for people who wanted to stop and listen to the discussion. A microphone was available for the dialogue participants to broadcast the discussion throughout the learning hall.

A faculty member introduced the session and explained its purpose. The student participants each introduced themselves and said how long they have been engaged in these types of conversations. A Muslim student read a passage from the Qur'an, and a Catholic student read a passage from the Bible. The students then discussed the wisdom and insights they gained from each of the readings. At the end of the dialogue we opened the conversation up to those who were gathered around for any questions for comments.

Possible Adaptations

The group can be adjusted to fit the demographic needs of the community. For example, we have a large population of Muslim students on campus, and we are a Catholic institution; therefore, we chose to begin with these two faith traditions. We hope to continue to grow and hold dialogues on other faiths. The dialogue group could also respond to various topics in the news or in a faith tradition.

Total Time

Fifty minutes.

Materials

Public space, table and chairs for dialogue leaders, audiovisual equipment (microphone and speaker), and holy books from the faith traditions.

Learning Goals

- Introduce the practices of respectful interfaith dialogue to the broader campus community
- Attract new members to our interfaith groups on campus
- Provide a counter narrative to the hateful rhetoric around different faith groups promoted by the media

Ground Rules

We begin the dialogue by reminding all present that each individual is speaking from personal experience and understanding and not on behalf of an entire faith community. We use Swindler (1983) as a guide before engaging in dialogue with one another. This provides participants with a greater understanding of the difference in discussion, debate, and dialogue.

Limitations

At Benedictine University we have a very supportive environment that fosters dialogue, which is important for sensitive conversations. It is helpful to also have a faculty member or faith leader present to firmly set forth the rules of the dialogue to open the event.

(Submitted by Carrie Roberts, director of campus
ministry, and Megan Benham, coordinator, Global and
Intercultural Program, Benedictine University)

Interfaith Thanksgiving, Friendsgiving

Description

Multiple faith-based groups and service-learning classes from Colorado State University join forces to create a space for dialogue, shared prayers, songs, and conversation during a shared meal. The menu always features kosher, vegan, gluten-free, and dairy-free options and is cooked by students. Preparation of the food begins a week in advance, and many dishes represent different religions. The event also features a variety of prayers and blessings from a range of religions spanning Judaism, Christianity, Islam, Bahá'í, Earth-based spiritualities, and many others. Activities include singing, facilitated table dialogues, and large poster boards where attendees are asked to write down what they are thankful for.

This event was initiated in 2015 by Hillel, the Jewish student organization. It continues to grow in cosponsors, participants, university support, and grants every year. In 2016 more than 160 people from various religious and spiritual groups around the university community participated. The event is designed to give students the opportunity to create community together by sharing a meal with intentional discussions across lines of difference.

The following is the program for the 2016 Interfaith Thanksgiving Celebration:

5:30–6:00 Ingathering
6:10 Welcome
6:15–6:30 Blessings and Prayers of Gratitude from various traditions
6:30 Eating and table discussion
7:45 Song: "Imagine" John Lennon
7:55 Closing

Total Time

One hour for planning per week, starting three months prior to the event (usually the event is the second week of November). Closer to the event, the time commitment varies. The following is a general outline of key preparation activities before the event:

1. Send e-mail invitation to groups the first week of August requesting participation. Make sure to include groups present at previous interfaith events. This e-mail invitation should include the following:
   a. Event explanation, date, purpose, and history of event
   b. Participation expectations for group involvement (i.e., not an opportunity to proselytize but to build relationships across lines of faith and belief, people to cook, set up, clean up, etc.).
   c. Name of their representatives for this event.
   d. First meeting date (second or third week of classes)
   e. Date when group should reply to indicate their interest in participating.
2. Hold a large-group meeting (every other week) in August, September, and October, where at least one rep from each organization must be present.
   a. Assemble groups (keeping diversity in mind) and determine project time lines.
   b. Set up individual group forums using social media connection (GroupMe or Google Docs work well).
   c. Elect team leaders for groups (marketing, programming, and food).
   d. Have someone take minutes at each meeting and post them on social media.
3. Everyone helps prepare the food during the four days before the event.

Materials
We keep a record of recipes, shopping lists, and shared cooking duties.

Ground Rules
The following suggestions are provided at each table to create intentional space:

> In this space, we ask all participants to engage in both guided and free-flowing interfaith conversation around a shared meal. We invite you to suspend judgment and agree to engage in conversations with respect and civility, allowing for a robust exchange of ideas and perspectives without demonizing or marginalizing any single voice or perspective. It is our hope to model compassionate and productive dialogue across lines of faith and belief. Thank you for your openness and participation.

The following are discussion questions for the tables:

1. What do celebrations of gratitude look like in your life?
2. Which of the blessings or prayers resonated with you?
3. Is America tolerant of religious and nonreligious diversity? How? How not? What can we learn from other cultural or countries about respecting such diversity?
4. What would you like others to know about your faith, beliefs, or traditions?
5. When and how have new avenues of understanding about faith, belief, and spirituality opened for you?

(Submitted by Elizabeth Sink, faculty, Communication
Studies, Colorado State University)

Interfaith Lunch and Conversation

Every Wednesday we invite our campus community to join us for a simple lunch of soup, salad, bread, cookies, and conversation. We choose a theme each year, such as Unity in Our Diversity, and seek students, faculty, outside groups, and occasionally a well-known expert or public figure to address a particular topic on what gives us meaning and purpose. We are intentional about the design and try to bring all points of view to the discussion. This year's theme was Flourishing in the Company of Strangers based on the film *Music of Strangers* (Neville & Rogers, 2015). One week we hosted a Buddhist nun and scholar, Ven. Jampa Tsedroen (Carola Roloff) who came as part of the Five College Robed Warriors series, highlighting four prominent Buddhist monastic women whose work has transformed contemporary Buddhist practice and the world beyond. Another week, we heard, using Skype, Sister Christine Schenk, a Catholic nun who was featured in the film *Radical Grace* (Alpert, Bernardi-Reis, & Sarandon, 2015) about a Vatican investigation into the work and lives of progressive American nuns.

Typically we explore topics related to religious and spiritual issues related to gender, sexuality, race, or politics. Our diverse student population ensures a lively discussion, but the most positive outcome is the trust and communication skills that are nurtured by having a weekly program that emulates a model of safe engagement on challenging topics. The community building that emerges from the weekly format is the gift of the time spent and the program.

The Interfaith Luncheon has had a powerful impact on our students who develop intimate relationships across cultural and socioeconomic lines.

The Interfaith Luncheon has become a bucket list item for students to experience before they graduate.

The Interfaith Luncheon has become so valuable to our diverse student body that the model of dialogue has been duplicated by alumnae who now live in Pakistan as part of a social movement they call #girlsatdhabas, which seeks to break the barriers of women in public squares. When interest to explore a topic more deeply is shown, smaller groups have been spawned with the support of Office of Religious and Spiritual Life staff.

Description
Lunch and discussion begins with a 20-minute interactive presentation. Conversations after the presentation often take place in dyads and triads of students; faculty and staff also participate with the students in this full community experience. The leaders will usually prepare questions related to their presentations and invite small-group discussions. The room is often referred to as the living room of the campus with its four large couches and dining tables. Many of the students take their lunches and sit on the floor because the room is packed. The cost of the meal, depending on number of participants, is roughly $300 per week for us.

Ground Rules
Active listening, no interrupting. Asking for clarification is encouraged. The staff and weekly participants work together to create a culture that welcomes everyone and where laughter and playfulness help too.

(Submitted by Annette McDermott, Division of Student Life,
Office of Religious and Spiritual Life, Mount Holyoke College)

Better Together Day Programming With Resident Assistants and Residents

This is an activity with the resident assistants and our residents on Interfaith Youth Core's (IFYC) Better Together Day each year in April.

Description
Encourage resident and assistants and students who live in residence halls to engage in conversations about their religious, spiritual, and secular identity to promote interfaith engagement.

Around the time of Better Together Day, we order wristbands. An interfaith conversation using the sample questions in this section takes place with each resident assistant to model the activity. They receive a wristband and one additional wristband to give to one of their residents after they engage in a similar conversation using the same questions. It is then hoped that their residents will talk to other residents on their floor or their peers across campus to learn from each other and share their stories. An e-mail is sent to the residents of the hall on Better Together Day to provide them with information and to encourage them to find another resident of the hall or a peer across campus to talk about their religious, spiritual, or secular identities. This is just a simple example, but it encourages a start to interfaith engagement for students and staff. The following questions can be used:

- How do you make meaning of the world?
- Do you identify with a particular religious, spiritual, or secular tradition?
- Do you know anyone whose tradition is different from yours?

Materials
IFYC We Are Better Together wristbands and T-shirts are free, although donations are appreciated. These items are not essential to the activity but provide a visual representation to spread awareness.

Limitations
You may encounter some resistance from a resident assistant or resident who may not feel comfortable engaging in a conversation centered on religious, spiritual, or secular beliefs or who resists interfaith cooperation. Although this has not been an issue, they could be encouraged to frame the conversation from a different perspective asking instead about how they make meaning in their life or if they have a favorite quote, for example.

(Submitted by Steven Sajkich, Residence Life,
University of Northern Iowa)

MuCh: Muslim Christian Interfaith Dialogue

MuCh (Muslim–Christian) Dialogue at New York University (NYU) is a student-led organization focused on bringing together Muslims and Christians of all ages, ethnicities, sects, backgrounds, genders, and levels of religiosity. They come together to discuss their faiths, life experiences, personal beliefs, similarities and differences, religious scriptures, ideas, and histories to facilitate and nurture a community that respects, cares for, and better understands those of different worldviews on matters of faith and spirituality. The club is a product of the friendship between Muslim and Christian undergraduates at NYU who met on an informal basis each week to discuss verses from the Bible and the Qur'an. Only three years in the making, the club now caters to undergraduate and graduate students, faculty, and community members in the entire NYU campus. The club has served as a platform for bridging the two large communities on campus. With MuCh opening the opportunity for friendships based on mutual empathy and a shared goal to serve God, active members from either community can be found attending the other group's events without feeling uncomfortable.

More important, under the guidance of Global Spiritual Life at NYU, MuCh has created a strong ally relationship between Muslims and Christians on campus. In times of large-scale religious discrimination or instances of hate crimes, both communities gather to share thoughts and prayers. The club has created an atmosphere in which a Muslim and Christian can easily have a conversation and build a mutual, respectful understanding of the other's walk of faith and recognize the challenges that come along with it. MuCh has served to foster a stronger and more inclusive spiritual community on campus, marking true progress for such a large university.

MuCh's signature events are the club's biweekly meetings. Every other week, MuCh members gather to discuss the scheduled topic for the night that the executive board carefully selects before the semester begins. Such topics have included Who is Jesus; Sin; God's Mercy and Forgiveness; the Afterlife; Prophets, Love, and Relationships; Marriage and Family; Noble Women; Purity; Miracles; and many others. The topics are malleable enough for anyone to provide insight and express thoughts.

Each meeting begins with a game (e.g., charades, 20 Questions, Jeopardy) for roughly 20 to 30 minutes, which serves as an icebreaker to get the participants relaxed, comfortable, and acquainted with the people attending that week's meeting. The game also prepares our attendees to slowly leave their comfort zones as many of them will share their stories, beliefs, questions and even challenges with the group. It is critical for attendees to feel safe and comfortable before anything else. The executive board facilitates a friendly and somewhat humorous atmosphere to allow participants the freedom and space for becoming vulnerable and empathetic toward others. After the game, the group gathers around food (often snacks or meals) paid for out of the club's budget. Although the game may sometimes be held in the lobby, the food portion of the night is always held inside a classroom around a discussion table. This is critical because it brings people together, makes speaking to a large group productive, and provides the group with adequate privacy.

While people are eating, the meeting kicks off with two guest speakers who introduce the theme topic. Guest speakers can be anyone who volunteers to be a guest speaker a few days in advance and has prepared a short opening speech. Some speakers present historical and academic introductions to the topic, whereas others simply share a personal journey relevant to the discussion. The guest speakers usually consist of one Muslim and one Christian undergraduate, chaplain, or staff member, but MuCh has had many members who do not identify with either religious tradition. Each speaker's presentation is about 5 minutes. After both guest speakers give their short introductions, the floor opens up to the rest of the audience, about 20–25 people on average. People begin to ask questions that may be directed specifically to the discussion leader, the general members of one religious community, or the audience members.

The Christian and Muslim copresidents have the responsibility of making sure anyone who wants an opportunity to speak has a fair chance. Thus, the executive board monitors the discussion and makes sure everyone is heard across the room. The executive board also keeps close attention in making sure no one is disrespectful of another's beliefs, unintentionally or not. The executive board further ensures that discussions stay on topic.

Although the session is normally held for 90 minutes, the time flies, and as such, many MuCh members find themselves continuing their discussions one on one throughout the night.

(Submitted by Selaedin Maksut and Arif Khalil, copresidents of MuCh Dialogue, New York University)

Finding Purpose: A Career and Major Selection Living-Learning Community With an Interfaith Approach

This program uses an interfaith approach to help second-year students choose a major or career aligned with their vocation. It was developed using Molly Schaller's (2005) research about the development of second-year students, which asserts that as students determine their futures, they pass through the following stages: random exploration, focused exploration, tentative choices, and commitment. Applying this knowledge in conjunction with the IFYC's pluralism and worldview engagement rubric (Interfaith Youth Core, n.d.-b) and the insights into the success of the purpose and vocation grants by the Lilly Endowment described by Clydesdale (2015), a unique path toward success can be identified.

Description

This program should be conducted with a living-learning community or a small residential community (fewer than 100 students in a facility) to maximize feelings of ownership and safety. Participants should be recruited from the pool of students who still do not have a declared major by the end of their first semester.

Once the roster is complete, members participate in preparatory, small-group activities, which should be designed to begin building trust among participants as well as to get the students to begin to reflect on their first year and their current vision of their future. For example, students could be asked to create a short journal about their experiences in the first year, specifically focusing on what felt meaningful. Once completed, the students could then be placed in small groups for an afternoon of icebreakers and discussion centered on the journal reflections.

Over the summer, the students participate in a common reading exercise using a book that demonstrates the application of personal values and beliefs to a successful life or career. Some possible examples include *Faithiest* (Stedman, 2012) or *Acts of Faith* (Patel, 2007). The reading should be used heavily in the fall semester to inform programming, conversations, and reflections.

In the fall semester, students participate in a series of values activities and dialogue experiences based on the speedfaithing activity from IFYC. In addition, students use assessments typically available through a campus career center. The fall semester also includes a biweekly speaker series, bringing successful campus partners and alumni or alumnae who model the application of personal values and beliefs to a successful life or career. The goal of this semester's work is to empower students to declare a major at a formal ceremony in November.

The spring semester proceeds into more focused career explorations with students while beginning to engage students in activities that further their sense of purpose, such as community service or research. The year can culminate in a career declaration ceremony.

(Submitted by Joseph Hawkins, Residence Life,
Miami University, Ohio)

Soulful Suppers

The religious student organizations on our campus rarely have the opportunity to meet with one another. Any gathering they had was often focused on administrative or organizational life on campus. The Office of Religious and Spiritual Life staff wanted to find a way to bring students together to discuss in meaningful ways the values, passions, and beliefs that drive them.

Description
During the 2015–2016 academic year, we hosted monthly dinner conversations around particular existential themes. In the spring semester we focused on love, uncertainty, and compassion. The dinners were open to all students,

but students from religious and spiritual life organizations were given individual invitations from the dean and chaplains or advisers. The goal was to assemble a diverse group of students to create a lively conversation in which students might learn more about one another and their traditions. Butcher block paper was placed on each dining table with crayons and markers. The theme question was written on the paper and students were invited to doodle or write throughout the course of the conversation as ideas and images came to them.

Possible Adaptations
These conversations could focus on a variety of values or existential themes. Themes could be chosen by season or current event. Students could also choose the themes and facilitate the conversation themselves.

Total Time
The agenda was as follows (60 minutes total):

- 15 minutes for dinner and informal conversation.
- 5 minutes for posing questions. One of the chaplains introduced the theme using a quote or textual reading, usually poetry or a recent article circulating on social media. For example, for the session on uncertainty, we read "Go to the Limits of Your Longing" (Rilke, n.d.) and asked where students experience beauty and terror and how they respond in a time of uncertainty. For the session on compassion, we did a brief loving kindness meditation from the Buddhist tradition and asked students where they have experienced compassion in their life, as the giver and receiver.
- 5 minutes for silent reflection, students reflect silently and write or draw their answers on the butcher block paper before beginning a group conversation.
- 5 minutes for pair and share, students turn to their neighbor and talk about what the question evoked for them.
- 25 minutes for large-group conversation facilitated by a chaplain using a list of conversation prompts created ahead of time.
- 5 minutes for closing the conversation by the chaplain and point students to resources on and off campus to further explore the topic of conversation.

Materials
A meal, butcher block paper, markers, pens, and copies of texts (poems, news articles, quotes), a series of conversation prompts.

Limitations

The conversations are only as rich as the diversity of those who attend. It is important to actively and intentionally recruit students from diverse communities on campus. Because sessions were only held once a month, and different students came to each, it was difficult to develop a strong sense of community. It was challenging for students to think critically and share deeply in just 60 minutes with other students they may not have met before.

(Submitted by Tiffany Steinwert, Office of Religious and Spiritual Life, Wellesley College)

Training

Speedfaithing for Resident Assistant Training

The Office of Religious Life is given the opportunity to lead a one-hour training session on religious diversity at the annual resident assistants (RA) training program. Recognizing that the session falls near the end of a long week, and the RAs have received more information than they can absorb, we conduct a training session that is as interactive as possible.

Description

As RAs enter the room for training on religious diversity, we distribute the Interfaith Literacy Quiz created by staff from the IFYC. When the RAs appear to have finished the quiz, we talk through the answers in a large group as a way to introduce the session. After introducing ourselves and offering a brief overview of the programs of the Office of Religious Life, we invite the RAs outside for an interactive experience called speedfaithing (Interfaith Youth Core, n.d.-a).

The students form two circles, one inside of the other and facing one another. Students are positioned across from one person and asked to discuss the following questions (the outside circle moves one person to the left after each question for a variety of conversation partners):

1. On a scale of 1 to 10, how fried is your brain right now and why?
2. How many group-building exercises have you done this week? Which was most fun?
3. Describe one childhood experience of faith or religion. (It can be positive or negative.)
4. Have you ever gotten into a heated discussion about religion or spirituality? If so, what was the topic?

5. What faith question would you ask if you were to lead this exercise in your residence hall?

After 20 minutes, students are invited to return to their seats for a large-group discussion. We lead a discussion using the following 3 questions:

1. What questions would you ask if you were to lead this exercise in your residence halls?
2. How might you invite conversation about religious diversity in your residence halls?
3. What anxieties would you have about doing that?

Materials

Copies of the Interfaith Literacy Quiz (www.ifyc.org/quiz), pencils or pens.

(Submitted by Kelly Burk, chaplain and director,
Quaker Life, Earlham College)

Interfaith Training for Staff and Student Leaders

We designed this session to introduce a safe space for student leaders to gain awareness and build a sense of cooperation through conversation on shared values. Our primary audience was student leaders in the residence life department at Fairfield University.

Part One: Opening Exercises

Share training goal. Participants talk about different kinds of spiritual, religious, and philosophical traditions and values with others who don't necessarily share those beliefs/values or ways of life.

Brainstorm agreements. What kind of agreements do you need as a group to have this conversation? Explain the difference between guidelines and agreements. The following are key agreements:

- Everyone has the right to pass
- Everything said is confidential
- Seek clarification if you don't understand something someone else is saying
- Make sure to listen to others without interrupting
- Be attentive to your own feelings and thoughts
- Use *I* statements
- Remember the importance of the other person's faith or ethical tradition in their lives

- Don't expect others to know everything about your own tradition
- Ask what agreements you'd like to add

Speed dialogue icebreaker (large-group activity): Participants begin to share information about their beliefs and get to know each other during this activity.

1. The facilitator asks students to form two circles, one inner circle and one outer circle.
2. Students in the inner circle face students in the outer circle.
3. The facilitator stands in the center of the inner circle and asks questions to the two groups. Students facing each other have two minutes each to respond to the question.
4. After each question, the students in the inner circle move to the left and continue to move to the left for each new question.
5. The speed dialogue questions we use are:
   a. What is your religious, spiritual, or nonreligious identity? Has your religious or spiritual identity changed over time? If so, what has influenced this?
   b. What is your favorite ritual, holiday observance, or celebration that is part of your religious, spiritual, or nonreligious background or identity?
   c. What is your earliest memory of contact with or awareness of people from a different religious, spiritual, or nonreligious group?
   d. What's your favorite ethnic or cultural food and why?
6. Debrief the activity with the following questions:
   - How did you feel participating in this activity?
   - How did your thinking and feeling change during the course of the activity?
7. Based on the answers to the questions, the facilitator asks the group members to individually decide what they value and how values affect their choices and personal beliefs system.

Values clarification team-building activity (small-group activity): Participants to articulate and prioritize their values during this activity.

1. Write down 10 values that are important to you or important to your tradition. Put each value on a separate piece of paper.
2. The facilitator asks students to look over their 10 values and remove 1 at a time those that are least important to each student.

3. The facilitator continues to guide students until they narrow down their values to their top two values.
4. The facilitator asks students to select the top value.
5. Discussion
   a. Facilitator should remind students that all the values are important but the focus is narrowing these values to one core value.
   b. Students write a clear meaning of their top value.
   c. Students reflect on the process of discarding their values and discuss what it was like them in their small groups.
   d. Students find other groups of students in the larger group who share the same value and reflect on why they chose that value as their top one.
   e. Students gather in a large group to hear what other students have to say about choosing their top 10 values, discarding each one, and what they learned from others who shared the same value.

Debriefing activity: To wrap up part one of the training, participants discuss their thoughts and feelings about the activities they have completed.
The facilitator asks the following:

- How did you feel participating in this activity?
- How did your thinking and feeling change during the course of the activity?
- What were your greatest frustrations or successes?

The facilitator helps student leaders to focus on how they will use their values and beliefs systems when forming inclusive communities. Areas of focus for the next section will be service and social responsibilities.

Part Two: Inclusive Community, Service, and Social Responsibility
Put students into groups of eight plus facilitators. At this point facilitators ask student leaders to create their own agreements based on their values and belief system for the community they envisioned by using the following questions:

- How does your personal belief system relate to your core value?
- How will your value and belief system help you to build an inclusive community?
- Did you hear anything you found challenging or helped you to think about your values or any particular value in a new way from others?
- Were there any moments that especially grabbed your attention?

- Reflect on how these agreements relate to your core value or one of your core values. How does it relate to your faith tradition or moral perspective?
- Explain that these agreements offer us a chance to think about how we interact and work with others who are different from us in light of our shared values.
- Use these agreements to begin a reflection on the value of service and social responsibility to frame a discussion on the shared values the group holds and engage in a conversation on how shared values can support or cooperate with different spiritual, religious, and philosophical traditions.
- Go further by asking student leaders to reflect on what inspired them to do this work. Was it something from their faith tradition or moral perspective? Give participants a chance to share these stories with one another.
- Ask participants to reflect on the connections, similarities, and differences they heard in each others' story.
- Facilitators can show participants texts from a religious or nonreligious, philosophical perspective as well as the Jesuit core values that exemplify or express acts of service and shared values.

Part Three: Strategies for Inclusive Programs and Practices
Students break into groups by residence hall. The focus of this activity is to provide strategies for student leaders to begin brainstorming how inclusive programming can be implemented on campus using the following questions:

- Think about the students you work with and how you can accommodate and promote cooperation based on their values, faith, or philosophical traditions.
  - Example: Programming
- Think about how you will include others when
  - advertising a pig roast when you have vegetarian as well as Jewish, Muslim, and many Christian students who don't eat pork and students in your area; serving meat on Fridays during Lent when many Christian students abstain from eating meat; providing a vegetarian option for Hindu students
  - looking at holiday programming, how do we celebrate and support each other? How do we include others in the celebration?
- Identify resources on campus that support interfaith endeavors to create change. How will you invite campus ministry into the residence halls?

Learning Goals

- Help student leaders discover the shared values across different spiritual, religious, and philosophical traditions through text, storytelling, and reflection on social action and responsibility.
- Encourage student leaders to explore their own spiritual, religious, and cultural practices, traditions, and identities, and what they value as they learn to listen to others.
- Build a sense of cooperation and collaboration among student leaders.
- Assist student leaders to explore and demonstrate skills to engage residents on interfaith pluralistic perspectives.
- Use our Jesuit core values to establish inclusivity that promotes spiritual, religious, and philosophical traditions.

(Submitted by Ophelie Rowe Allen,
Residence Life, Fairfield University)

Scenario Discussions at Residence Assistant Training

The Office of Religious Life is given the opportunity to lead a one-hour training session on religious diversity at the annual RA training. Recognizing that the session falls near the end of a long week, and the RAs have received more information than they can absorb, we lead a session that is as interactive as possible.

Description

After introducing ourselves and briefly describing the religious demographics of the college, we invite the RAs to divide into groups of 4 and discuss the handout containing 5 residence life scenarios created by staff of the IFYC. Volunteers read the 5 scenarios aloud for everyone to hear. Then each group is given 20 to 25 minutes to discuss how members would respond to each scenario in their roles as RAs. The session concludes with a large-group discussion in which each group shares thoughts on how RAs might best respond to each scenario.

Materials

A handout that includes the following five scenarios:

1. It is the middle of the fall semester and classes, midterms, and activities are in full swing for students. One night you get an e-mail from another RA telling you that one of her female first-year students, Emily, has approached her concerning her roommate. The student says that her roommate, who is Muslim, has asked her not to bring visitors

by their room at night after she has taken off her hijab. Emily says she is very social and thinks it's unfair that she can't have friends over after 10:00 p.m., the time her roommate often takes her hijab off and gets ready for bed. Emily thinks her roommate is just too shy, especially around boys, and should "loosen up because after all this is college."

2. As a part of an awareness campaign, a group of students in an evangelical Christian a capella group get approval to put up flyers in their residence hall advertising their next concert. The flyers quote a Bible verse and mention that the group is Christian. A few days later, a secular students group puts up flyers in the building advertising their next meeting. The flyers include the tagline: Science Flies You to the Moon; Religion Flies You into Buildings. A day or two later, you hear that some students are upset about the flyer. The next day some of the a capella group members approach you and say they are offended by the flyers and feel they are aimed directly at them. They want them taken down immediately because of their offensive language.

3. With the semester approaching midterm, some residence hall directors are helping plan a study break kind of get-together for students in their buildings. During the night of the study break, a swastika is spray-painted on the side of a larger residence hall. In the morning a lot of students walk by and see the swastika, and even though it is soon cleaned off, word gets out about it and the student newspaper writes an article on the incident. A group of students want to organize some kind of response as soon as possible. A few students tell the newspaper reporter that because the residence halls are their home on campus, they need to be reassured of their safety. A group of fellow residence hall directors approach you with the same idea to do something.

4. At the end of the spring semester, with finals approaching, a group of residence halls is holding a big cookout for students. Using some outside grills, burgers and hot dogs are prepared, along with vegetarian burgers. A student approaches you and asks for a moment of your time. The student has noticed that the veggie burgers are being prepared on the same grill as the other burgers. He says that he doesn't feel right eating any of the food off the grill, and consequently there is really nothing he can eat at the party. He has already talked to an RA, but the RA recommended he talk to you. The student asks if there is anything you can do about the situation, especially because he said he can't really choose what to eat and not eat; it's his religion.

5. After a staff meeting with some RAs, one of the RAs approaches you one on one in the hall. She tells you that in her political science class earlier

that day the professor and students had been discussing a news story about a new law in Utah expanding gun ownership rights. The course focuses on state legislatures, which is how the story was initially brought up, but toward the end of the discussion the professor commented, "And this law is one of the many reasons I don't live in Utah. That, and the crazy underwear!" Most of the class laughed at the comment. However, the RA, who is Mormon, tells you that she felt personally attacked by the comment. She also brings up how many of the students on her hall don't like her because she enforces the rules as written, whereas other RAs are a little more lenient. She thinks other students think that because she is Mormon, she is stricter than a typical RA. She tells you that RAs are always talking about bias, but she feels her clear bias is never addressed.

(Submitted by Kelly Burk, chaplain and director, Quaker Life, Earlham College)

Advocacy

Syrian Refugee Awareness Week

This student-run initiative aims to educate, advocate, and create a conversation on campus about the Syrian refugee crisis. Students of all faiths can address this important issue of social justice, bringing them together around a common cause. Several events are hosted throughout the week that give context and offer ways for students to engage in community service on the issue. Students are encouraged to do research and invite those in the local community or on campus who have experience working with refugees or advocacy. Examples of events could be conversations between chaplains and nonprofit leaders and student panels to share volunteer experiences.

The following is a sample lineup of weekly events that were used at NYU one year:

- Monday: Information panel on the conflict in Syria, which is a one- to two-hour event featuring panelists who inform the audience about the conflict from a political and humanitarian perspective. The idea is to have Syrian panelists if possible, to center their voices.
- Tuesday: Faith in action, a service event where people from multiple faiths work together on a local level to raise awareness about the crisis and to form coalitions based on common faith-based values.
- Wednesday: Political action, which can be calling local representatives to ask them to resist Islamophobia and xenophobia through language

and law, a political demonstration in solidarity with Syrians: an outdoor musical performance, and so on.

- Thursday: Fund-raiser for assisting local Syrian refugees and organizations working in countries like Turkey or Greece involves directly asking for funds and selling stickers and other artwork that could be displayed on a backpack, with proceeds going to refugee aid.
- Friday: Next steps event or panel, which if possible, should continue every semester or perhaps start a club on the issue or even organize a school-sponsored trip to go Greece, Turkey, or Germany to work with refugees.

In a day and age where Islamophobia, xenophobia, and anti-refugee rhetoric have become common discourse in our social and political arenas, it is all the more important to have a program like this on college campuses. Faith leaders of various backgrounds should be strongly encouraged to take part. The program can take different forms depending on the funding available, number of volunteers, various types of resources, and the different types of activities that are possible. Students should be encouraged to work with others at their university to receive sponsorship, funding, and assistance from staff. At NYU, the Global Center for Spiritual Life served as the sponsor. This event could take place over a longer time period and could also focus on other critical interfaith issues throughout world, such as criminal justice reform; lesbian, gay, bisexual, and transgender equality; and racial justice.

(Submitted by Asad Dandia and Madeline Dolgin, student leaders, Global Spiritual Life, New York University)

Can It!

As part of President Barack Obama's Interfaith and Community Service Challenge, Syracuse University and Georgetown University collaborated to raise funds and awareness about the issue of hunger. The project was student-led as part of the Better Together campaign and involved many different departments across each university. The event was so successful, administrators at Syracuse University decided to continue the event without Georgetown after Syracuse moved to a different athletic conference, thus ending the friendly rivalry that was the basis for the campaign.

Description
Students collaborated with peers at a rival campus to coordinate two canned food drives and fund-raisers during basketball games. Each campus used the games to collect canned goods and funds for a local food pantry. During

pregame festivities, students hosted an informational booth with games and prizes to raise awareness about the issue of hunger and IFYC's Better Together campaign and collected food and funds. During the game, students handed out Better Together T-shirts, created videos to run during time-outs and commercial breaks, and created a half-time event that highlighted the issue of hunger and interfaith efforts to combat it. The two campuses used the competition between the schools as motivation to combat hunger and collaborate across faith differences.

Total Time
Planning for Can It! required biweekly one-hour meetings during the fall semester and weekly meetings during the spring semester in preparation for the game. Students worked with administrative staff members from religious life, residence life, athletics, facilities, civic engagement offices, public affairs, and student affairs, as well as with off-campus nonprofit organizations to make the event a success. The event itself began four hours prior to the start of the game and lasted one hour after the game. Students then worked to coordinate food pickup the following week.

Materials
Students asked local companies to donate T-shirts and prizes for promoting the event. At the students' request, nonprofit organizations contributed collection barrels for the food and plastic cases for monetary donations. Students produced promotional videos in conjunction with the university public affairs office.

Limitations
The event required collaboration across many different offices and departments in the university as well as with a rival institution, requiring regular meetings and the willingness of the institutions to support and promote the event. It risks framing interfaith cooperation as charity versus justice work and may reduce wider efforts to develop deep relationships and meaningful conversations in a one-and-done service event. This event must be connected to broader interfaith efforts on and off campus.

(Submitted by Tiffany Steinwert on behalf of
Hendricks Chapel, Syracuse University)

Conversation, Action, Faith, and Education Preorientation Program

The Conversation, Action, Faith, and Education (CAFE) Interfaith Social Justice Preorientation Program is a dynamic experience for incoming Tufts

University undergraduates interested in learning more about diverse religious and philosophical expressions, developing leadership skills, and connecting with other students who value self-exploration and social change. The program is supported by the university chaplaincy department and is one of six preorientation programs students can elect to attend in addition to the formal Tufts Undergraduate Orientation program.

CAFE was first offered in August 2009 and conducted in the summers of 2010 and 2011. After the program was discontinued for three years, a student and staff planning committee met in the spring semester 2015 with the goal of bringing back a revamped and reenvisioned CAFE in August of that year. The planning committee created the following mission statement for CAFE:

> The mission of the CAFE Preorientation Program is to welcome, gather, equip, and network with the religious, spiritual, ethical, and interfaith leaders of the incoming class—leaders who are committed both to mutual inspiration and to making positive change in the world. The program involves
> - exploration of self and others,
> - identifying strengths in religious and philosophical literacy and room to grow,
> - consciousness-raising about issues of social justice on campus and in the wider community, and
> - training on how to make a positive change through community organizing and activism.

Although this program provides an introduction to local issues and organizations working to address them, it is not focused on direct service but rather on using systemic analysis, advocacy, and action to change adverse ecosocial circumstances and promote well-being. This program explores the connections between inspiration and action, and the integration of the life of the mind and that of the heart to improve and liberate oneself and the world.

The university chaplaincy hired a student coordinator to help plan the program during the summer in collaboration with university staff. The chaplaincy also hired 12 to 14 peer leaders in the preceding spring semester to lead students through the program and facilitate conversation while also fully participating in all aspects of the program. In August 2015 the CAFE preorientation hosted 19 incoming students, received positive feedback from participants and partners, and was awarded the 2016 Outstanding Spiritual Initiative Award from the NASPA–Student Affairs Administrators in Higher Education Spirituality and Religion in Higher Education Knowledge Community.

Description

The CAFE program is six days long, leading into Tufts Undergraduate Orientation at the beginning of the academic year. We believe the unique niche of CAFE is that it is an introduction not only to the vibrant religious and philosophical life at Tufts and in Boston but also to the ways these communities and others engage in social justice and the resources and opportunities for activism on campus and beyond.

Program highlights from the 2015 program include the following:

- Training opportunities for peer leaders
  - Facilitation training led by Boston Mobilization, an organization dedicated to developing the next generation of social justice leaders through training, community organizing campaign work, and mentorship of young leaders
  - Pluralism and Interfaith Engagement Workshop led by the university chaplain, Rev. Greg McGonigle
  - Exploring Leadership Style Training led by the university chaplaincy program manager, Zachary Cole
  - Identity Exploration and Leadership Workshop led by the Tufts Lesbian, Gay, Bisexual, and Transgender Center director, Nino Testa
  - Peer leader training sessions on alcohol and other drugs, mental health, and sexual misconduct led by relevant campus partners
- Field trips and spiritual practice opportunities
  - Jumah prayer, Islamic Society of Boston Cultural Center
  - Shabbat service and dinner, Tufts Hillel
  - Mindfulness meditation and service, Cambridge Zen Center
  - Harvard Square Sunday services: Friends meetings at Cambridge, Old Cambridge Baptist Church, St. Paul's Catholic Church, and University Lutheran Church
  - Interfaith meal packing and conversation with the the assistant Humanist chaplain, Vanessa Zoltan, Harvard Humanist Hub
  - Harvard Divinity School conversation with the chaplain and director of religious and spiritual life, Rev. Kerry Maloney
  - Visits to Boston-area community organizations: Asian Task Force Against Domestic Violence in Chinatown and City Life, Vida Urbana in Jamaica Plain
  - Tour of Sri Lakshmi Hindu Temple, Ashland, Massachusetts
- Other highlights
  - Mapping Your Religious or Philosophical Journey activity led by the university chaplain, Rev. Greg McGonigle

- ○ Visits from the university president, chief diversity officer, dean of student affairs, and religion department chair
- ○ Social Identities Exploration Workshop led by Boston Mobilization
- ○ Working with Community Organizations Workshop led by the Jonathan M. Tisch College of Citizenship Public Service
- ○ Dinner and panel with the university's chaplains (Catholic, Humanist, Jewish, Muslim, and Protestant)
- ○ Self-care workshops led by CAFE peer leaders
- ○ Icebreakers, bowling, scavenger hunt, and introduction to local eateries
- ○ Program conclusion with a Boston Harbor boat cruise
- ○ Introduction to the Massachusetts Bay Transportation Authority (MBTA) system, Davis, Harvard, and Central Squares, and various neighborhoods of Boston

Possible Adaptations

This program fits nicely into the preorientation offerings at Tufts, but it could be adapted for different times of the year such as over a long weekend or January or over spring break to provide an opportunity for current students in addition to new incoming students to participate in the CAFE program. It is ideal to have a multiday program to build community among the participants, establish trust, share personal reflections, and visit multiple religious and philosophical sites.

Depending on the goals, different components of the CAFE program could take place during different periods in the semester. Site visits, activities, training sessions and workshops, reflections, and other activities could be spread out over the course of a semester or year as part of a longer curriculum.

Total Time

CAFE peer leaders move in on a Monday and attend a social event that evening. The next two days (Tuesday and Wednesday) are training days for the peer leaders. Incoming students move in on Thursday, and the program begins that evening. The program runs through the evening of the following Tuesday with undergraduate orientation beginning on Wednesday. The program begins early to accommodate Jumah prayer and Shabbat services on Friday.

Materials

Primary materials include the following:

- • Meals, snacks, and plates and utensils
- • Program folders (schedules, contact information, and other resources)

- Office supplies for self-care sessions and other activities (paper, colored pencils, scissors, craft supplies, white T-shirts for decorating, etc.)
- CAFE T-shirts
- CAFE buttons

Limitations

CAFE is funded through participant fees, the Tufts preorientation office, and a contribution from the university chaplaincy programming budget. Depending on the size and length of the program, significant financial resources are needed.

Another challenge is representing the breadth of different religious and philosophical traditions and community organizations in just six days. Some choices have to be made regarding site visits. It is important to seek feedback from students and partners and to ensure that the needs and practices of incoming students and peer leaders are taken into consideration when planning site visits.

(Submitted by Rev. Greg McGonigle, university chaplain,
Tufts University, and Zachary Cole, program manager,
University Chaplaincy, Tufts University)

Campus Collaborations

Colorado State University's Multifaith and Belief Student Council

Many universities and colleges have student councils, such as a Greek Council. The advantage of councils is that they can advocate on behalf of their student organizations and organize collaborative efforts. This is a description of how Colorado State University (CSU) developed a Multifaith and Belief Student Council. CSU has many organizations for students from a variety of faith and belief traditions. Several factors provided the motivation for the formation of this council at CSU. Some students wanted to promote the positive experiences of faith-based organizations and the interfaith cooperation that was already taking place between groups. It became clear that a council could help solidify these efforts. The university administration decided that students could advocate for emerging needs by organizing their own multifaith council. Finally, CSU's student government wanted to create representation for students from faith-based groups.

Description

An important step in developing the council was to identify student leaders and organizational partners. Toward the end of the spring semester 2016, a short survey was mailed to community faith and belief partners who serve students and to students who had attended past interfaith events to determine the level of interest. Meetings were held with several students in the summer to develop the scaffolding and direction for the organization.

In fall 2016 a faculty member in the School of Education served as the founding adviser with two students who became founding officers. The founding leadership team wrote a constitution (see www.ramlink.ollegiatelink .net/organization/Faith_and_Belief_Council) and submitted the paperwork to become a student council. The council was created as "a network of representatives from faith, belief, and spiritual student groups that create a positive presence on campus, including campus advocacy, cultivating relationships between groups rooted in respect and compassion, and pointing students to groups in good standing."

The founding leadership team began to meet with first-year students in fall 2016 in an interfaith academic class taught by a faculty member. The interfaith students helped develop pieces of the organization, including publicity materials. The interfaith class was also leading programming, including a film series and an interfaith thanksgiving. A poster was developed to promote these interfaith events and the newly formed council. The founding leadership team also set up an online platform (see www.facebook.com/ CSUMultifaithBelief) through Facebook and the university website, which enabled others to join the council.

In spring 2017 we invited faith-based student organizations and faith and belief community partners to send their students to bimonthly meetings. We had an enthusiastic response, and students have been regularly attending meetings representing a variety of groups. We have four committed officers on the council, most of whom continued into the next academic year. The council continues to work on supporting interfaith programs as well as developing new initiatives members of the council have suggested. The council is regularly posting on social media and also received funding from the campus student government to support the Better Together Day, which is coordinated by the interfaith academic class. We were able to elect our first student government representative by the end of the first year as an organization. All these successes have contributed to realizing our aspirations to strengthen our positive contributions and presence in our diverse community.

Limitations

Development of a new student council can be a time-intensive effort, especially at larger universities. For CSU, the level of unmet needs (for faith, belief, spiritual, and religious-based student organizations) and the access to funding and resources were major motivations to invest time and energy in this effort. One of the challenges in our first year was to set manageable priorities, knowing that we would be able to take on more later. Another challenge was finding a time to meet that does not conflict with too many other groups' meeting times. Also, some of the faith groups have less motivation and time for the council. To represent multiple perspectives, we need to find ways to keep groups included in the council's efforts. We hope to continue to expand our efforts as a council in the coming years.

> (Submitted by Viviane Ephraimson-Abt, manager, Resiliency
> and Well-Being Initiatives, Health Network and adjunct
> faculty, School of Education, Colorado State University)

A Foundation for Student-Led Interfaith Dialogue on Difficult Topics

University of North Florida (UNF) is a public university in the northeastern part of the state with 18,000 undergraduate and graduate students. The UNF Interfaith Center hired Tarah Trueblood to serve as its first director in 2011. In 2012 the center hired Rachael McNeal as the current coordinator. Since then we have forged a foundation for students to engage other students in civil discourse on difficult topics across religious, spiritual, and nonreligious identities (or worldviews). That foundation was built on the following:

- A high-impact student interfaith leadership mentoring program. In our experience, two factors are essential for training and empowering student leaders. The first is engagement in the center's Better Together Interfaith Leadership Development Program (B2GIL), which was developed with the center's affiliated student organization, Better Together at UNF (founded by a UNF student). We define *interfaith leadership* as a relational and ethical process of people together attempting to accomplish positive change across diverse religious, spiritual, and values-based worldviews; we adapted this definition from Komives, Lucas, and McMahon (2013). The second essential factor is participation at the IFYC Interfaith Leadership Institute, which connects students to the larger, national interfaith student movement, provides unique opportunities for national student leadership, and offers a host of campus resources.
- A framework for engaging in civil discourse across difference. Center staff and its student leaders developed a set of guidelines for civil discourse. Students in the B2GIL program internalize these guidelines to the point that they find themselves applying them in daily work and their personal life with very positive ends. It is impossible to overemphasize the importance of this framework. The guidelines are a

way of reminding people how to be respectful because mutual respect is the foundation for dialogue and cooperation across difference. The guidelines provide rules for listening, speaking, and context (no debating and no proselytizing or converting).

- Regular student-led (staff-directed) programs and events. Students need multiple opportunities to practice facilitating dialogue across difference and leading cooperative community service projects that advance the common good. The center provides a framework of regular programs for students to acquire basic leadership skills and opportunities for students to develop and lead special programs and events such as interfaith community service projects as required for students in the B2GIL program. Some of the programs that the center provides are

  o a weekly coffee and conversation session (55 minutes) during which a student, staff, faculty, or community storyteller shares his or her spiritual, religious, or secular beliefs and the journey to those beliefs;

  o a bimonthly lunch discussion (55 minutes) about religious and secular worldviews and how they intersect with gender and sexuality;

  o a monthly dinner (two hours) where students can try new food while celebrating the intercultural, interfaith, and international environment on UNF's campus; and

  o a monthly dine and dialogue program (two and a half hours) focused on sacred and secular texts.

- A community of empowered students from diverse worldviews. As a direct result of the center's B2GIL program, consistent use of UNF's *Guidelines for Civil Discourse* by students and staff at virtually all programs and events, consistent and regular student-led interfaith programming on campus, and the emergence of a strong community of students equipped with skills in interfaith dialogue, the center is able to engage the wider campus community on more challenging issues. In our experience, students are very eager, even hungry, to participate in respectful dialogue on current, difficult topics. Examples of high-profile events involving difficult topics include the following:

  o Coffee & Difficult Conversation: Black Student Stories (2016)

  o Candlelight vigil for Paris, Beirut, and Baghdad (2016)

  o One-Islam (2016)

  o Jewish Freedom Seder (2016)

  o Coffee & Difficult Conversation: Being Black and Agnostic (2016)

  o Coffee & Difficult Conversation: Would Mohammad Approve His Cartoon? Where Free Speech, Satire, & Religion Collide (2015) o Coffee & Difficult Conversations—A Lament for Peace: Hamas & Israel (2014)

(Submitted by Tarah Trueblood, director, Center for American and World Cultures, Miami University, Ohio)

Vigils: Space for Communal Healing

One of the most important roles that the Office of Global Spiritual Life serves at NYU is to convene vigils in response to national and international tragedies that have an impact on the emotional and spiritual health of our students. These vigils are nondenominational and create the time and space for anyone from any walk of life, regardless of religion or background, to join a community and heal.

Creating a successful vigil involves five key steps. First, a vigil should always be initiated by a student group that feels connected to the tragedy rather than by an official university office. This helps mitigate the challenge of deciding which global tragedies are deserving of a vigil and how to avoid prioritizing the pain of one community over another.

Second, the vigil should be held in a public space that is easily accessible for anyone to attend. At NYU vigils are held on the steps of our student activities building, which can accommodate about 200 participants.

Third, a diverse set of offices and campus partners should cosponsor the vigil. For example, at NYU we send an e-mail asking for cosponsorship to all our partners around the university including the Center for Multicultural Education and Programs, The LGBTQ Student Center, the Bronfman Center for Jewish Student Life, the Islamic Center, the Catholic Center, the Protestant Life Affiliate Network, and any specific communities that are directly affected by the tragedy. This diverse set of cosponsorships allows the entire NYU community to be invested in the vigil and to make sure speakers are representative of NYU's full diversity.

Fourth, possibly the most challenging aspect of the vigil is to select and prepare speakers. At NYU we usually ask two or three chaplains to speak and one or two students with connections to the tragedy to share reflections and personal experiences that relate to the tragedy. They are usually from the region where the tragedy took place or from the community of people targeted. To prepare the students, we ask them to reflect on the following questions before composing their remarks: How are you connected to the tragedy? Can you share a testimonial from the heart that will explain your personal experience? Chaplains should be asked to speak using similar guidelines. Each speech should be no longer than 2 or 3 minutes, which allows 5 to 7 speakers in an event of 30 minutes.

Fifth, the vigil should have a prominent place on social media so those who are not generally connected to spiritual life at the university can have access to the event. This outreach is best done by the student group organizing the event with support from the various administrative offices that cosponsor the vigil.

Throughout the past few years, these vigils have become institutionalized elements of NYU's response to tragedy, serving a critical role in the broader NYU community. We have held vigils for terrorist attacks in Paris, the shooting in the Pulse nightclub in Orlando, and the earthquakes in Nepal, among many other tragedies that have affected our student body.

(Submitted by Ariel Ennis and Yael Shy, Office of
Global Spiritual Life, New York University)

References

Alpert, D., Bernardi-Reis, N, & Sarandon, S. (Producers), & Parrish, R. (Director). (2015). *Radical grace* [Motion picture]. United States: Interchange Productions & Kindling Group.

Clydesdale, T. (2015). *The purposeful graduate: Why colleges must talk to students about vocation.* Chicago, IL: University of Chicago Press.

Interfaith Youth Core. (n.d.-a). *How to hold a speedfaithing event.* Retrieved from https://www.ifyc.org/resources/how-hold-speedfaithing-event

Interfaith Youth Core. (n.d.-b). *Pluralism and worldview engagement rubric.* Retrieved from https://www.ifyc.org/resources/pluralism-and-worldview-engagement-rubric

Komives, S. R., Lucas, N., & McMahon, T. R. (2013). *Exploring leadership: for college students who want to make a difference* (3rd ed.). San Francisco, CA: Jossey-Bass.

Neville, M. & Rogers, C. (Producers), & Neville, M. (Director). (2015). *The music of strangers* [Motion picture]. United States: The Orchard & Participant Media.

Patel, E. (2007). *Acts of faith: The story of an American Muslim, in the struggle for the soul of a generation.* Boston, MA: Beacon Press.

Rilke, R. M. (n.d.) *Go the limits of your longing.* Retrieved from https://onbeing.org/blog/go-limits-longing/

Schaller, M. A. (2005). Wandering and wondering: Traversing the uneven terrain of the second college year. *About Campus,* 10(3), 18–24.

Stedman, C. D. (2012). *Faitheist: How an atheist found common ground with the religious.* Boston, MA: Beacon Press.

Swindler, L. (1983). Dialogue decalogue: Ground rules for interreligious, interideiological dialogue. *Journal of Ecumenical Studies, 20*(1), 1984.

9

INTERFAITH ACTIVITIES INTEGRATED INTO ACADEMIC COURSES AND PROGRAMS

Kathleen M. Goodman and Mary Ellen Giess

Although specific examples of academic minor subjects are not included in this chapter, it should be noted that academic minors and other course sequences in interfaith studies are becoming quite common. Although such programs are often housed in religious studies departments, most programs are intentionally interdisciplinary and may be housed in surprising locations, such as the interfaith studies program in the School of Economics and Business Administration at St. Mary's College in Moraga, California. In recent years, a cross-section of institutional types has also taken up this effort, with programs launching at public campuses (e.g., California State University, Chico and University of Toledo); private, secular institutions (e.g., Elon University and Illinois College); and religiously affiliated institutions (e.g., Dominican University and Concordia College, Moorhead). Elizabethtown College in Pennsylvania announced the first interfaith studies major in the country. These academic programs frequently include an experiential learning component in the requirements, making them an ideal collaborative opportunity for integration with cocurricular programming.

However, even institutions without such programs have abundant opportunities to create interfaith learning experiences that span the curriculum and cocurriculum. The programs described in this chapter illustrate that the student affairs profession is committed to student learning and partnerships to foster that learning. ACPA–College Student Educators International (1996) encouraged student affairs practitioners to create partnerships with faculty and others in academic affairs to create a seamless learning environment. The need for collaboration was repeated in ACPA (1998) and again in ACPA and NASPA–Student Affairs Administrators in Higher Education (2004). Religious diversity and interfaith engagement are ideally situated at the nexus of academic and student affairs, given the personal nature and relationship to identity (typically student affairs territory) and the need to understand the history and experiences of many religions (typically academic affairs territory). This chapter is a compilation of programs, described by educators from across the country, that take advantage of this nexus in pursuit of strengthened learning experiences for students.

Souljourners: Interfaith Service-Learning Program

Souljourners is an interfaith service-learning program sponsored jointly by the University of Southern California's Office of Religious Life and the Joint Educational Project. Using the Joint Educational Project's service-learning model, Souljourners develops students' interfaith engagement skills by forming partnerships with academic courses to facilitate interfaith engagement opportunities for undergraduate students.

Souljourners works with faculty members to facilitate specific intercultural and interfaith experiences most relevant to the goals of the class and to tailor assignments to guide students' written reflections. The most successful collaboration has been with an upper-division business course focused on diversity in the workplace. The professors teaching the course recognized that students' participation in Souljourners could supplement their skills on issues of religious diversity in professional spaces. Souljourners uses intentional interfaith experiences and reflective writing assignments to encourage students to consider how faith may influence their personal and professional development.

Students participate in Souljourners for about eight weeks out of the semester, participating in up to two hours of intercultural or interfaith experiences outside regular class time and completing written reflection assignments based on those experiences. Souljourners staff adapts assignments and project content to align with the learning goals of each course. Faculty grade each assignment, and Souljourners staff provide feedback to the students. Each of the assignments aligns with a specific learning goal of the program.

Week 1: Preparatory Reflection Assignment

Souljourners seeks to support students' exploration of religious, spiritual, or secular identity by encouraging students to consider their own beliefs and worldviews. To accomplish this goal, students discuss their current religious or spiritual identity in a written reflection assignment prior to their first interfaith event or experience. This assignment allows students to share as much as they feel comfortable with about their upbringing and how their childhood, parents, and family may have influenced their current beliefs. Students are also asked to describe their prior experiences with individuals from other faiths, including personal interactions, friendships, and exposure to other faiths through academic study.

Weeks 2 and 3: Intercultural Interaction Assignment

Souljourners seeks to help our students bravely engage religious difference. For the intercultural interaction project, students are asked to interact with a different culture or faith and then discuss issues of diversity, inclusion, and ecumenicism in a written reflection assignment. To help them accomplish this goal, students are provided with relevant information prior to their interfaith experiences and are encouraged to research the group or event before attending. This includes in-class discussions of current relevant topics as well as suggested resources from the Office of Religious Life. Offering students positive and accurate information about the group they will be interacting with helps dissuade some of their initial concerns.

Weeks 4 and 5: House of Worship Assignment

Souljourners seeks to enhance students' awareness of religious diversity, particularly greater consideration of the experiences of religious minorities. One of the primary projects is to have students visit two houses of worship and compare their experiences at each. Students can select any religious service to attend; however, many students take the opportunity to visit the mosque near campus to learn more about the Islamic faith. Despite initial hesitation to participate in religious services, students are able to gain insight into the experiences of other faiths. Students report the experience encourages them to consider their own beliefs as well as the potential saliency of faith for their peers and future colleagues.

Weeks 6 and 7: Fortune 500 Research and Reflection Assignment

Souljourners seeks to develop students' professional skills related to religious diversity in and beyond their academic field of study. The staff works with each professor to create a reflection assignment tailored to the specific needs and goals of the academic course. For the business course, for example, students research a *Fortune* 500 company to examine their policies regarding religious or spiritual identity and expression. They provide evidence of their findings and consider how the company's policies may affect its employees as well as customer perceptions. The assignment also connects the in-class lessons and discussions by asking students to consider the professional skills needed to thrive in a religiously diverse workplace.

Week 8: Final Reflection

Souljourners seeks to cultivate students' proclivity toward interfaith engagement through the final reflection assignment of the program. Students reflect on their experiences in Souljourners and discuss how the insights gained through the program might have influenced their knowledge, attitudes, and relationships with individuals from other faiths. This reflective assignment challenges students to consider the implications of their own faith or secular identity in their own personal development.

> (Submitted by Sable Manson, Office of Religious Life, Souljourners program director, University of Southern California)

Case Study for Students Returning From Off-Campus Study

The Office of Religious Life is given the opportunity to present an interfaith case study to a semester-long class designed for students returning from off-campus study. An event in which religion plays a key role was chosen—the *Charlie Hebdo* shooting incident in Paris that had occurred the previous month. In the shooting, masked gunmen killed 12 staff members of a satirical newspaper. One week in advance of the class discussion, we provide copies of two articles (Al Jazeera Staff, 2015; Bilefsky & de la Baume, 2015) that present different cultural perspectives on this tragic incident. The case study invites rich discussion on matters of xenophobia, religious extremism, and free speech. The purpose of the discussion was to invite students to express their perspective on the role religion plays in various cultures.

After introductions and a brief description of the day's topic, we invite the class into small groups to discuss the two articles assigned in advance for careful reading. We ask the following questions:

1. What are the facts of the incident? What happened on January 7?
2. What is the context and setting of this incident? Who are the stakeholders?
3. How would you compare and contrast the two articles?
4. What are the underlying themes and issues going on here?
5. What stance or position do you identify with or find difficult to understand?
6. What questions do you have?

After 20 minutes of discussion, the class is brought back together for a large-group discussion based on these questions. We then shift focus to the following questions designed to encourage reflection on the role religion played in their off-campus study program:

1. What did you notice about the religious climate in your off-campus study experience?
2. How large a role did religion play in the culture? What were the dynamics?
3. How did you deal with the religious dimension of the culture? What did you learn about yourself or your own culture by doing so?
4. Did anyone have a spiritual or religious experience during off-campus study you would be willing to tell us about?
5. Now that you are back in the United States, what do you notice about the role of religion in this culture?

We divide the 80-minute class session into the following segments:

- 30 minutes for introductions and small-group discussions of the 2 articles
- 20 minutes for large-group discussion of the 2 articles
- 30 minutes for large-group discussion of religious climate during off-campus study experience

(Submitted by Kelly Burk, chaplain and director, Quaker Life, Earlham College)

Many Faiths, One Humanity Interfaith Travel Experience

The idea for this activity was conceived by Thomas V. Wolfe when he served as dean of Hendricks Chapel at Syracuse University.

> He said, We wanted to put a human face on the issues of how diverse faith communities have historically shared and continue to share life together. . . . On campus and beyond, we hope our experience will increase awareness of the three faith traditions' contemporary issues and spark renewed dialogue toward understanding and cooperation.

The first trip took place in 2003 with students traveling to Spain. Since then, students have traveled to Turkey (2007), Jerusalem (2009), London (2011 and 2013) and San Francisco (2014). Under the leadership of Dean of Hendricks Chapel Tiffany Steinwert, the program expanded beyond the three Abrahamic faiths and beyond a one-week travel experience. The program became a four-credit undergraduate course that included an immersive travel experience to London (2011 and 2013) and San Francisco (2014). The course integrated the use of art (contemplative video, drawing, and poetry) with community service to facilitate interfaith dialogue.

Participants in this program registered for a one-credit travel seminar and a three-credit semester course, Intergroup Dialogue, cross-listed in women and gender studies and education. Throughout the semester, students gathered to share personal experiences, explore historic and contemporary religious pluralism, and finally travel together to London or San Francisco. In both cities students participated in living communities of many faith traditions and life stances and learned concrete strategies for collaborative action.

In London, students worked alongside our artist in residence, Zah Rasul, using the art of writing and drawing to discover different perspectives. Their creative work allowed them to rediscover the world and see the extraordinary in the ordinary. It also provided a platform to share their points of view with one another as well as with those students they met as they traveled in London and later at home as they developed a collaborative art installation on campus.

In San Francisco students used community service as a lens to explore the intersection of faith and social justice. Based at Glide Memorial United Methodist Church, students volunteered in various programs at the church and visited diverse communities of faith asking the members how their tradition addresses issues of social justice, including systemic racism; addiction; lesbian, gay, bisexual, transgender, and queer civil rights; and poverty.

Through this program students learned to build intentional and constructive relationships across difference, enabling them to imagine new ways of being that break down destructive barriers of prejudice, stereotypes, and mistrust.

The immersive travel seminar could occur on its own as in previous years. In that version of the program, students met only a few times prior to the travel experience as part of a cocurricular, non-credit-bearing activity. Students traveled over spring break and gathered following the trip for critical reflection. The locations and foci of the trip could vary. However, the ideal is a semester-long course with a one-week travel seminar. It could have monthly one-hour meetings prior to and following travel and a one-week travel seminar.

There are some challenges related to developing and leading travel experience as I have described. The program is labor and resource intensive. Costs per student ranged from $1,200 to $4,000, depending on the site. The program also requires collaboration with an academic department, which can pose its own challenges. Travel logistics can be difficult, particularly if the site is in an area of conflict. For example, the planned trip to Jerusalem had to be postponed because of international travel restrictions.

(Submitted by Tiffany Steinwert on behalf of
Hendricks Chapel, Syracuse University)

Case Study for Business and Nonprofit Management Class

The Office of Religious Life is given the opportunity to present an interfaith case study to a business and nonprofit management course. The case study focuses on tensions that arose in a meatpacking plant in Nebraska when Somali immigrant employees requested special breaks for Muslim prayers. Racial and ethnic tensions surfaced throughout the community, providing an excellent case study for business students to discuss the complexity of religious pluralism in the workplace. Do businesses need to accommodate the religious practices of its employees, or should employees be expected to adapt to the workplace? One week in advance of class, an article (Semple, 2008) describing the Nebraska situation is distributed to the students.

On the day of the class, after introductions and a brief description of the day's topic, we invite the students into a large-group discussion of the case study assigned in advance for careful reading. We ask the following questions:

1. What happened in Grand Island, Nebraska?
2. Who were the key players and what was their perspective?
3. What do we know about Somalia?
4. What are the underlying theme and issues going on here?

After 15 to 20 minutes of discussion, the class is divided into groups of 4 and asked to write a speech to be delivered in Grand Island in 2008 from 1 of 3 perspectives: as mayor speaking to the community, as pastor or imam speaking to his or her congregation, as coach speaking to a local sports team. Each speech should be 3 to 4 minutes long. The groups are given 30 minutes to prepare and practice their speech.

The speeches are presented one after the other, which takes about 15 minutes depending on the size of the class. We then conclude the class with a large-group discussion on additional thoughts, questions, or scenarios they could imagine where religious diversity would affect the business world.

(Submitted by Kelly Burk, chaplain and
director, Quaker Life, Earlham College)

References

ACPA–College Student Educators International. (1996). *The student learning imperative: Implications for student affairs.* Retrieved from http://www.myacpa.org/files/acpas-student-learning-imperative.pdf

ACPA–College Student Educators International. (1998). *Powerful partnerships: A shared responsibility for learning.* Retrieved from http://www.myacpa.org/files/taskforcepowerfulpartnershipsasharedresponsibilityforlearningpdf

ACPA–College Student Educators International & NASPA–Student Affairs Administrators in Higher Education. (2004). *Learning reconsidered: A campus-wide focus on the student experience.* Washington, DC: Author.

Al Jazeera Staff. (2015, January 7). Hunt for gunmen after 12 killed in Paris attack on satirical magazine. *Al Jazeera America.* Retrieved from http://america.aljazeera.com/articles/2015/1/7/at-least-10-deadinshootingatparissatiricalmagazine.html

Bilefsky, D., & de la Baume, M. (2015, January 7). Terrorists strike *Charlie Hebdo* newspaper in Paris, leaving 12 dead. *The New York Times.* Retrieved from https://www.nytimes.com/2015/01/08/world/europe/charlie-hebdo-paris-shooting.html

Semple, K. (2008, October 16). Somali immigrant workers test a Nebraska town. *New York Times.* Retrieved from https://www.nytimes.com/2008/10/16/world/americas/16iht-letter.1.17008659.html

USING CASE STUDIES TO ENGAGE WITH RELIGIOUS DIVERSITY AND BUILD INTERFAITH LEADERSHIP

Cassie Meyer

Engaging religious and worldview diversity is not limited to responding to crises or healing tensions; indeed, there is enormous positive opportunity in mobilizing students from diverse religions and worldviews for common action on issues they find meaningful. This priority aligns with higher education's broader call to educate the next generation of civic leaders. Indeed, worldview identity is a powerful motivator for involvement in social change and civic engagement. Additionally, in a majority of professions or community roles that students will take on after graduation, knowledge and skills for engaging religious diversity are imperative. A doctor working in a diverse hospital, a teacher with a classroom of students from many backgrounds, or a community leader in a small city with growing religious diversity will all need to be attentive to religious diversity to do their jobs well.

The work of engaging religious diversity to ameliorate tensions or respond to discrimination as well as to build a healthy, thriving civic space is carried out by people described as interfaith leaders. An interfaith leader is someone who has the vision, knowledge, skills, and qualities to respond to the challenges and opportunities offered by religious diversity. An interfaith leader seeks to build interfaith cooperation, developing spaces where individuals can express their own religious or secular identities, build relationships across lines of difference, and come together around shared common goods (Patel, 2016). Case studies offer a useful approach for addressing these questions in common campus settings, such as student leadership training sessions, professional development workshops, or the classroom.

Case Studies as an Effective Educational Tool

Case studies are particularly effective for educating people on interfaith topics on campus, in and out of the classroom, for several reasons. Case studies help create a sense of urgency and opportunity around the priority of interfaith cooperation. Because issues related to religious tolerance and interfaith cooperation are becoming more present in campus and public life, case studies can help make the ways interreligious relations might play out on their campus real for student and campus leaders. Case studies help concretize the issues raised by religious and worldview diversity and help individuals understand how religion and worldview might affect their local community or their life as professionals. At the same time, the case study as an educational methodology works from the assumption that solutions are possible and provides the chance to think creatively and collaboratively toward solutions. Individuals are thus given agency to solve interreligious problems, even as this practice of problem-solving continues to help hone their skills.

Furthermore, case studies can emphasize that although there are skills specific to interfaith leadership, many of the skills effective campus leaders use for organizing and community building are also applicable to interreligious situations. At Interfaith Youth Core, we have found that many students and student affairs professionals fear engaging religious and worldview diversity because they worry they do not know enough about the manifold religious identities that may be present on their campus. An inclination to know everything about diverse worldviews, then, becomes a barrier to engagement.

In contrast, case studies require individuals to focus on what they need to know to foster positive relationships, build a sense of community, and organize common projects. Engaging worldview diversity effectively does not necessitate becoming a scholar of world religions, although such knowledge is of course helpful; instead, it requires activating community-building and leadership skills and seeking the knowledge about diverse traditions which is relevant and necessary for those efforts. As those working through the cases begin to think toward practical solutions, they can identify their personal and collective strengths as well as challenges or opportunities for growth. This results in a sense of empowerment and agency for individuals learning to engage these issues proactively on campus and in the classroom.

How to Use Case Studies

The following are some examples of times when case studies might be used on campus to foster conversation, leadership, and skill building on interfaith topics.

1. In a student leadership training session, educators can use case studies to help students think concretely about what interfaith action looks like on their campus, what assets and skills they have for creating interfaith cooperation, and areas in which individuals and the group may need additional learning or skill building.

2. In professional development training (whether formal sessions, departmental conversations, or even one-on-one coaching), case studies can help illustrate ways that religious dynamics or sensibilities might be at play in the campus environment. For those who have less experience dealing directly with religious diversity, case studies can help them identify professional skills useful for dealing with religious and secular identities as well as skills that still need to be developed.

3. In an academic course focusing on religious diversity, pluralism, or religious diversity and professional contexts (e.g., including graduate courses in student affairs administration), case studies can be used to help students think about the practical applications of theories and terms they are using, as well as explore how the topics they are considering in the classroom are relevant beyond campus.

Using the Cases in This Book

Chapters 10 through 14 contain case studies for use in a variety of campus contexts. Some cases are longer with multiple parts that raise opportunities for in-depth conversation and problem-solving. Shorter scenarios are also included to help groups explore several different issues related to religious diversity and identity on campus in a shorter time frame. The following is a brief synopsis of the cases in this text as well as suggestions for how to use them in a campus context.

Chapter 10: Study or Indoctrination?

Do religious texts have a place as required texts in the curriculum at public institutions? This case explores tensions around teaching Sells's (1999) *Approaching the Qur'an* at the University of North Carolina at Chapel Hill.

This case can help prompt questions about the separation of church and state and the role of interfaith engagement at public universities in addition to exploring dynamics related to Islamophobia on campus. Additionally, faculty may find it helpful to discuss this case together to explore the opportunities and challenges of taking on potential hot topics regarding religious and worldview diversity in their classrooms.

Chapter 11: Coercion or Conversion?

Can religious groups with exclusive truth claims or commitments to proselytizing be a part of interfaith efforts on campus? Staff at the University of Illinois at Chicago explore these difficult questions and seek a way forward together in this case.

This case can be helpful for any campus administration that has wrestled with inclusion of evangelical Christians or other groups with exclusive truth claims. Additionally, administrators asking questions about "all comers" policies or seeking to develop formal structures or policies regarding staff and representatives of diverse traditions might use this case as a starting point for examining the issues at play.

Chapter 12: Secular Students on the Prairie

At Concordia College, a Lutheran-affiliated liberal arts college in Minnesota, secular students are eager to organize an official student group that will allow a space for nonreligious students to gather with one another and to organize secular students into being more involved in interfaith efforts. The students receive positive feedback on their efforts and thus are shocked when they find their application for recognition has been rejected because of a perceived conflict with the college's mission.

This case may be useful for campuses seeking to be inclusive of students who identify as atheist, agnostic, or nonreligious as well as for religiously affiliated campuses whose administrators are thinking about religious and worldview inclusion issues. This case can also help student leaders think concretely about how to make a case for interfaith cooperation on their campus and how to constructively solve problems when faced with roadblocks.

Chapter 13: When Causes Collide

At fictional Kinnamon University, students working to organize in support of the Black Lives Matter movement encounter an unexpected conflict when the Jewish Student Association offers to cosponsor an upcoming event.

Commitments to social justice can come into conflict when diverse religious and worldview identities are at play. This case can be useful for student affairs professionals seeking to explore these kinds of conflicts more deeply, as well as for groups that want to better understand the complex issues raised by engaging with worldview diversity. This case would also be helpful for students working to build broad coalitions, helping them to anticipate potential pitfalls.

Chapter 14: Engaging With Religious Diversity on a Regular Basis

These nine short scenarios cover a broad swath of fictionalized moments when worldview diversity becomes a flashpoint on campus. From the residence hall to the classroom, from orientation to cocurricular community engagement, these scenarios help educators explore the opportunities and challenges posed by worldview diversity. Consider using these in a variety of settings, such as a retreat for student leaders of the campus interfaith group, a professional development training session for student affairs professionals, or a diversity training for student leaders and educators charged with thinking about diversity, such as residential advisers, orientation leaders, and students involved in multiculturalism efforts.

Discussion Questions for Case Studies

Although many educators, student affairs professionals, and student leaders will develop their own questions or discussion topics, the following questions (Suomala & Interfaith Youth Core, 2013) are useful for engaging groups in a case study. For case studies that have two parts, the group working through the case should read the first part prior to the meeting or at the beginning of the gathering. Then, as a large group, depending on group size, or in small groups of four to six individuals, groups members can consider the following questions:

- What is the issue or problem in this case?
- Who are the stakeholders in this case? In other words, who has an investment or interest in the outcome?
- What is the context of the problem? What is the setting, situation, and so on?
- What information is missing? What information would you like to have?
- Is there an individual or group in the case with whom you strongly identify? Why or why not?

- Whose stance or position do you find the most difficult to identify with or understand? Why? How widespread do you think these views or positions are on campus? In society more broadly?
- Can you imagine something like this happening on campus?
- If this issue occurred on our campus or in our community, what solution would you recommend and why?
- For your proposed solution, think about the following:
  - How would your solution foster interfaith cooperation?
  - What groups would need to be involved in the solution?
  - What relationships would you need to build to make your solution a reality? Who are your allies on campus who will support you in your vision?
  - What skills and assets are present in you or in this team that are relevant to seeking your solution? Where might we need to grow?

If participants worked in small groups, consider bringing them back to a large group to share highlights from their conversations. If relevant, pass out part two of the case, which contains the resolution of the situation. After reading it, consider the following questions:

- What do you think about what actually happened? Are you satisfied with what happened? Why or why not?
- How close is the actual solution to the solution you recommended? What might be the impact or consequences of the solution?
- Given what we have discussed and uncovered through this case study activity, what should our next steps be for fostering and building interfaith cooperation?

Consider wrapping up your conversation with a growth question that prompts individuals to think about their own interfaith leadership moving forward. Participants might write in journals or reflect silently on these questions before gathering again for discussion in small groups.

- Based on what we discussed today, how do you understand your own interfaith leadership?
- What skills, experience, or perspective do you have to offer your campus when it comes to fostering a positive campus climate concerning religious diversity or building interfaith relationships?
- Where do you feel like you still need to grow? For example, what knowledge or skills do you want to continue honing? What do you want to learn more about? What do you need to grow in these ways?

References

Patel, E. (2016). *Interfaith leadership: A primer.* Boston, MA: Beacon Press.

Sells, M. (1999). *Approaching the Qur'an: The early revelations.* Ashland, OR: White Cloud Press.

Suomala, K., & Interfaith Youth Core. (2013). *Case studies for exploring interfaith cooperation: Classroom tools.* Retrieved from https://www.ifyc.org/sites/default/files/Case%20Studies_small_0.pdf

STUDY OR INDOCTRINATION?

Teaching the Qur'an at the University of North Carolina

Karla Suomala

Growing up Unitarian Universalist outside Philadelphia, Mary Ellen Geiss was shocked by what she saw as she settled into the University of North Carolina (UNC) community. "Religion was suddenly in my face in a way that it had never been before," she recalled (M. Giess, personal communication, February 2, 2010). She discovered it was not just religion in general but conservative Christianity in particular. "I had friends in high school who were more conservative than me religiously, but I guess we just overlooked those kinds of differences. At UNC, though, religion was impossible to ignore."

One day when she was walking through the center of campus, Mary Ellen recalled seeing two men holding signs listing all the different kinds of people who were going to hell. "It was a profound moment for me," notes Mary Ellen. "Even though some people tend to think of UNC as a very hippy-liberal place, over 80% of the student body comes from North Carolina, which tends to be a lot more religiously conservative. It was the first time that I encountered this type of religious expression."

Mary Ellen didn't have to wait long to see the central role that religion played on campus and in the region. As one of 4,200 incoming first-year and transfer students at UNC in the fall of 2002, she was required to read *Approaching the Qur'an: The Early Revelations* (Sells, 1999). New students were asked to read the book over the summer and write a 1-page response essay on it. All students were expected to participate in small-group discussions of the text that would take place in August.

Carolina Summer Reading Program

Each year the Carolina Summer Reading Program (CSRP) selects a book that all incoming first-year and transfer students are required to read over the summer. This program is intended to introduce new students to the intellectual life at UNC through discussion and critical thinking about a current topic. The program directors also hope to create a sense of community among incoming students by providing a common experience.

Immediately following the events of September 11, 2001, educators across the country were considering ways to teach students about Islam. Carl Ernst, a religious studies professor at UNC, was approached by the CSRP committee to recommend a good translation of the Qur'an. Ernst (2003) said, "I immediately thought of Sells' book. . . . I cannot think of any other translation of the Qur'an that I would have recommended" (para. 2).

In the Spotlight

"What could be a better way to start a college career than by reading from a Good Book?" asked Michael Park (2002) of *Fox News*. "Plenty, if the book in question is the Qur'an and your country has been attacked by Muslim terrorists" (para. 1–2). *Fox News* announced that the Family Policy Network [FPN] was "taking aim at the University of North Carolina at Chapel Hill for requiring all incoming freshmen . . . to read a book about the Qur'an, the holy book of Islam" (Park, 2002, para. 3), thus putting UNC's book selection in the national spotlight. Terry Moffitt, FPN chairman and UNC alumnus, argued that UNC's book selection "amounts to state support for one religion over another." Moffitt, who said he had not read the book, worried that "students will get an incomplete picture of Islam, a politically correct view formed by [reading] only part of the entire holy book" (Park, 2002, para. 8–11).

Media attention grew exponentially after Fox's report (Park, 2002) in print and on television, and the FPN indicated it would file a lawsuit. UNC's CSRP website was updated to indicate that students could opt out of reading the book using their one-page essay assignment to explain why they did so and could be excused from attending the discussion sessions. University officials defended their choice of the book for the CSRP, saying that "the book is an academic text rather than a religious one. It was chosen specifically to address issues related to the September 11 terrorist attacks and to educate students on Islam" (Park, 2002). Sue Estroff, chairwoman of UNC's faculty, added "I think it was a terrific choice of topics for us to take up this year. To me, all the uproar bolsters the case of why we have to do this" (Park, 2002).

Incoming Student Orientation

"I was going into my sophomore year that summer when incoming students were reading *Approaching the Qur'an*," said UNC student orientation leader Amir Thomas.

> When I first heard that the Qur'an book was chosen, I wasn't really surprised. There was a lot of backlash or resistance toward the Muslim community because people didn't really understand or like this religion. In our training we were told that there might be some concerns about the book and some of our training involved conflict resolution. They gave us some specific discussion points that we could use in case we encountered students who were resistant, to try to encourage them to be more open to the book. (A. Thomas, personal communication, May 9, 2010)

Throughout the summer, Amir and other orientation leaders met with groups of first-year students who came for orientation. "We would talk about the book and give them more information about what to expect in the discussion sessions when they came to the campus in the fall." Amir didn't hear many strong reactions from incoming students toward the reading, either positive or negative. "Mostly there were questions about whether or not students needed to read the whole thing, and some lighthearted joking about the assignment" (A. Thomas, personal communication, May 9, 2010).

UNC and the Establishment Clause

On Monday, July 22, a lawsuit was filed in the U.S. District Court in Greensboro, North Carolina, on behalf of three unnamed incoming first-year students and the FPN. The lawsuit alleged that UNC's reading assignment violated the establishment clause, pointing to those portions of the clause that prohibit the government from giving precedence to one religion over another and from interfering with the free expression of an individual's religious beliefs ("University Sued Over Islam Reading Assignment," 2002).

A few days later, attorneys for the plaintiffs also asked a judge to issue an order to halt the program. Named as one of the defendants in the case, UNC Chancellor James Moeser responded to the suit in a statement issued on Thursday, July 25: "There is no proselytizing here. We'll be leading our students into asking questions. We are being faithful to our motto—Lux, Libertas [Light, Liberty]. We are shedding light and we are defending freedom" (Ferreri, 2002a).

Jen Daum, UNC's student body president, agreed:

What is a university if it is not a place where students can read about a largely foreign topic and engage in dialogue? For students who think they find the Qur'an offensive, I challenge you—at least read the book and make up your own mind. (Ferreri, 2002a, A1)

Bashar Staitieh, UNC's Muslim Society president, was also very supportive of the book choice, saying, "People just really need a different image of Islam and it's programs like this that are going to give it to them," he said (Severson & Davis, 2002, para. 28).

Politicians Take a Stand

The controversy continued to grow. In an amendment to the budget, the North Carolina House Appropriations Committee voted 64 to 10 on August 7 to bar funding for the CSRP (Ferreri, 2002b). One of the amendment's supporters, State Rep. Gene Arnold, Nash County, said that UNC Chancellor James Moeser "knew the general public had an attitude that is anti-Arabic because of the 9/11 incident. . . . I think the chancellor is totally, completely out of step with what the people of North Carolina want and expect out of its university" (Ferreri, 2002b, A1). Moeser issued a statement that read in part,

> It's unfortunate that people have misinterpreted this reading assignment as a form of indoctrination. We are offering the summer reading program this year in the spirit of seeking understanding—not in advocacy of Islam over Christianity or Judaism or any other religion. (Ferreri, 2002b, A1)

Day in Court

As August 19, the day incoming students would meet in small groups, loomed large, it was still not clear to UNC faculty, administration, and staff whether the sessions would even be held. In the first phase of the lawsuit filed by the FPN, lawyers sought an injunction for discussions that focused on the Qur'an, basing their arguments on the same precedents that banned prayer and Bible readings in public schools. They told the judge that the establishment clause should also apply to UNC's summer book selection just as it did in cases involving school prayer. They argued further that by requiring the book, a public university was indoctrinating students with deceptive claims about the peaceful nature of Islam. This, they said, was a clear violation of the establishment clause, which prohibits government actions that might give precedence to one religion over another (Ross, 2002).

"The Establishment clause doesn't prevent teaching [people] about religion," said Celia Lata, associate attorney general representing UNC (Ross,

2002, A9). Noting that more than 100 courses offered at UNC deal with religion in one way or another, Lata said that the plaintiffs

> object to Dr. Sells' book because it conflicts with their religious beliefs. They alleged that the assignment is pro-Islam because it isn't sufficiently anti-Islam. This is really not about protecting religious freedom, it is about the censorship of ideas. (Ferreri, 2002d, A1)

Attorneys for the university also pointed out that the reading program was not in fact mandatory.

On August 15, the judge ruled in UNC's favor, denying the request that was made by the plaintiffs to stop the upcoming discussion sessions (Ferreri, 2002e). FNP appealed this decision, so by the morning of August 19, it was still not clear whether the discussion sessions would be held.

PART TWO

Students Stream Into Chapel Hill

Throughout the summer UNC students did not have a lot of opportunities to weigh in on the debate because regular classes weren't in session. But as they arrived on campus in the days before the academic year started, they walked into a media frenzy. Mariah Hoffman, a first-year student, told a reporter from the *Durham Herald-Sun*, "It was valuable to read about a religion I didn't know much about." She added, "School is a place where you learn about the world; so if the purpose is for learning then I don't think [the book] is a bad thing" (Ferreri, 2002c, B4). Student Nadav Ariel agreed in part, saying, "Students should be ready to come to a university to learn about other cultures instead of being close-minded." But, he wondered, maybe "requiring all first-year students to read about the Qur'an and not about the culture is a bit too close to forcing religious values" (Ferreri, 2002c, B4).

Andrew Synn, another first-year student, thought that the FPN did have a case because "the [book has] sensitive material in it regarding religion. So if you're a religious person, you won't like it. But the book isn't trying to convert anyone" (Ferreri, 2002c, B4). In fact, Synn noticed similarities between Islam and his own religious tradition, Christianity. "The book reminds me a lot of the [Psalms] and Proverbs that the [Bible] had" (p. B4).

Finally Approaching the Qur'an

The FPN's final attempt to stop the discussion sessions from taking place was denied by a federal appeals court (Ahmad, Bukhari, & Nyang, 2012).

Incoming students at UNC would have the opportunity to meet and talk about Sells's (1999) book. "As orientation leaders we were encouraged to read the book so we could participate in the discussion groups," Amir Thomas recalls. "In my group, students asked questions, and they had thoughtful and insightful things to say. Everyone participated." Later, when Amir and his fellow orientation leaders talked about the discussions, the consensus was that they had gone well. "But we also had the sense that the whole thing had been over-hyped," he said (A. Thomas, personal communication, May 2010).

"I enjoyed reading the book because I knew nothing about Islam," recalls Mary Ellen Giess, the student who had been so shocked by the role religion played on the UNC campus. "It was like understanding scripture for the first time, and how powerful it could be. It gave me a new perspective on scripture in general." However, the discussion session was also a letdown for Mary Ellen. "I think that it was partly because we were all freshmen. We had no idea what we were doing." But, she added, "Part of it was not being pushed to engage at a deeper level" (M. Giess, personal communication, May 4, 2010). She had hoped for more. Although the media, political, and legal drama continued, the CSRP was over as far as UNC's incoming class of 2002 was concerned.

References

Ahmad, M., Bukhari, Z., & Nyang, S. (2012). *Observing the observer: The state of Islamic studies in American universities.* Herndon, VA: International Institute of Islamic Thought.

Ernst, C. (2003). From the heart of the Qur'an belt. *Religious Studies News.* Retrieved from http://www.unc.edu/~cernst/rsnews.htm

Ferreri, E. (2002a, July 26). UNC chancellor defends required Qur'an assignment. *Durham Herald-Sun*, p. A1.

Ferreri, E. (2002b, August 9). Qur'an ban bid miffs some UNC officials. *Durham Herald-Sun*, p. A1.

Ferreri, E. (2002c, August 12). Several incoming UNC students see book discussion as healthy. *Durham Herald-Sun*, p. B4.

Ferreri, E. (2002d, August 16). Judge upholds readings at UNC. *Durham Herald-Sun*, p. A1.

Ferreri, E. (2002e, August 20). UNC students discuss Qur'an book. *Chapel Hill Herald*, p. 1.

Park, M. (2002, July 6). University's Qur'an reading stirs controversy. *Fox News.* Retrieved from http://www.foxnews.com/story/2002/07/06/university-quran-reading-stirs-controversy.html

Ross, K. (2002, August 18). Making the case. *Chapel Hill News*, p. A9.

Sells, M. (1999). *Approaching the Qur'an: The early revelations*. Ashland, OR: White Cloud Press.

Severson, L., & Davis, D. (2002, September 12). Qu'ran at UNC. *Religion & Ethics Newsweekly*. Retrieved from http://www.heraldtribune.com/article/LK/20020912/News/605238287/SH/

University sued over Islam reading assignment. (2002, July 24). *CNN.com Law Center*. Retrieved from http://www.cnn.com/2002/LAW/07/24/islam.unc.lawsuit/index.html.

II

COERCION OR
CONVERSION?

Grappling With Religious Difference at
the University of Illinois at Chicago

Karla Suomala

Nick Price arrived at University of Illinois at Chicago (UIC) as a new staff worker for InterVarsity Christian Fellowship, an evangelical Christian ministry that works with students and faculty at colleges and universities across the country. Nick had just completed a two-year training program with InterVarsity, and he was excited about his new position and getting to know the UIC community. Since InterVarsity is a primarily student-led organization, Nick's job involved training students to lead small-group Bible studies, implementing outreach events, and creating service opportunities on and around campus. "Basically," he explained, "we're the ones behind the scenes training and equipping students to lead the ministry on campus" (N. Price, personal communication, December 7, 2009). In addition, Nick said he looked forward to meeting and collaborating with staff from other religious groups at the university through an interfaith organization called the Religious Workers Association (RWA).

Although UIC is a public institution and doesn't sponsor any particular religious activities or groups, it does make a place for the religious life of students on campus. Set up by the dean's office, the RWA allows the professional staff of different religious organizations on campus to come together and discuss what they are each doing with students. In addition, members of the RWA work with the university administration to address concerns that can arise in the religiously diverse community. To join the RWA and become registered with the university, an organization must sign a covenant or agreement committing to a number of goals, including "fostering a sense of human community at UIC around humane concerns"; "making known to all at UIC the availability of religious counsel, fellowship, and worship offered by the UIC RWA communities"; and "cooperating with University administrators in services to the UIC community." Each member agrees to follow a set of guidelines for the way religious groups can operate with each other and with members of the campus community.

Considering Campus Crusade for Christ

At the first RWA meeting that fall, the chairperson of the group informed fellow members that Campus Crusade for Christ (Cru), an evangelical Christian organization, had expressed interest in joining the RWA. The chair also indicated that he had taken the preliminary step of meeting with Cru staff to review the RWA's covenant. He reported that Cru staff responded positively to all of the RWA's commitments, except for one. Specifically, Cru was concerned about committing to the line in the RWA covenant that read, "We will . . . not initiate personal religious opportunities designed to draw persons from another religious community into [our] religious community." As an organization whose primary aim is to share the gospel and invite people to have a relationship with Jesus Christ, they felt that agreeing to this statement in its current form would limit their ability to live their calling. The chair asked how the RWA should respond to this situation.

Nick vividly recalls this meeting because hearing about the situation with Cru, he was taken by surprise. He remembers thinking, "Does this statement basically mean that as members of the RWA, we cannot share our faith with anybody of another tradition?" (N. Price, personal communication, December 7, 2009). Nick was torn. He had long been involved with interfaith work, and the RWA seemed like a good place to further this interest. However, he wondered whether as an InterVarsity staff member dedicated to sharing the Christian message he should be a member of the RWA with this commitment. Nick expressed concern about the clause in question, saying, "[InterVarsity]'s Christian faith demands that we share what we believe with others" (N. Price, personal communication, December 7, 2009). Nick also pointed out that the imperative to share one's theological beliefs was in fact shared by Islam. A number of the other RWA members, however, were adamant about keeping the clause, which meant denying membership to Cru.

An Uncomfortable Conversation

The conversation broadened to the larger question of how to deal with religious groups for whom proselytizing (the attempt to convert a person from one religion, belief, or opinion to another) and evangelizing (communicating the key messages of one's religious tradition to others) were central aspects of religious identity. In the meantime, RWA members realized they were not going to be able to settle the Cru matter quickly. Over the course of the academic year, the RWA reconsidered the language in its membership covenant. What became evident was that a level of discomfort existed about how to accommodate religious groups that hold very specific truth claims and think these claims should be shared with others. According to Nick, the RWA conversation moved away from the logistical question about what to do with a particular clause to the much deeper question of how people with different theologies gather and talk through differences.

Marla Baker, director of UIC Hillel for Jewish students at UIC, was very aware of the challenge that Nick and some of his colleagues were experiencing. "But," she said, "it's [a] gray area, and we all live with some amount of discomfort around these issues" (M. Baker, personal communication, May 17, 2010). Proselytization itself isn't much of the issue for Marla but rather the way groups spread their message.

> When, for example, a religious group puts out signs inviting everybody to a really nice pizza party and a volleyball game, but then afterward gets everyone together to talk about their religious beliefs and what they stand for, it's problematic . . . because they are not being up front about who they are and what they're trying to accomplish. They don't indicate that this event is about evangelization. (M. Baker, personal communication, May 17, 2010)

Marla recalls situations like this on campus that bordered on coercion because some groups were not honest when they approached people.

Sometimes, however, situations are not necessarily as clearly defined. For example, what about a group of students putting up a sign inviting hall residents to play basketball, and at some point during the activity or afterward, the conversation turns toward religious matters? Could this be considered coercive behavior? Or situations in which staff workers of religious organizations such as InterVarsity meet one on one with students? If students were genuinely open to talking about religion if it comes up in conversation, then there isn't really any danger of coercion. As for the one-on-one meetings, they are an important part of Nick's job. They offer opportunities for Nick to get to know students better and accomplish some of InterVarsity's training and leadership development goals.

When They Won't Take No for an Answer

Coercive behavior isn't the only problem that is connected to groups that proselytize, notes Marla. There are some religious groups that make it difficult for students to disengage once they've attended a few events. She points to instances on the UIC campus when a group has been unwilling to take no for an answer.

Nick agreed with Marla and other members that coercive or harassing behavior on the part of religious groups was unacceptable. He was concerned, however, that they were equating proselytization or evangelization with coercion and that they were simply assuming that groups that held exclusive truth claims were coercive. "At InterVarsity, we don't want to see any high pressure tactics being used with students," Nick said. "We want them to feel the freedom to safely question and choose" (N. Price, personal communication, March 4, 2010). That being said, however, Nick asked, "Do we want to see people come to know Christ? Absolutely. That's [an] important part of who we are as an organization. We're not going to be shy about that. But if they don't, we want to honor that choice too." Nick is accepting of other religious groups that want to win converts or invite people to join their tradition. "The UIC has one of the largest Muslim student groups in the United States," says Nick, "and every year they host an Islamic Awareness Week where they make it very clear that they are sharing the message of Islam and trying to help people look at Islam with new eyes, with the hope that people will become Muslims. And you know what? I'm OK with that" (N. Price, personal communication, March 4, 2010).

Up Front and Open

The bottom line for Marla was that she wanted groups to be up front and say,

> This is what we represent, and we'd like to have a conversation with you about it. . . . [College is] a place where students have an opportunity to be exposed to all different kinds of things and make up their own minds. (M. Baker, personal communication, May 17, 2010)

Marla reflected that on a personal level, her problem with proselytism is

> the same problem I have with any fundamentalism, which is that students are in college so they can learn to do critical thinking, to live with gray area[s], to make decisions for themselves about how they approach those things. Any tradition that reduces things to black-and-white answers or says, "We have the truth and you don't, so listen to us," whatever the truth might be is really problematic because it's not in keeping with the university's mission and goals. (M. Baker, personal communication, May 17, 2010)

The kind of atmosphere that Marla describes—open and honest and where students have the opportunity to reach their own decisions about religion, among other things—is also important to Nick. Being able to ask questions and come to his own conclusions has been central to Nick's religious path. "I remember trying to figure out if I fit into a particular religious category," Nick said. "Eventually I began seriously exploring Christianity and learning everything I could about it." By his junior year in high school, Nick became a Christian when he "came to the conclusion that Christ was who he claimed to be, that he was God, and that he'd come to live among us and to save us" (N. Price, personal communication, December 7, 2009).

Well-Worn Tracks

Nick's problem with the RWA's conversation about groups that proselytize on campus was that it seemed to be running along the well-worn tracks of religious progressives versus conservatives. In a blog article he wrote about evangelicals and interfaith engagement, Nick pointed out that progressives increasingly hold that evangelicals "represent an outdated and intolerant worldview which cannot constructively add to religious dialogue between different faith traditions" (Price, 2009). Nick asked, "How can a group say, 'We are open; we accept everyone,' but then show such hostility when somebody with an exclusive truth claim shows up?" (N. Price, personal communication, December 7, 2009).

On the other hand, Nick acknowledged that it is often true that evangelicals are just as wary of progressives and interfaith dialogue because they fear they will be pressured "to accept the theological truth claims of other faiths that directly contradict their own deeply held spiritual beliefs" (N. Price, personal communication, March 4, 2010). Nick admits that when he first became involved in interfaith work, many of his evangelical Christian friends asked him how he was able to maintain his own beliefs while still respecting the faith of others. They wondered if he was being superficial or maybe even hypocritical. "That being said," Nick said, "there are many evangelicals who are interested in building bridges. . . . For interfaith engagement to be authentic, it must be able to accommodate groups with these kinds of exclusive truth claims" (N. Price, personal communication, March 4, 2010).

Making a Decision

When it came down to making a decision about the RWA covenant, RWA members deliberated about the best course of action to take. They considered how they might change the wording of the clause in question or whether they should keep it at all.

PART TWO

"I think a lot of fruit came out of our conversations," Nick said of the RWA's year-long process, "and I feel as if a lot of trust was built over the year that we talked about this issue" (N. Price, personal communication, December 7, 2009). In terms of the covenant, the RWA membership finally decided to change the language of the clause that started the whole discussion. Now the clause in the RWA covenant is more specifically focused on the use of coercive tactics to draw students away from various faith communities:

> We will not target students of other faith traditions to undermine their faith traditions for the purpose of recruiting them to our own faith communities. Instead, we will promote mutually enriching conversation about religion (both in our similarities and differences) with respect, integrity, and transparency.

As Nick reflected on the revision, he said,

> Basically, we were able to articulate what we really intended to say in the first place. The way that the RWA came to terms with groups that proselytize was to say that, "We know that people from some faith traditions feel that they need to invite students to explore their tradition, and possibly convert." What we don't want to see is one faith community specifically focusing on another faith community with the intent to convert the entire community. We want students to have the space to freely question, explore, and choose. (N. Price, personal communiation, March 4, 2010)

Cru staff then looked at the revised clause and agreed to the language and suggested they'd like to move forward with membership to the RWA (N. Price, personal communication, December 7, 2009). But when the RWA came together to make a final decision about Cru's membership, there was still no consensus among members about the group's admission, which was basically no by default. So despite the progress that Nick felt the group made in terms of building trust and dedicating time to the issue, there wasn't as much resolution as he would have hoped for.

> I'm sure that this isn't the end of it, but I guess that right now, we are at the point where we are going to continue to work together and foster the relationships we have built with each other. Hopefully, in the future, we can take the conversation about what to do with groups like Cru, with truth claims they feel they must proclaim openly, a little bit further. (N. Price, personal communication, December 7, 2009)

Reference

Price, N. (2009). All nations before God's throne: Evangelicals in an interfaith world. *CrossCurrents Magazine, 55*, pp. 404–413.

SECULAR STUDENTS
ON THE PRAIRIE

Welcoming Secular Students at
Concordia College, Moorhead

Karla Suomala

Arriving from Norway as a new student at Concordia College, in Moorhead, Minnesota, it didn't take Bjoern Kvernstuen very long to figure out that "religion was a big deal" on campus (B. Kvernstuen, personal communication, December 14, 2009). Even though he was aware of Concordia's Norwegian Lutheran heritage, Kvernstuen hadn't imagined that the religious side of this inheritance would be so significant. In Norway today, the Lutheran churches that dot the Norwegian landscape "are more cultural than religious," said Kvernstuen (B. Kvernstuen, personal communication, December 14, 2009). At Concordia, however, religion seemed to play an important role in the lives of many of his new classmates and was central to the identity and mission of the institution. Although worship attendance on campus is voluntary, all students are required to take at least two religion courses as part of the college's core curriculum.

Growing up in a small village outside Lillehammer, Kvernstuen noticed the active religious communities of recent immigrants to Norway, making him curious about religious practices and ideas. His interactions with religion grew in Afghanistan during military service. His experience there allowed him to see religion and violence connected in ways that troubled him. "It was odd," he said, "seeing American soldiers with biblical inscriptions on their guns and praying before they went out to the field." At the same time, "there were suicide bombings and other brutal acts also being carried out in the name religion. Everywhere you looked, religion was at the center of the conflict" (B. Kvernstuen, personal communication, December 14, 2009).

Claiming a Secular Identity

Once at Concordia, though, Kvernstuen learned to think critically about religion and learned more about himself. He was also able to see where he fit in the picture and to more fully claim his secular identity. "At first, it seemed a little black and white," he said. "On the surface it appeared as if everyone was a Christian, and even more specifically, Lutheran" (B. Kvernstuen, personal communication, December 14, 2009). As he spoke with fellow students, however, Kvernstuen discovered many were Lutheran by culture. He also found that half the student body came from other religious traditions but was primarily Christian. With many groups on campus to meet the needs of students from a variety of religious traditions, Kvernstuen wanted secularists like himself to be represented at Concordia as well.

A Club for Secular Students?

Kvernstuen first started thinking about forming a secular student group in the summer of 2009. Through word of mouth and Facebook, Kvernstuen identified a core group of interested students who, like him, were interested in having an "open, welcoming place to discuss their varying views on faith" (Paulson, 2011). But to reserve rooms on campus for meetings and to advertise meetings and events, a student group or organization at Concordia must be officially recognized by the institution. Therefore, Kvernstuen and a few classmates set about making this happen.

As part of the process, the group leaders and founders had to declare their intention to start an organization by filling out an application that required the name of a faculty member or staff adviser. It took more time than they expected to find someone willing to fill this role. "We had several interested people," said Kvernstuen, "but when it [came] to actually putting your name down and making it formal" people became more hesitant (Dalrymple, 2009, para. 8). Richard Gilmore chair of the philosophy department, eventually agreed to be the official adviser. "It seems to me that it's healthy to have a counter voice, a space for a different way of talking about values," noted Gilmore (Dalrymple, 2009, para. 10). With Gilmore on board, the Secular Students of Concordia (SSC) moved forward and submitted a completed application by late fall.

In Conflict With the Mission of the College

The group was informed on December 17, 2009, that it would not be recognized by the college. Concordia College spokesperson Roger Degerman said the application was denied because "Concordia organizations cannot be in conflict with the mission of the college or the ELCA [Evangelical Lutheran Church in America]." Concordia is 1 of 26 Lutheran colleges and universities in the United States associated with ELCA. According to Degerman,

> The proposed constitution from the secularist organization stated that it wanted to present "secular values as adequate alternatives to religion." That stated goal is in opposition to the mission of the college and the ELCA. . . . Concordia does not prescribe that its community members adhere to certain beliefs and practices. However, the college should not be expected to sanction and fund any group or organization that is in direct conflict with its mission and purpose. (Davila, 2010, p. 1)

Degerman also noted that "a new proposal would only be considered if it included fundamental purpose changes that were not in conflict with Concordia's mission" (Dalrymple, 2010, p. 1).

What College Standards Don't Atheists Meet?

Kvernstuen, Gilmore, and other students were shocked and disappointed by the decision. Even though they were aware that not everyone in the Concordia community was happy about having a secular student group, they hadn't met with any formal opposition (Dalrymple, 2010).

Many students at Concordia publicly disagreed with the college's decision. "The Lutheran academic tradition promotes the freedom to search for truth . . . and, most importantly, the engagement of faith and learning as a creative dialogue," said junior Theodor Rinell in an interview with the *Concordian* (Davila, 2010, p. 1). In an editorial that appeared in the same newspaper, Jake Johnson asked, "What 'college standards' do atheists not meet? Are we not equal members of the Concordia community?" (Johnson, 2010, p. 5).

Although there are similar clubs at nearby institutions, SSC's request to be recognized created quite a stir outside the Concordia community. *The Forum of Fargo-Moorhead* ran a front-page article at about the time that SSC submitted its final application and ran another follow-up on the administration's decision not to recognize SSC (Dalrymple, 2009, 2010). The story was then picked up by commentators around the country. Humanist interfaith activist Chris Stedman wrote on his blog, "As a graduate of another college affiliated with the ELCA, I can tell you that religious diversity was present at my school, including many secular folks. [Concordia's] decision is ridiculous and I hope that they will reconsider" (Stedman, 2010).

The publicity was helpful to the SSC. After receiving a gift from an anonymous donor and a letter from a Lutheran congregation in Minneapolis–St. Paul expressing support, the group was confident it had a goal worth pursuing.

Kvernstuen felt that perhaps the college administrators had misunderstood the purpose of the group. "It is not in our nature, nor in our interest, to evangelize our point of view," Kvernstuen emphasized (Dalrymple, 2010, para. 15). The student members of the Facebook group gathered signatures of support from fellow students and worked on a second application.

"It took [Kvernstuen and Gilmore] . . . a long time to figure out what it exactly was about the SSC that didn't meet ELCA and college standards since the rejection rationale was so generally stated and rumors were heavily circulated," Paulson (2011, para. 4) reported in the *Concordian* a year later when the group had submitted its second application. After talking to several administrators to sort out the issue, Kvernstuen discovered that two main reasons seemed to fuel Concordia's rejection of the SSC's application: "The organization only included atheists in the mission statement and stipulated that SSC members must also be members of the national organization American Atheists" (Paulson, 2011, para. 4).

Concordia's Future and Student Diversity

Once they were able to elicit this more specific rationale, Gilmore said that he could understand the college's initial concerns about the group, telling the *Concordian* "that other clubs were also rejected for similar reasons [the previous] year, including The Remedy, a non-denominational organization that was rejected for its literal fundamentalist view of the Bible, which is contrary to the views of the ELCA" (Paulson, 2011, para 7). Rev. Tim Megorden, a campus pastor at Concordia during that time, explained that even better known groups such as Cru were not allowed to organize because Concordia was concerned about the influence that nonstudent leaders from outside groups could exert on campus (T. Megorden, personal communication, August 29, 2016). Off campus, however, students were encouraged to participate in religious or nonreligious organizations of their choice. Concordia's main campus worship service had always taken place on Wednesdays rather than Sundays so that students could "go local" (T. Megorden, personal communication, August 29, 2016).

Megorden noted that despite the college's decision not to recognize the group, the administration under the leadership of President Pamela Jolicoeur was not necessarily opposed to having a secular student group on campus. "Pam was aware of the changing dynamics of the Lutheran church and Christianity more broadly," Megorden said, "and believed that Concordia's future depended on engaging the religious diversity of its students" (T. Megorden, personal communication, August 29, 2016). She was excited about creating partnerships across these kinds of boundaries and was convinced that that by doing so, Concordia would be a stronger and more creative community. In practice, however, the institution did not have guidelines for communicating and cooperating with other religious organizations. Up to that point, decisions had been made on a case-by-case basis, and this was quickly becoming untenable. Jolicoeur realized that the administration would need to create a more comprehensive policy.

Back to the Drawing Board

To understand more clearly how they should revise their mission and constitution, SSC leaders looked carefully at Concordia's mission statement, which stated that "students who are eager to address big questions, open to the complexity of our multicultural world, and passionate about making a difference in their communities are welcome to be full and active participants in the life of Concordia." Even more specifically, the statement highlighted the institution's commitment to "freedom to search for truth, with nothing off-limits for inquiry and critique" (Concordia College, 2018).

Kvernstuen said that as they prepared to submit a second application, the group revised the mission statement to make it more inclusive. "Although I initially began the club to raise awareness of atheism, that changed somewhat along the way. The organization was becoming more about asking critical questions and including all points of view" (B. Kvernstuen, personal communication, December 14, 2009). They also changed the constitution so that students were not expected to join any other organization except the SSC. The revised goals for the group included the following: participation in interfaith dialogue, cooperation with the Campus Ministry Commission, bringing speakers to campus, and hosting movie discussion nights where students could get together for open conversation (Paulson, 2011).

Over the summer of 2010, however, Jolicoeur died unexpectedly. The community as a whole experienced the grief of losing Jolicoeur while trying to figure out what would come next. The college administration still intended to develop a comprehensive new policy about student organizations that would better recognize and embrace the growing diversity of students. Given the circumstances, though, many decisions were put on hold until a new president was in place.

PART TWO

A year passed and the SSC's second application was still awaiting a decision. Over the summer of 2012, Concordia welcomed a new president, William Craft, along with a new vice president and dean of student affairs, Sue Oatey.

As Oatey prepared for the arrival of students, her staff informed her about the efforts of the SSC to be recognized as a student organization (S. Oatey, personal communication, September 8, 2016). By this point, most of the students who were part of the original group had graduated. In addition, there was still no policy in place to work with unaffiliated religious and secular organizations.

Despite the leadership transition, the college continued with efforts to be more inclusive and to broaden the campus conversation. Part of that commitment was evident in professor of religion and director of the Forum on Faith and Life Jacqueline Bussie's new efforts to initiate a campuswide interfaith initiative. Many students had begun to participate in these opportunities to talk about their beliefs and about the kind of community that Concordia should be.

Partly because of the energy of these interfaith efforts, the administration decided it was time to more formally consider the role and place of student organizations on campus and to think about how a secular student organization would fit at Concordia. Over the course of a year, Craft formed a group in which he, the cabinet, Oatey, and Pastor Megorden engaged in a process to more systematically discuss these questions. This involved learning more about the Concordia context and history. As they worked toward a decision, Oatey said that they thought carefully about the kind of message they wanted to communicate about diversity and openness at Concordia to the campus community as well as to the larger community beyond. "The students were remarkably patient with us throughout that time," she added (S. Oatey, personal communication, September 8, 2016).

Meanwhile, a new group of students revived the SSC cause. Andreas Rekdal was a senior that year, and he and his fellow students decided to start from scratch on a third application attempt. They looked more carefully at the positions of a national organization, the Secular Student Alliance (SSA), and found that they were "uncomfortable with SSA's emphasis on pure science being the only dimension that humans can know anything about and that all other perspectives were disregarded" (A. Rekdal, personal communication, September 15, 2016). What they wanted instead, he said, "was a place where you could freely speak about and explore philosophy and ethics from a non-religious perspective but that was also open to people who were religious."

As the students shaped this third application, they tried to be as inclusive as possible so that anyone who participated, regardless of religious affiliation, would feel safe and welcome. In addition, they opted for a relational approach to the application. By the end of the 2012–2013 academic year, the administration determined that the application made by Rekdal and his classmates was in line with Concordia's mission and vision. The SSC was formally recognized as a student organization.

References

Concordia College. (2018). *Called to make a difference*. Retrieved from https://www.concordiacollege.edu/about/our-mission/

Dalrymple, A. (2009). *Concordia students starting secular club*. Retrieved from http://www.inforum.com/retrieve/concordia%20students%20starting%20secular%20club/1/relevance

Dalrymple, A. (2010). Concordia secular club wants school officials to reconsider. *Forum of Fargo-Moorhead*. Retrieved from http://www.inforum.com/content/concordia-secular-club-wants-school-officials-reconsider

Davila, B. (2010, January 22). Approval denied to secularist organization. *Concordian*, p. 1.

Johnson, J. (2010, January 15). Atheist students silenced. *Concordian*, p. 5.

Paulson, M. (2011, March 4). Secular group applies for college recognition again. *Concordian*. Retrieved from http://theconcordian.org/2011/03/07/secular-group-applies-for-college-recognition-again

Stedman, C. (2010, February 12). Religion (and secular) roundup: Secular students, fundamentalist atheists, postage stamps. Retrieved from http://nonprophetstatus.com/?s=secular+students+of+concordia.

13

WHEN CAUSES COLLIDE

Exploring Intersectionality and the Middle East Conflict

Megan Lane

Listening to Nia Adams and Rachel Cohen talk about their experience at Kinnamon University prior to the controversy that erupted over social justice movements, they almost could have been speaking for each other. "Kinnamon gave me a voice and an opportunity to express my identity in a new way," Nia said. Rachel echoed similar themes. "I feel like I discovered who I was and how my identity intersected with the world in an empowering way," she said. Both students recalled how their first years on campus provided them with the opportunity to encounter difference in a productive way, which deepened their commitment to their individual identities while providing opportunities to encounter difference.

For some, this might have happened by accident. For Rachel and Nia, this was by design. Kinnamon University's five-year diversity strategic plan, Faces of Kinnamon, launched two years before these two students set foot on campus, establishing an ambitious vision for diversifying the student body while building capacity across the institution to use that diversity in new and exciting ways. However, through the experiences of Nia and Rachel, the individual experiences and the strategy of this prestigious university were about to be tested as student groups on campus became embroiled in a controversy on racial social justice movements and their intersection with religious identity.

An Ambitious Campus Strategy

Kinnamon University is an elite private institution on the West Coast. Founded in 1890 with 10,000 undergraduate and 12,000 graduate students,

Kinnamon boasts a faculty of world-renowned scholars and a global reputation for research scholarship. Kinnamon also has a rich history of student activism and social justice. From women's suffrage to civil rights to lesbian, gay, bisexual, and transgender equality, Kinnamon students were on the front lines throughout the university's history. The combination of academic excellence and emphasis on active citizenship presents a variety of unique challenges as students navigate the intersections between the drive for success and the desire to speak out.

Precisely because of this compelling history, Kinnamon was at the cutting edge of diversity engagement when it announced its ambitious multi-year strategic plan to proactively address the challenge of diversity in higher education. The complex strategy included diversifying the student body, building new learning experiences for students to encounter diversity and develop the skills to live those experiences productively, and providing professional development training for all members of the campus community to equip leaders to make a lasting impact on diversity issues on campus. Kinnamon President Rebecca Sellers proudly proclaimed, "Over the next five years, Kinnamon will be a role model in what it means to engage with America's diversity proudly and confidently."

Students were widely committed to this work and commended Kinnamon's efforts. "It's part of what drew me to Kinnamon," Nia said. "I wanted to be at an institution that cared about my identity and helped me be a leader for social change."

Students Take the Lead

Given the university's strong history of student activism and orientation toward engaging with diversity, no one on campus was surprised when a growing number of students became involved in the Movement for Black Lives. In response to a barrage of recordings of police shooting Black men in the summer of 2014, the movement organized to advocate for institutional change and demand the end of racism and violence against people of color (Movement for Black Lives, 2016). Nia said, "What is happening in our country provided a concrete opportunity for us to utilize the skills that Kinnamon claims to want to teach us." Quickly, the Black Student Union (BSU) began to plan events to support the national Movement for Black Lives, often with the support of students from other cultural and religious groups on campus.

The fall semester began as it typically did, with welcome festivities and events to introduce students to ways to get involved on campus. As a way to communicate to the campus that activism is essential to its programming, the

BSU planned a peaceful #blacklivesmatter march to introduce new students to the movement and invite new participation. As incoming BSU president, Nia was particularly excited about this decision. "To me, this event was perfectly in line with the diversity strategy that Kinnamon was undertaking," she said. "I thought this was a way to share our Kinnamon values with the world."

As part of the march, the BSU also invited several other student organizations to participate as cosponsors. Knowing that the march would draw attention from the media as well as alumni, Nia requested time to discuss the march at the next meeting of the Student Activities Council, which consists of the formal leadership of Kinnamon's registered student organizations. Nia intended to solidify the list of cosponsor organizations for the event. When called on to speak at the meeting, Nia spoke eloquently about the goals of the march.

Listening to Nia, Rachel was thrilled and energized. As the president of the Jewish Student Association (JSA), Rachel was actively looking for opportunities to engage in social justice activity. "When I heard Nia speak, I knew we had to get involved," Rachel said, adding, "As a Jew, I am called by the idea of *tikkun olam* [healing the world] to engage in social activism." Given the JSA's past history of social justice efforts, Rachel knew the JSA leadership would be in support of the march. As Nia concluded her presentation, she asked if any of the other groups would be willing to cosponsor the march with the BSU. A handful of organization presidents volunteered, including Rachel. According to the BSU's constitution, cosponsorship of major events requires a majority vote of its executive board. Nia collected the volunteering organizations' names and promised to obtain BSU board approval as soon as the board met.

BSU Executive Board Meets

Members of the BSU executive board Casey Burt, Rynell Washington, Ebonie Smith, and Heather Jones, along with Nia, met to discuss and vote on cosponsors for the Black Lives Matter march. Nia described how the Student Activities Council met and suggested the partner organizations' names for consideration. The board voted to approve three organizations— The LGBTQ Alliance, the Women's Center, and Students for Peace in Palestine—before coming to the fourth organization, the JSA. Nia recalled thinking that the JSA was a natural choice for cosponsorship. "The JSA has been really involved in many social justice issues on campus, and tons of BSU members are friends with JSA folks and regularly attend each other's events," she said.

As Nia called for the vote, however, a conversation began as Casey raised his hand to speak, saying, "I want to point out that the JSA is a Zionist organization, which publicly supports Israel. How can we allow the JSA to cosponsor when the Movement for Black Lives is clearly in support of the Palestinian people?" Casey opened his laptop and read directly from the Movement's platform:

> Israel is an apartheid state with over 50 laws on the books that sanction discrimination against the Palestinian people. Palestinian homes and land are routinely bulldozed to make way for illegal Israeli settlements. Israeli soldiers also regularly arrest and detain Palestinians. . . . Palestinians are forced to walk through military checkpoints along the US-funded apartheid wall. (Movement for Black Lives Platform, 2016)

Casey continued, "We march to stand in solidarity with marginalized and oppressed peoples of color like the Palestinians. We'll look like hypocrites if we have a pro-Israel organization cosponsor."

Heather interjected and offered her support for the JSA: "You think Jewish people don't understand oppression? Regardless of the political stance of the national umbrella of their organization, they've been a solid support to us and our programming for years." Ebonie, also an active member of Students for Peace in Palestine, offered a different perspective:

> The Movement for Black Lives is built around advocacy for the rights of peoples of color. The truth of the matter is that Jews, while certainly oppressed in the past, have access to Whiteness. If the purpose of our march is to spark dialogue about racial inequality on campus, we need to acknowledge that the people of Palestine are people of color, and our support is for them first.

With meeting time running short, the executive team decided to go ahead with the vote to confirm or deny JSA cosponsorship. In a three to two vote, the executive team voted to deny JSA's cosponsorship of the march.

The Fallout

Nia was devastated by the decision but determined to be clear that the vote intended to avoid divergence from the official platform of the Movement for Black Lives, not to delegitimize the JSA as an organization. After the vote, she sent an e-mail to Rachel to inform her of the BSU's decision to deny the JSA's cosponsorship, explaining the BSU's decision did not intend to cut off the JSA from future cosponsorship but that this event needed to stay aligned with the movement's national platform. Nia also made it clear that members of the JSA were welcome to attend the march as participants.

Rachel recalled the moment she received Nia's e-mail, sitting in the library between classes. She said, "I could tell Nia was trying to be really careful and caring in her message. At the same time, I couldn't help but feel hurt." She immediately forwarded the message to her fellow JSA executive committee members, knowing that her fellow student leaders would react strongly.

The JSA secretary, David Weiss, immediately wrote an opinion piece for the *Kinnamon Post*, in which he said,

> Jews have—over the course of centuries—been persecuted and marginalized. The only reason I exist is because my grandparents were able to escape communist Romania for Israel when my mother was small. Israel is our sacred homeland as Jews and the savior of my family. Calling it an "Apartheid State" is anti-Semitic.

Nia checked her Facebook feed not long after David's piece was published to discover that Kinnamon had erupted in debate over the BSU's decision. She read the following comments from many of her fellow students that illustrated a wide diversity of opinions:

> I identify as Jewish, liberal, Non-Zionist, and a person of color. Drawing all these lines in the sand between who is welcome and who is not dilutes the message of Black Lives Matter. To assume that all Jews are of one opinion about Israel is an unfair generalization; there are groups of young American Jews who are actively working to end American support for the Israeli occupation of Palestine. (Little & Weiser, 2016)

Another Facebook comment read,

> Jews have been involved in support of African American rights for decades. Rabbi Abraham Joshua Heschel, a Holocaust survivor who marched beside Martin Luther King in Selma in 1965, later said that participating in the march made him feel like "[his] legs were praying." Would Dr. King have asked Rabbi Heschel if he was Zionist and turned him away if he said 'yes'? I seriously doubt it. (Richardson, 2016)

Yet another Facebook comment read,

> I can't believe David said that the Movement for Black Lives is "anti-Semitic"! You can be pro-Palestine without being anti-Jew. Conflating

Israel with Jewishness and implying that any critique of Israel equates to bigotry is grossly unfair. And whether David wants to admit it or not, Israeli treatment of the Palestinian people has been violent, oppressive, and dehumanizing for nearly 70 years. We can't just ignore that because his family lives there.

The final post Nia read was written by Rachel's friend Amal:

Last year, my mosque was spray painted by vandals with anti-Muslim slurs. I—along with many members of the Muslim community—was afraid for my safety and questioned the stories I'd heard growing up in Syria about America as a land of welcome and tolerance. As I struggled to understand how to make sense of it all, the first call I received was from my friend Rachel, a Jew. She immediately made herself and the JSA available to help clean up the graffiti, and more importantly, offered us their support and friendship. I understand that the BSU is bound by the platform of their national organization, as is the JSA, but when it comes to Kinnamon we are all on the same side and we need to stand together as a community against violence and racism.

Nia printed all the posts and gave them to the BSU adviser, Pamela Hawkins, prior to the march. Hawkins and the adviser for the JSA, Rabbi Daniel Rosen, met to discuss the best ways to address the situation and heal the rift among the students they advise.

PART TWO

During their conversation, Hawkins and Rosen decided to focus on ways to move forward with the march at the time and later with their students over the longer term. They contacted campus police to coordinate security for the day. They also wrote a joint statement to the *Kinnamon Post* as advisers of the two groups, describing the nuances of the conflict and stressing the importance of maintaining relationships in the face of deep disagreement. They also set up a standing meeting for the two of them to continue to connect and planned to encourage their students to be in conversation with one another. When the time was right, they brought together the executive teams of each group to discuss ways to move forward.

The march proceeded as planned. Members of the JSA attended the events as participants, but the group was noticeably smaller than the groups the JSA usually provided for BSU events. Some students carried provocative signs such as "I'm a Jew and I support #blacklivesmatter" and "Pro-Black Lives/Pro-Israel." A few tense words were exchanged between students with the Peace in Palestine group and members of the JSA, but there were no major disturbances during the event.

A few months later, the JSA planned an event for Sukkot, a Jewish holiday celebrating the harvest. As part of the event, JSA members typically invited members of other student organizations to help them build a *sukkah* (a temporary shelter or tent built during Sukkot) on the quad, where people can stop by to learn more Jewish practice during Sukkot. Noticeably absent from the JSA's list of invitations was the BSU.

Editor's Note

Although all the other case studies in this book are fully researched based on specific campus incidents, this is a hypothetical case that draws on a variety of experiences from campuses across the country. When developing the case study section, we wanted to include a case addressing the ways the Middle East conflict affects U.S. campuses given the ongoing challenges it poses to many institutions. However, as we contacted representatives from a series of institutions to request their involvement in this project, each one declined to be profiled because of concerns about aggravating ongoing tensions in the community. Hearing this from our campus partners only underscored how fraught with tension this topic can be and reinforced the importance of including a case study addressing it. We compiled this case based on our experiences working with campuses navigating tensions on the Middle East conflict; however, the institution we call Kinnamon University, the characters, and stories are entirely fabricated.

References

Little, A., & Weiser, M. (2016). *Don't like Black Lives Matter? Get ready to lose young Jews like us*. Retrieved from http://forward.com/opinion/346901/dont-like-black-lives-matter-get-ready-to-lose-young-jews-like-us/

Movement for Black Lives. (2016). *About us*. Retrieved from https://policy.m4bl.org/about/

Movement for Black Lives Platform. (2016). Retrieved from https://policy.m4bl.org/invest-divest/

Richardson, V. (2016, August 15). Black Lives Matter blindsides Jewish supporters with anti-Israel platform. *Washington Times*. Retrieved from http://www.washingtontimes.com/news/2016/aug/15/black-lives-matters-anti-israel-platform-blindside/

14

ENGAGING WITH RELIGIOUS DIVERSITY ON A REGULAR BASIS

Short Scenarios

Megan Lane

The short scenarios laid out in this chapter cover a broad cross-section of fictionalized moments when worldview diversity becomes a flashpoint on campus. From the residence hall to the classroom, from orientation to cocurricular community engagement, these scenarios were designed to help educators explore the opportunities and challenges posed by worldview diversity. We encourage educators to use these scenarios to cultivate skills among all campus leaders in engaging worldview diversity on campus. Consider using these in a variety of settings, such as a retreat for student leaders of the campus interfaith group, a professional development training for student affairs professionals, or a diversity training for student leaders and educators charged with thinking about diversity (e.g., residential advisers, orientation leaders, and students involved in multiculturalism efforts). Reflection questions are offered for each scenario to prompt reflection and skill-building. Review the introduction to part four of this book for a more in-depth introduction to using case studies for professional development and learning.

Scenario 1: Roommates in Interfaith Conflict

A pair of students living together in your residence hall come to you in conflict over the Buddhist altar that one of them built in their room. The Buddhist student insists that the altar is an important part of his religious observance needs, whereas the other student, an atheist, says with equal sincerity that the altar makes him feel uncomfortable and unwelcome in the space as a nonreligious person. The two students do not report any other issues with their living arrangements but can't come to an understanding about this divergence in beliefs and the significant negative effects it has on their relationship. Both students feel that their belief systems are under threat by their living situation. The following are potential discussion questions:

1. What is your role in this situation as a student affairs professional?
2. What questions will you ask the students?
3. What are the goals of your conversations with these students?
4. Do you move the students to other rooms? Why or why not?

Scenario 2: Culture and Religion—Mutually Exclusive?

As adviser for the Multicultural Student Council, you serve a supporting role for students planning the annual Diversity Festival on campus. As an element of the festival, students want to include a fashion show showcasing different modes of dress in different cultures. One of the outfits proposed is traditional Muslim dress, including the hijab and abaya. When the outfit is proposed, disagreement erupts among the students on the council. Some argue that the hijab is religious wear and shouldn't be trivialized in a fashion show, and others believe the show provides a valuable opportunity to educate the campus on the significance of different forms of religious attire. A barrage of anti-Muslim events on campus makes you unsure about how this element of the festival should be framed and presented. The following are potential discussion questions:

1. What is your responsibility in this situation?
2. What teachable moment presents itself here?
3. What questions do you pose to the group?
4. What is the difference between appreciation and appropriation?

Scenario 3: Town and Gown

As part of the annual programming for the Office of Service-Learning and Civic Engagement, a group of students you advise plan an interfaith-focused project to work with the local Habitat for Humanity in the city surrounding campus. On the first day of construction, a student approaches you during a break to tell you that during conversation with a community member, he talked a bit about the Hindu values that motivate him to serve his community. The community member responded by telling him he that he wasn't going to Heaven because he hadn't been saved by Jesus Christ. The student is no stranger to this type of comment but was still rattled by the blunt nature of the exchange. He is at a loss on how to proceed and approaches you for your advice. The following are potential discussion questions:

1. What is your responsibility in this situation?
2. How should students be prepared for these kinds of conversations?
3. What perspectives do you encourage the student to take in this instance?
4. How can you help guide the student to focus on relationship building in the face of his discomfort (and articulate his values unapologetically and with respect)?

Scenario 4: Teaching Students About Religion

As a part of the annual professional development retreat for your division, you are incorporating elements of religious literacy and interfaith engagement into the diversity training curriculum you are planning. The curriculum focuses on demographic data you've collected about the religious and worldview makeup of your student body and students' perceptions of campus climate and accommodations for their religious observance. During the retreat you present the data, and although most of the audience is receptive to the findings, one particularly vocal audience member said rather strongly, "Worrying about how people observe their religion is inappropriate, and endorsing religion at a public institution violates the separation of church and state. I worry we're getting into a legal gray area as educators here." The following are potential discussion questions:

1. Does this person make a valid point? Why or why not?
2. What information would you offer to address his concerns?
3. What role do you play as an educator when it comes to religion and worldview?
4. How do you respond?

Scenario 5: Out of Sight, Out of Mind

An upper administrator visits your office to express concern over the accommodations provided for Muslim students for prayer. She came across a group of Muslim students praying in a stairwell and says she was appalled to see that students had nowhere else to go to recite their prayers. She asks you what the university is required to provide to students in terms of their religious observation and what accommodations are already provided. She also mentions that she is willing to provide support, financial and in staff time, to develop a new space. Where do you begin? The following are potential discussion questions:

1. How do you find the information you need about requirements for religious accommodations?
2. Who can you talk to on campus about providing accommodations for different students' needs?
3. What is your first step in creating a new space?
4. What factors do you need to consider when planning for the space?

Scenario 6: Education Versus Values

A student who is a member of the Church of Jesus Christ of Latter-day Saints tells you that his film studies course requires viewing a movie with explicit sexual content that makes him uncomfortable. He is unsure how to approach the faculty member teaching the course in fear that his opposition to the subject material will be misinterpreted and rejected by the professor. He understands that the thematic elements are an integral part of the character development in the story, but the depictions of extramarital sex go against his values as a Mormon. The following are potential discussion questions:

1. How can you articulate in your own words, as an educator, the conflict in this situation?
2. What questions would you use to coach this student?
3. Would you consider approaching the faculty member? How might you do so?
4. What takes precedence in this situation—learning or adhering to one's values?

Scenario 7: Suffering Differences

A Jewish student tells you that a faculty member claimed in class that what the Palestinians are suffering under Israeli occupation is worse than the Holocaust. The student understands the professor's reasoning behind this opinion, particularly given that the professor has family members living in the West Bank. Nevertheless, she is shocked and dismayed by the professor's stark position, and you know from a previous conversation that her grandparents were Holocaust survivors. The student is unsure how she can continue in the faculty member's class knowing his opinion, but the course is required for the completion of her major, and he is the only one who teaches it. The following are potential discussion questions:

1. What will you do to support this student?
2. How would you coach her on how to move forward?
3. Would you approach the faculty member? Why or why not?
4. What additional information would be helpful for you to have as context for this situation?

Scenario 8: Summer Events and Religious Observance

You are organizing a back-to-school welcome event including a cookout for families of students. The day before the event a student tells you he is Muslim and it is the last week of the holy month of Ramadan, so he and his family will be fasting, and they won't be needing food. His comment is completely benign and meant to inform, but you are devastated that you accidentally planned an event revolving around food when there will probably be a number of families who cannot eat. The following are potential discussion questions:

1. What are possible solutions to this problem?
2. How can you include those fasting during the event?
3. How can you find out what other religious holidays involve fasting (from various traditions)?
4. On a similar note, what kinds of food should you avoid serving to create interfaith friendly menus?

Scenario 9: Relationships and Rejection

A group of students from the Atheist, Agnostic, and Freethinker Society are organizing a service event to aid victims of a hurricane that affected local communities. They are interested in cosponsoring the project with members of other student organizations, including the religious groups on campus. A student leader with the organization asks for your advice when their invitation is rejected by one of the more conservative religious groups on campus saying its members weren't interested in working with immoral atheists. The students are hurt by the rejection and question whether they should even do interfaith projects. The following are potential discussion questions:

1. How would you frame your conversation with this student?
2. What is important for this student to know, feel, or understand?
3. Would you or how would you approach the members of the other group?
4. What kinds of relationship building would you plan or encourage the atheist students to undertake?

PART FIVE

FOUNDATIONAL KNOWLEDGE: WHAT MATTERS AND WHY?

Mary Ellen Giess

Lack of knowledge about religious traditions is one of the most common concerns we hear from higher education professionals when considering religious diversity on campus. "What if I misspeak or overgeneralize?" people wonder. "What if I say something that offends someone?" This concern, in our opinion, comes from a place of deep care and concern about saying or doing something that might cause harm to someone else. It also comes from a genuine place of respect for individuals, traditions, and indeed, the idea of expertise itself.

This fear is also not unfounded. Although research shows that the United States is among the most religious countries in the world, Americans are largely uninformed about the basic facts about religious communities: their beliefs, practices, history, and leading figures (Pew Research Center, 2010). Prothero (2007) argued that this religious illiteracy limits our ability to be effective citizens in an increasingly religiously diverse country and world.

If higher education is a microcosm of the broader American society we collectively envision, then it is incumbent on educators to start with themselves in gaining foundational knowledge about the religious diversity present on our campuses. This is no doubt an overwhelming task, and, we believe, it is a lifelong project as there is always more to learn about the religious identities and communities present on campuses. However, it is hoped that this part of the book serves as a starting point.

Part five gathers contributors who have a high degree of personal experience and expertise in working with some of the most prevalent religious communities on our college campuses. Although we are deeply concerned about stereotyping and essentializing traditions, communities, and individuals (each contributor continually emphasizes the diversity in his or her community), we nevertheless recognize that we must start somewhere in providing concrete knowledge and information to equip educators in supporting students. Rather than focusing on traditions or histories, the question at the heart of each of these chapters is, "What do educators need to know to support students in this community?" Please read these chapters simply as a place to begin and know that great complexity lies beyond each word in the pages that follow.

References

Pew Research Center. (2010). *U.S. religious knowledge survey: Executive summary.* Retrieved from http://www.pewforum.org/2010/09/28/u-s-religious-knowledge-survey/

Prothero, S. (2007). *Religious literacy: What every American needs to know—and doesn't.* New York, NY: HarperCollins.

15

UNDERSTANDING CHRISTIAN STUDENTS ON CAMPUS

Katie Brick, J. Cody Nielsen, Greg Jao, Eric Paul Rogers,
and John A. Monson

Christian students make up the majority of religious students on college campuses in the United States; nevertheless, there is a great deal of diversity in the Christian tradition. Precisely because we live in a Christian majority country, it is easy to assume we know and understand the Christian tradition, but often our assumptions are not entirely accurate. This chapter presents the experiences of some of the most common Christian identities on campus—Roman Catholic (by Katie Brick), mainline Protestant (by J. Cody Nielsen), evangelical Protestant (by Greg Jao), and Mormon (by Eric Paul Rogers and John A. Monson).

Roman Catholic Students

More than a billion people worldwide are Catholic, half of all Christians. According to the 2015 Cooperative Institutional Research Program (CIRP) Freshman Survey, 24% of first-year students at U.S. baccalaureate institutions identified as Catholic (Eagan et al., 2015). Depending on your campus' demographics, roughly 1 in 4 students who walk through your door could be Catholic, that is, a person who was baptized in the Catholic Church or received into the Catholic Church after a valid Christian baptism. Demographically, of the 17% of U.S. Catholics who are millennials between 18 and 29 (about 8.7 million people), 44% are White, 44% are Latino, 5% are Black, 5% are Asian, and 2% are of other ancestry (Pew Research Center, 2015b).

The pope is perhaps the only entirely unique aspect of Catholicism among the many Christian traditions; some other characteristics strongly associated with Catholicism include a belief in saints who can intercede on behalf of believers, the observance of seven sacraments, a belief that Communion bread truly becomes the body of Christ, an obligation to attend weekly Mass, and the call to live a moral life as outlined by the teachings of the Catholic Church and wisdom of the Bible. Catholic students recognize these things as being part of their tradition, even if the importance they place on them varies.

The Roman Catholic Church prides itself on being a global church with a centralized hierarchy, a common liturgy, and clear teachings. However, that does not mean one can make assumptions about the beliefs and sensibilities of Catholic college students.

Catholic Identity and Worldview

Catholics often feel that their denomination and identity are unique. They make inside jokes about priests and nuns, Mass, fish-fry Fridays, and Catholic guilt. Young people who leave the tradition may later desire to have their children baptized Catholic. The pope is still regularly newsworthy when few other religious leaders are. Many Catholics feel they have the most accurate understanding of the Christian tradition.

As with all other traditions, there is a range of expression in how Catholic students understand and embody their faith. For a growing number of evangelical Catholics, who can be perceived as more traditional in practice, Catholic identity means living the missionary identity of the Church and engaging students in worship and education on Catholic orthodoxy. For Catholic students focused on social justice, Catholicism entails living the ideals of Catholic social teaching (explained later in this section) and living their religious identity through service and social justice work. Other students may be ambiguous about their tradition and on the verge of leaving it. For Catholic students of all stripes, Catholicism may be just one of many identities seen through the lens of their family and culture (including ethnic background).

Michael Galligan-Stierle (2009), president of the Association of Catholic Colleges and Universities, cautions against an overly reductive view of millennial Catholics. He proposes 12 categories to better understand students, which include the following:

- Church culturals, students who were raised Catholic, often tied to a political, cultural or national identity but with a fairly limited understanding of Catholicism as their adult faith

- Church apologists, students with a keen intellectual understanding of Catholicism who often seek to educate people about (and defend) the Church
- Church in service, students who engage in direct volunteer service and work with marginalized communities to live out the principles of Catholic social teaching as an expression of their faith
- Church prophetics, students who seek systemic justice, perhaps through social advocacy work
- Church all inclusives, students open to a variety of prayer and practice regardless of tradition and who often defend those who are not Catholic and value individual spiritual growth over the Church's truth
- Church eclipsed, perhaps the largest group, students who are former Catholics and have parted with their tradition

This framework gives a sense of the range of beliefs and practice among Catholic students, and many students may identify with multiple categories at the same time. Ask questions and listen to understand where your Catholic students may be coming from.

Catholic Worship and Practice

Regardless of the different approaches among students, it will benefit student affairs educators to understand some of the central tenets of Catholicism.

Mass Attendance

Catholics are expected to attend weekly Saturday evening or Sunday Mass (religious services). Data on Catholic Millennials report that 28% attend Mass weekly, whereas 53% of young adult Catholics attend Mass from once or twice a month to a few times a year (Pew Research Center, 2015b). A small number of Catholic students may also attend daily Mass. Catholic students, churchgoers or not, would probably be taken aback if higher education professionals scheduled activities that precluded people from going to weekly Mass without consideration.

In addition to the Sunday Mass requirement, there are periodic holy days of obligation when Catholics attend Mass even if it is not a Sunday. These dates can be found on the U.S. Council of Catholic Bishops website (www.USCCB.org) and include All Saints Day (November 1), the Feast of the Immaculate Conception (December 8), and Christmas (December 25). Easter is not on this list because it is always on a Sunday. Various ethnic Catholic groups also commemorate special holy days such as El Día de

Los Tres Reyes (Three Kings' Day) celebrated at Christmas by several Latin American countries and Spain; there are also various regional celebrations of saints important to particular areas.

Catholic students can typically find local churches or campus ministry groups to fulfill their worship needs. Regardless, educators can always explore whether the institution is providing necessary space, resources, referrals, and such for students to fully exercise their religious practice.

Other Observances

There are relatively few dietary or gender-influenced practices for Catholics. One dietary exception is Lenten observance, a time of communal preparation for Easter, lasting from Ash Wednesday until Easter, during which Catholics are invited to pray, fast, and give alms. This period typically falls between mid-to-late February or early March and goes through late March or early April. During Lent, Church teaching dictates that Catholics abstain from eating meat on Ash Wednesday, Good Friday, and all Fridays during Lent; Ash Wednesday and Good Friday are also fast days, which include fasting from midnight to midnight with one main meal and possibly two small meals during this time. Special events held on these dates should be sure to have fish or vegetarian fare available, and campus dining services should consider offering ample fish and vegetarian options on Fridays.

Prayer

There are many forms of Catholic prayer: individual, including informal and spontaneous praying to saints; contemplative, or other specific devotional practices; and communal, including blessings before meals, reciting the rosary, and morning and evening prayers. According to Pew data, 68% of millennial Catholics pray daily or at least weekly.

Common Catholic Beliefs and Attitudes

Catholics are not in lockstep agreement on theological and social issues. The institutional Church has teachings and belief statements that are very important and provide a common framework, but how Catholics incorporate these beliefs in their daily lives varies. Some adherents see the Catholic Church as being out of touch and judgemental (either from their own experience or that of their parents), and they part from the Church on various issues without leaving it. Others take great comfort from getting clear directions from the Church in a world that seems so morally ambiguous. The following provides an indication of how Catholics weigh in on some main issues, based on data from the Pew Research Center (2015).

Morality

Although many think of Catholicism as very rule oriented, ideally the Church is about connecting people to God, not enforcing rules. Main moral themes underpin many Catholics' moral perspectives on the world. Some of these themes include the ideas that God and creation are good, people are given the freedom to choose between right and wrong, and Jesus is God incarnate who calls us to love one another.

At the same time, there are many levels of Church teachings on morals and ethics that have evolved over time and can be confusing, which may be why the Pew Religious Landscape study (Pew Research Center, 2015b) found that only 21% of millennial Catholics say they consciously look to their religion for guidance on right and wrong. Official Church doctrine speaks with authority, but authorities in the church such as individual bishops or priests and important church documents can contradict one another. Many Catholics stop formal Catholic education around age 13, when they go through a confirmation process that welcomes them as adults into the Church, and it's not unusual for Catholics to be out of step with or contradict formal Church teachings despite the incredible confidence they might have when telling you, "But the Church says . . . !" Educators can always ask respectful questions of Catholic students and kindly point out possible contradictions for them to reflect on. Catholicism proclaims itself supportive of faith and reason, so exploring assumptions and conclusions with students is reasonable.

Latinx Catholics, who make up 45% of millennial Catholics, tend to be more aligned with the Church than White Catholics, according to a Pew study ("U.S. Catholics Open to Non-Traditional Families," 2015). Despite this tendency, experience on campus has shown that one cannot assume that Latinx Catholics are necessarily more traditional than non-Latinx (Martínez, 2015). Their perspectives can sometimes bring them into conflict with their parents' generation and lead to conversations necessitating expertise in multiculturalism and intersectionality.

There is a great intellectual tradition in the Church calling on Catholics to rely on their conscience, which can lead to some real worldview differences among Catholics who feel that being unquestioningly obedient to formal Church teachings is following one's conscience, whereas others believe one's conscience can conflict with Church teachings. Regardless, Catholic tradition dictates that people should rely on an informed conscience rather than a gut feeling or shallow understanding. Educators would do well to encourage Catholic students to authentically explore complex moral and political issues including what their tradition's teachings say and why.

Sexuality and Birth Control

It is not possible to assume a Catholic student's perspective on sex and marriage. The institutional Catholic Church is clear that there should be no sex outside marriage and that marriage is between a man and a woman who are open to having children. Nevertheless, many unmarried Catholic college students are sexually active, and four out of five U.S. Catholics say cohabitation outside marriage is acceptable even if some don't find it optimal ("U.S. Catholics Open to Non-Traditional Families," 2015).

Some college Catholics have no issue with having sex outside marriage. Others feel caught between Church messages and pressure to experience sex with a partner. Some Catholic students feel comfortable conforming to the Catholic ideal of chastity before marriage as a time-tested spiritual practice or perhaps as a way to opt out of pressure to have sex. As with many college students, Catholic students are learning about their sexuality and have differing relationships with their tradition's formal teachings on the matter. Referral relationships with Catholics (a priest or knowledgeable layperson) can be useful for Catholic students seeking such input.

The Catholic Church opposes any use of artificial birth control for a host of relational and moral reasons. However, the majority of young Catholics do not agree, with 68% of Hispanic and 72% of White Catholic millennials believing using artificial birth control is morally acceptable (Cox & Jones, 2015).

Abortion

The Catholic Church is categorically opposed to abortion. Young U.S. Catholics are split on abortion with 52% believing it should be legal in all or most cases and 46% believing it should be illegal in all or most cases (Pew Research Center, 2015b). Some of the staunchest pro-life leaders are Catholics, and the Catholic Church strongly supports life from conception to death (not just prior to birth). At the same time, there are also national groups of Catholics that support abortion, contrary to Church teaching.

Same-Sex Relationships and Marriage

The church defines *marriage* as between a man and a woman, but Catholicism's core belief in human dignity asserts that gay people are not inherently sinful, are not a self-constructed fiction, and deserve respect and love. According to Church teaching, gay people should remain chaste (like their unmarried straight counterparts), but most U.S. Catholics do not concur with Church teachings on this topic. Eighty percent of young adult Catholics say homosexuality should be accepted, and 72% are strongly in favor of same-sex marriage, with some recent polls putting that number as high as 85% (Lipka, 2014).

However, not all college-age Catholics part with the Church over same-sex relationships. Students tend to be firmly committed to their perspective no matter which side they are inclined toward. Regardless, Catholic ideas of love, respect, and human dignity are universal for all regardless of sexual orientation.

Increasingly accepting views on same-sex relationships does not negate the fact that the Catholic Church has caused some real hurt on issues of sexual orientation. Some Catholic families may be uncomfortable with their own child coming out, and more traditional Catholic families may accuse their child of being sinful and then compromise their relationship with them. Catholic students in the process of coming out may confront these challenges, and university support and solid referrals are very important in these situations.

Women

There are ongoing tensions in the Church about the appropriate leadership role for women. Women are formally barred from the priesthood but can hold other leadership roles in formal Church structures. Many Catholics continue to grapple with what they see as gender inequality in the Church. For some, the Church's understanding of women as complementing men with nurturing and domestic support makes sense. However, many others are frustrated with the Catholic notion of gender complementarity, particularly given that women constitute the majority of Catholic Church members, often serve as lay parish leaders, and lead flagship Catholic organizations (Hannum, 2016). With that said, many women have found in Catholicism a rich spirituality, community, and faith identity whether they differ with the Church on gender issues or not.

Ecumenical Concerns

When asked whether they are Christian, some Catholics respond, "No. I am Catholic." Many Catholics see the Christian question as an attempt to discover whether they have accepted Christ in a way that is more representative of a Protestant or evangelical experience. Saying, "No, I'm not Christian" can also be a way to assert a student's distinctively Catholic identity, even though they know Catholics are Christian because they believe in Christ. Relatedly, Catholics are not considered Christians by some other Christian denomination because of differing theologies and particularly differing perspectives on the pope.

If Catholics are told that Catholics are not Christian, not saved, and are going to hell, it can be anguishing for them and for students who are no longer Catholic but whose family and friends are. Catholic students are known to be at risk for proselytization (attempts to convert) as they can be less informed about their tradition and the Bible than other Christian sects. Campus policies around proselytization or general solicitation can address proselytization in residence halls or other campus locales.

Catholic Social Justice and Activism

It's not unusual to find Catholics among the strongest conservative and liberal activist students on campus, often on opposite ends of issues. Some have a sense that secular society is at war with Church values and that conservative voices are being silenced. These students often lead more conservative political or social campaigns because of their deeply held Catholic values and may feel oppressed and disrespected because of their Catholic identity. With these students, higher education professionals can explore the question of whether such students are experiencing discomfort or actual oppression.

At the same time, a body of thought known as Catholic social teaching inspires other Catholics to advocate for and serve people on the margins. These students engage in volunteer community service and work on behalf of systemic justice in ways that are perceived as liberal or antiestablishment. They are more likely to be in sync with the Church's stance against war, the death penalty, materialism, destruction of the environment, and its support for immigrants and the elderly, and so forth.

Interestingly, students on both sides of the political spectrum have a robust history and theology to draw on in the teachings of the Church. How students prioritize church teachings according to their consciences likely affects their choices for political and social action.

Campus Support for Catholic Students

Most campuses have some form of support for Catholic students. Catholic colleges usually have a campus ministry staff employed by the university who serve Catholics and others in the campus community. Newman Centers are a network of hundreds of independent residence and Catholic ministry centers at non-Catholic universities. Some emerging evangelical Catholic groups such as Fellowship of Catholic University Students (FOCUS) are establishing a presence on campuses as well.

Do some research before referring a Catholic student to Catholic resources. Some are welcoming to lesbian, gay, bisexual, transgender, queer, and other students and others may not be. Some take a more traditionalist view about the role of women, spiritual practice, and liturgy, whereas others may be part of a social justice–focused community or have a more modern liturgical expression. Catholic students may have particular interests or needs that align with the Catholic resources available in the community, and Catholic staff, faculty, and students can be good sources of information about nuances of various parishes and organizations.

Additional Resources

- Dignity USA, www.dignityusa.org
- FOCUS, www.focus.org
- Local dioceses and parishes, www.thecatholicdirectory.com
- Newman Centers, www.newmanconnection.com
- U.S. Council of Catholic Bishops for links to beliefs and teachings, prayer and worship, scripture readings, www.usccb.org

Mainline Protestant Students

Protestantism began around 1517 when Martin Luther published his 95 Theses, which marked the split between himself and the Catholic Church (alongside others like John Calvin and Huldrych Zwingli). The Great Reformation, as it has come to be called, was one of the most historically significant splits in the Christian Church and led to significant growth of the primary branches of the Christian Church (now Orthodox, Catholic, and Protestant). In general, the founders of the Protestant Reformation were concerned with the assertion that humans gain salvation through faith alone rather than through works (the term referring to the importance of good behavior, *salvation through works*, is generally considered a Roman Catholic belief). Additionally, Protestant reformers emphasized the authority of Christ as head of the Christian church rather than a papal authority.

Research indicates that the number of mainline Protestants (differentiated from evangelical Protestants, discussed later in this chapter) globally is around 800 million (Pew Research Center, 2011). Unlike the Catholic Church with its unified structure and papal authority, Protestants have broken into more than 9,000 denominations globally, the largest being Anglicanism (Alt, 2016). These denominations have grown out of one another, at times multiplying in such a rapid succession that historians have had difficulty keeping up. From issues related to theological questions on the nature of Jesus to social issues like slavery and the role of women in ministry, Protestants seemed to divide themselves at every turn over the smallest to the largest issues of concern. Needless to say, these branches of the Protestant church speak to a much divided structure of belief and thus a difficult-to-generalize population.

Protestantism in America includes a significant number of these denominations, including mainline traditions such as the Episcopal Church,

Presbyterian Church (USA), Presbyterian Church in America, American Baptist, Cooperative Baptist, Southern Baptist, Disciples of Christ, United Church of Christ, United Methodist, Evangelical Lutheran Church in America, and Missouri and Wisconsin Synod Lutheran. These few among many are the most likely Protestant denominations college students will identify with, although isolated pockets of others exist on individual campuses.

It's worth noting that there is a remarkable history of African American Protestantism in the United States, which is, at times, culturally distinct from other Protestant communities. Although many typical Protestant denominations and churches are racially and ethnically diverse, Martin Luther King Jr. notably called Sunday morning "the most segregated hour in Christian America" (King, 2010[1958], p. 202), and this is still largely true, with 73% of Whites attending all or mostly White churches and 71% of African Americans attending all or mostly Black churches (Gallup, 2002). Although many lament this continued division, predominantly African American churches can serve as a source of inspiration, empowerment, and hope in a community that has been historically marginalized. Denominations such as the African Methodist Episcopal, the African Methodist Episcopal Zion, and the Christian Methodist Episcopal churches fuse religious communities with African American culture, including distinct worship styles and historical roots from the time of slavery (Glaude, 2014).

Data suggest that 11.57% of incoming first-year students in fall 2015 identified as mainline Protestant. Protestant college students come from a variety of racial backgrounds, although nearly 75% of Protestant students are White with an additional 8.5% identifying as African American and 6.58% as Asian or Pacific Islander. As a result of this racial makeup, Protestant ministries are not nearly as diverse as some other religiously affiliated groups on campus. Protestant college students also appear to be politically left-leaning or moderate, with 32% identifying as liberal or very liberal, 43% as moderate, and only 25% as conservative or very conservative (Mayhew et al., 2016).

Protestant Role in Higher Education

Protestantism has played an essential role in U.S. higher education since the founding of Harvard College in 1636. Designed to train clergy, Harvard, alongside many of the early institutions of higher education, often included chaplains or religious professionals on faculty for the education of young men. This emphasis on the religious component of higher education led to a proliferation of religiously affiliated institutions, a dynamic that continues to mark U.S. higher education today. The centrality of Protestant leadership remains on many of the private university campuses across the country, especially through the Office of the Chaplain (Jacobsen & Jacobsen, 2012).

Public university students can find a variety of Protestant ministries available for support, including Methodist Episcopal, Lutheran Campus Ministries, the Wesley Foundation, Westminster Houses, and Baptist Campus Ministries. In addition to these church-affiliated campus ministries, a few ecumenical (interdenominational) ministries such as United Campus Ministries, or others with similar names, exist at some college campuses.

Protestant Worldview

With so many denominational branches, mainline Protestants, and particularly mainline Protestant college students, can have difficulty in articulating the differences among themselves. Students on campus may have attended churches of one or more Protestant denominations, likely with little information on the theological differences between each. Perhaps the easiest way to begin to separate mainline Protestants from Catholics and evangelical Christians is in their views related to worship and the Eucharist or Communion.

Worship

One of the principal defining characteristics is the focus of worship as being on the *Word* through a sermon or lesson. Therefore, in Protestant churches, the clergy is often given more time to speak on the specific lessons being offered. Protestant churches are likely to worship using a traditional hymn book and a liturgy, as compared to their evangelical counterparts who are more likely to use worship bands and more contemporary worship styles. However, Protestant communities have in the past 10 to 20 years become more likely to use more styles of worship that some previously considered evangelical in nature. African American Protestant communities in particular often have a distinct worship style, using certain musical traditions, call-and-response praise and worship, and an established rhetorical tradition of preaching (Glaude, 2014).

Communion

Whereas the Catholic tradition's most important part of the worship service is the Eucharist, which is celebrated at every Mass, U.S. Protestant churches are more likely to celebrate the Eucharist only once a month, frequently on the first Sunday.

Theologically, Protestants differ from Catholics based on their beliefs on Communion and the nature of the Eucharist (Del Rosario, 2014). Whereas

Catholics believe in Transubstantiation (the belief that the bread and wine transform during the Eucharist to become the actual body and blood of Christ), Protestants have a variety of beliefs about the nature of the Eucharist, ranging from simply believing that the meal is a symbol and reminder of Jesus's final meal with the disciples to believing that the Eucharist coexists as bread and wine and the body and blood of Christ (a theological argument known as Consubstantiation). Although many Protestant students may not understand the definite beliefs of their particular denomination, many will be able to understand that they and Catholics have differing beliefs regarding the Eucharistic meal (Del Rosario, 2014).

Although other theological differences exist between Protestants and others in the Christian Church, they are less visible on campus. Should administration wish to dive deeper into issues that separate denominations, they should consider contacting religious life staff, who can offer a plethora of additional information.

Mainline Protestants and Social Issues

The mainline Protestant Church and its denominations range across the spectrum of social issues in the United States, depending on geographic location and individual ministries. In general, mainline Protestant churches tend to be more progressive in comparison to evangelical churches, although not always. Across the continuum of liberal to conservative, members of the United Church of Christ are often seen as the most progressive, and Southern Baptists (who some would argue identify closer with evangelicals than mainline Protestants) are on the conservative end. The breadth of stances on particular social issues is one of the more important points for higher education professionals who want to understand mainline Protestants and the students who claim these worldviews.

In the past, Protestant denominations were among the most liberal organizations on campus; Protestant ministers were particularly active in protests related to civil rights and Vietnam. Many Protestant leaders have also served as catalysts for interfaith dialogue and have values associated with pluralism. These leaders can be strong partners for student affairs professionals trying to build coalitions around religious, secular, and spiritual beliefs on campus.

Sexuality

Protestant denominations, much like other Christian denominations, have struggled regarding their beliefs related to lesbian, gay, bisexual, transgender, queer, intersex, and asexual (LGBTQIA) individuals. Since 1969 the United

Church of Christ has been "open and affirming" ("Open and Affirming in the UCC," n.d.) and remains one of the most likely denominations where LGBTQIA clergy and laity are employed, ordained, and affirmed as members ("Resolution on Homosexuals and the Law," 1969). A variety of Protestant denominations in U.S. culture have more recently seen shifts in their stances regarding LGBTQIA people. Since 1991 the ELCA Lutheran Church has welcomed LGBTQIA individuals but only since 2010 has been willing to ordain clergy who openly profess a LGBTQIA identity ("Stances of Faiths," 2015).

Denominations have wrestled with the question of conducting marriage ceremonies for members of the LGBTQIA community. It should be noted that Protestant denominations are not at all unified on this issue and often remain divided even after changing policy, causing rifts and what appears to be the beginnings of major denominational schisms that may occur over the next few years.

Among college students who claim a Protestant denominational background, there is significant support for LGBTQIA inclusion (Murphy, 2015). Those who claim a more conservative belief structure may be likely to drift into more evangelical groups, whereas their liberal or progressive peers will seek communities that are inclusive of various sexual orientations and gender identities.

Women in Ministry
Largely affirmed by most Protestant denominations, with the exception of Southern Baptists, female clergy remain a relatively new occurrence, especially in the southern United States. Women represent the largest gender identifying population of Protestant ministries on campus at nearly 65% (Mayhew et al., 2016). This population is helping to strengthen the role of women in ministry among Protestant denominations. Administrators seeking support for liberal- and progressive-leaning religious women on campus might contact Protestant ministry staff to help find welcoming communities for these women.

However, it should be noted that on many campuses south of the Mason–Dixon line, female clergy from Protestant ministries may represent the only female-identifying member of the religious staff, especially in public universities. On these campuses, female-identifying clergy may feel ostracized and pushed out of conversations by male colleagues and peers.

Abortion
Protestants are not of like mind on the issue of abortion, a significant topic of concern in the Christian Church today. Protestant ministries on campus will most likely offer a much more progressive viewpoint of abortion than their

evangelical or Catholic counterparts, with portions of the Christian religious community seeking communities that have a more pro-choice stance. These communities have been more vocal over the past few years on particular campuses and can be great assets to women's health centers on campus. But pockets of more pro-life students remain involved in Protestant ministries, and thus these communities may have ongoing discussions related to this topic.

Race

Protestants in the past have been some of the forerunners of race relations on campus and represent a significant number of students involved in organizing and supportive work. Yet, because the population of Protestants remains significantly White in its identification, challenges may exist on whether Protestant groups are the best candidates to lead movements on campus regarding the racial climate.

The notable exception to this is, of course, the African American Protestant church, which has played a leadership role in U.S. movements for Black liberation. During the civil rights era, in particular, African American Protestant churches and individuals provided an anchoring leadership role in galvanizing a religiously diverse movement. Black churches continue to draw on their theological commitments to fuel ongoing social action for Black equality (Glaude, 2014).

Current Challenges of Protestant Denominations on Campus

Perhaps the biggest threat to Protestant ministries is their sources of funding and the demands of the constituents and bureaucracies that oversee them. Over the past 20 years, Protestant ministries, especially public university campus ministries, have seen significant funding cuts and the closure of hundreds of historic ministries, many of which have stood on or near campus for decades. At religiously affiliated institutions, Protestant ministers have been the most likely staff to be engaged in widespread support of a university's mission and vision, often because of historical ties between the chaplaincy and the institution. Lately, changes in perspective have, at times, diminished the historic relationships between Protestant ministry professionals and those working in higher education. Nevertheless, these staff remain committed to the vision of higher education and are well placed to support Protestant students and institutional priorities at large.

Support for Protestant Students on Campus

When supporting mainline Protestant students, it is important to consider their varieties on campus. Referring Protestant students to specifically

Protestant denominations may or may not be appropriate and because of this or other concerns, higher education professionals may wish to seek more information before making a referral. Religious life professionals on campus can be helpful in this regard.

Support of mainline Protestant students may also include helping those students in gaining a wider perspective. Because of the challenges of privilege (with the vast majority of Protestants identifying as White), administrators may be able to give guidance and support for these students to engage in issues related to individuals with other identities. There have been incidents on college campuses where Protestant ministries remain complacent on issues related to racism largely because students did not see themselves as part of the ongoing work. For students who need a vantage point beyond their current community, educators may find it beneficial to focus their attention on encouraging students from these communities to be more engaged.

Additional Resources

- Association for College and University Religious Advisors, www .acuraonline.net
- Association of Presbyterian Colleges and Universities, www.presbyterian colleges.org
- Higher Education and Leadership Ministries (Disciples of Christ), www.helmdisciples.org
- Lutheran Campus Ministry Network, www.lumin-network.com
- National Association of College and University Chaplains, www .nacuc.net
- National Campus Ministry Association, www.campusministry.net
- Network of Evangelical Lutheran Church in America Colleges and Universities, www.elca.org/colleges
- UKirk (Presbyterian) Campus Ministry, www.ukirk.org
- United Methodist Church Office for Collegiate Ministry, www .gbhem.org/education/collegiate-ministry
- Young Adult and Campus Ministries (Episcopal Church), www .episcopalchurch.org/blog/YoungAdult

Evangelical Protestant Students

Defining *evangelical* is a cottage industry among academics (Balmer, 2016; Noll, 2000), pollsters (Newport, 2005), and theologians (Naselli & Hansen, 2011), and the movement incorporates a bewildering variety of people and practices that manifest themselves on campus in various configurations based on ethnic, historic, doctrinal, and ecclesial differences. Evangelical students come from storefront urban churches and suburban megachurches, historically Black denominations, traditionally nonevangelical denominations, campus groups (as conversions occur), and international students who are a part of the global expression of evangelicalism (Pew Research Center, 2011).

Evangelicals represent about 31.9% of the U.S. population (Pew Research Center, 2015a), suggesting that nearly 1 in 3 students on campus could have an evangelical background. They represent every ethnic group and many nationalities on campus; the evangelical organization InterVarsity Christian Fellowship states that in 2015–2016, 46% of its students identified as White, 17% as Asian American, 13% as Black, 7% as Hispanic, 4% as multiracial, 1% Mideast American, 1% Pacific/Native American, and another 12% were international students They include students from most denominations.

What unites these disparate groups, which may share little by way of politics or praxis or history? Although evangelicals affirm the historic creeds (Apostle's Creed or Nicene Creed) of all Protestant, Catholic, and Orthodox churches, British historian David Bebbington (1989) defines *evangelicals* as Christians who share four emphases:

1. Crucicentrism: a focus on the death of Jesus Christ on the cross, achieving the redemption of humanity from sin and triumphing over evil.
2. Conversionism: a belief that God transforms human lives through a born-again experience, which results in ongoing change and service as people follow Jesus.
3. Biblicism: an embrace of the Christian Bible as the ultimate authority in defining Christian belief and practice and to obey its teachings.
4. Activism: an expectation that all Christians should engage in evangelism (spreading the Christian gospel) and social reform efforts (e.g., caring for the poor, fighting human trafficking, etc.).

It is important to recognize that evangelicals primarily self-identify along these criteria, rather than denominational, political, or behavioral similarities. Given the diversity of this group, it can be difficult to identify shared characteristics beyond these doctrinal emphases.

Campus Expression

On campus, evangelical students tend to create programs that reflect these theological emphases. Typically, most student groups sponsor weekly Bible discussion groups (biblicism), evangelistic and community service activities (activism and conversionism), and weekly meetings for campuswide worship and prayer, often focusing on the life, death, and resurrection of Jesus (biblicism and crucicentrism). Some groups also sponsor times for urban or global service or evangelism projects during spring break or summer (activism).

Evangelical students organize or participate in these types of religious activity in five different (although potentially overlapping) ways.

1. Student groups affiliated with national or regional *parachurch* organizations: These student groups are affiliated with national (e.g., Cru, formerly Campus Crusade for Christ, InterVarsity Christian Fellowship, the Navigators, etc.) or regional (e.g., Brothers and Sisters in Christ, Coalition for Christian Outreach, etc.) organizations. They may be organized by primary ethnicity of the participants (e.g., Asian American Christian Fellowship), vocation or activities of the participants (e.g., Fellowship of Christian Athletes), or common areas of interest (e.g., Christian fraternities and sororities). These groups are frequently interdenominational. *Parachurch* organizations most frequently are 501(c)(3) organizations that operate under the authority of an independent board of trustees. They frequently support student groups by providing campus ministers, resources, programs, conferences, and so on. These groups do not think of themselves as churches, and the students typically participate in local churches as well.

2. Student groups affiliated with denominations: These student groups are affiliated with denominations (e.g., Chi Alpha is the campus ministry of the Assemblies of God). The denomination often provides campus ministers, resources, programs, conferences, and such. Although sponsored by churches, these groups do not think of themselves as churches, and the students typically participate in a local church as well.

3. Student groups affiliated with local churches: These student groups may be the campus ministry of a local church. They may or may not operate like student groups in that their primary leadership comes from the local church's pastoral staff, and they primarily serve as a means to sponsor Bible studies or other programs on campus.

4. Student groups that function as a local church: These student groups are, for all intents and purposes, local churches led by pastors whose primary congregants are students. They may function like traditional student groups, although their primary function is to provide the church's meeting place and activities. These groups serve students in the same way that Hillel or Chabad does for Jewish students.

5. Student groups without other affiliations: These student groups operate like traditional student groups. They rarely have ministerial input,
although local pastors may be available to provide advice. This category
includes many Gospel choirs and a capella groups, in addition to some
Christian publication groups on campus. These students usually also participate in local church programs.

It should be noted that these differences demonstrate why many campuses
have multiple evangelical groups (and why campus restrictions on groups
with similar purposes may be misguided). Each group reflects a particular
tradition, history, people, and emphasis, even if they all share a similar ethos.

Tension Between Evangelical Student Groups and Campus Administration

Colleges and universities experience four primary areas of tension with evangelical student groups.

Campus Ministers and Staff and Student Affairs

Because of their ability to provide campus ministry staff, evangelical student
groups often do not work with student activities offices or other campus
services. They effectively create a parallel program, often to the frustration
of campus administrators, who see the ministers as external influences with
no accountability to the campus and who disengage students from support
and programming.

It is true, and it is a failure on the part of evangelical student groups.
Many evangelical group leaders on campus recognize that we often engage
with student activities offices as little as possible, and our programming often
keeps students too busy to participate in other campus programming.

A better way forward: Consider treating campus ministers and student
leaders as your partners on campus.

- Create opportunities to meet with campus ministers each term to
exchange aspirations for your work. Most campus ministers would be
eager to hear your perspectives and would be honored to contribute
their insights.
- Invite them to engage in campuswide initiatives on community
service and justice in ways that fit their religious traditions (with
adequate planning time).
- Offer them training on campus policies or certification to act in
formal roles on campus. Invite their participation in times of crisis
or tragedy.

- Work with them to explore mental health, meaning-making, and community service issues with broader constituencies that might appreciate a religious voice.
- Because many students of color come from evangelical traditions, invite campus ministers to work with you to create safer, more supportive communities for those students.
- Ask them to mobilize community volunteers.
- Offer them parking passes or office space to facilitate their work with students.

Evangelism and Anti-Proselytization Regulations

All evangelical student groups share a common religious commitment to evangelism (i.e., inviting others to convert to Christianity). This is a faith requirement shared by other Christian traditions and many world religions. Some universities have adopted strict anti-proselytization requirements designed to limit this kind of activity, using different configurations.

These requirements usually reflect a laudable desire by administrators to reduce potential religious conflict and to protect vulnerable students from emotional or relational manipulation. They also may reflect a less laudable relativistic worldview that disapproves of any religion's ultimate truth claims. It should be admitted that every religion or worldview, including atheism or Secular Humanism, makes ultimate truth claims that are irreconcilable with truth claims of other religions. Despite the appropriate concerns, these restrictions are often perceived as overly paternalistic, restrictive of free speech, violations of the free exercise of religion, and dismissive of religious belief.

A better way forward: Rather than proscribing religious activity and conversation, universities and colleges could do the following:

- Reaffirm the university's intention to be a marketplace of ideas, where robust but respectful disagreement is necessary and valued and where conversions (intellectual, religious, emotional) are to be expected. This means training to learn to speak respectfully with and about other groups with whom one may disagree without minimizing the differences and requires protecting venues as well as cultivating aspirations for confident pluralism on campus (Inazu, 2016).
- Equip students (through programs developed with religious advisers) to identify manipulative behaviors that are inappropriate in religious conversations. (This would be valuable for other political and social conversations as well.)
- Work with religious student groups to develop a code of ethics for evangelism or proselytization that affirms the right of religious

students and groups to invite others to change their faith identity but expects them to do so in ways that make their intentions clear, rejects any attempts to engage in emotional manipulation by bypassing the intellectual faculties of the individual, and speaks respectfully of other beliefs, even when expressing disagreement. InterVarsity Christian Fellowship (2018), for example, has adopted a Code of Ethics for Christian Witness that universities have adopted.

- Create interfaith initiatives focused on community service that do not minimize religious differences (or avoid the possibility of conversion) and mutual religious advocacy; as an example, see the declaration of evangelical student groups to Muslim student groups after the 2016 presidential election (InterVarsity Christian Fellowship, 2016). These initiatives help create a respectful religious community on campus that can support healthy religious conversation.

Nondiscrimination Policies and Religious Belief Criteria

On a number of campuses, evangelical student groups have been derecognized because they require their leaders to share their group's doctrinal commitments (most groups are happy to have nonevangelicals as a part of the general membership). Campus administrators assert that this violates nondiscrimination and inclusion policies and values, which require all student groups and leadership positions to be open to any student. This requirement is problematic for evangelical student groups. Theologically, the Christian scriptures require leaders to be adherents, and they desire to be faithful to 2,000 years of Christian tradition. Pragmatically, students lead the religious functions of most evangelical student groups (Bible studies, prayer meetings, worship times, etc.). Participants expect their religious leaders to actually believe what they are teaching to be true. Ironically, the very policies that should protect religious groups that want to retain their distinctive religious identity end up penalizing those groups for wanting to retain their religious identity.

This has led to a number of conversations between evangelical group leaders and campus administrators along these lines:

Question from campus administrators: Is this just a proxy for preventing LGBTQIA students from becoming leaders?

Answer: No. In the vast majority of cases since 2010, campus administrators have argued that any requirement for leaders to share the beliefs of the group is discriminatory. On some campuses, even a doctrinal requirement as minimal as believing that Jesus is Savior and Lord has been deemed discriminatory. Many evangelical organizations employ

LGBTQIA staff and (try to) welcome LGBTQIA students as members and leaders.

Question: Don't we have the constitutional right to implement all comers policies? You cannot claim that your leadership requirements are protected by the First Amendment.

Answer: Respectfully, the relevant ruling, *Christian Legal Society v. Martinez* (2011) is quite limited. The court held that if a campus applied the all-comers policy to all groups, without exception and without bias, it might pass First Amendment scrutiny. But here are two observations. First, a campus that allows organizations with gender-specific or ability-related requirements (e.g., same-sex a cappella groups or athletic clubs) has not implemented an all-comers policy without exception. Second, and perhaps most important, a campus that prohibits religious student organizations from using the religious criteria required by their religious beliefs to select their religious leaders may not value religious diversity and inclusion as deeply as administrators may believe. Respect and inclusion for religious groups includes creating space for their distinctly religious requirements and beliefs. Inasmuch as campuses (rightly) create accommodations for prayer spaces, schedule test taking around religious holidays, provide swimming times or classes for religious students (and employees), it should create parallel accommodations for the leadership of religious student groups.

Question: Are members of evangelical student groups really worried that nonadherents will ask to lead the group?

Answer: In fact, this happens all the time. Many evangelical groups involve large numbers of students who do not identify as Christians. These folks often love the community, participate actively (including inviting their friends), but do not yet identify as Christians. Because they do not, they are not yet qualified to lead prayers, Bible studies, or religious worship. Similarly, because students change religious beliefs, it is an issue of integrity for most religious groups for their leaders to be required to step down if they no longer believe.

Question: Would it not be enough to require a test of Bible knowledge or some other objective or nonreligious criteria? That would screen out most people.

Answer: It might, but it would lack integrity if we were to pretend that our processes were open to all when in fact they were designed to be restrictive. Equally important, knowledge is not the key issue for most religions. Belief is. Belief is the sine qua non of almost every religious group. To be led by someone who does not believe this to be true would undermine the very purpose of the group and would not be accepted by most religious students.

Question: But what you are asking for is incompatible with the school's commitment to inclusion.

Answer: We affirm the school's commitment to inclusion, and we hope our groups reflect that value in their membership and activities. Where it does not, leaders of evangelical groups invite the help of campus administrators so that we can become more inclusive. We also hope your commitment to inclusion extends to religious students who want to find a religious community on campus that supports their religious convictions. We also ask you to recognize that other types of student activities do not demonstrate full inclusion. Fraternities and sororities, single-gender a capella groups, and intercollegiate athletics limit membership along gender lines. Although this might be permissible under Title IX (1972), gender-restrictive activities are not required by Title IX. The campus permits these because it chooses to value the contributions made by those organizations. Athletic groups and performance groups (e.g., music, drama, etc.) are often ableist, using tryouts and practices that prevent those differently abled from fully participating. This kind of restriction, though, is not inappropriately discriminatory. The restriction goes to the very nature of the activity and group as does belief for a religious group. Muslim and Orthodox Jewish groups are permitted to segregate their prayer meetings along gender lines, if they wish. Catholic groups can restrict participation in the Eucharist to Catholics. Evangelical student groups should be able to require their leaders to be evangelicals so they can preserve the evangelical nature of their group.

A better way forward: Numerous university systems (e.g., Ohio State, Florida, Texas, etc.) have adopted nondiscrimination policies that require membership to be open to all students but allows religious groups to limit leadership to those who share the group's religious beliefs. This minimal accommodation actually advances the campus administrators' desire for greater diversity (including religious diversity) and avoids inadvertently penalizing a group protected by the policy.

Human Sexuality, Particularly With LGBTQIA Students

Evangelicals largely, although (regretfully) not universally, recognize our complicity and agency in creating a culture and system that demonized LGBTQIA individuals. This resulted in severe personal distress for many and in violence directed against the LGBTQIA community. Many evangelical leaders know we need to ask forgiveness of the LGBTQIA community. We need to renounce and repudiate language and actions that denigrate LGBTQIA individuals. Evangelicals should recognize the inherent dignity and value of each member of the LGBTQIA community. We are grateful that some actions along these lines have begun (Marin, 2009), and we wish more would happen. We also are grateful for the growing voices of LGBTQIA evangelicals who affirm the historical reading of scripture while building bridges with the broader LGBTQIA community (Hill, 2016; Shaw, 2015).

Like some Catholics, Orthodox Christians, Orthodox Jews, Muslims, and members of the Church Jesus Christ of Latter-day Saints, many evangelicals hold to a sexual ethic that restricts genital sexual activity to a monogamously married heterosexual couple. This is part of a larger, comprehensive sexual ethic that also addresses heterosexual premarital sexual activity, pornography, divorce, and so forth, but many evangelical leaders acknowledge our culture's heightened scrutiny on LGBTQIA people and understand that this culture is created at least in part because of the sins of the evangelical community described in the preceding paragraph. Evangelical student groups do employ LGBTQIA staff, but those employees are expected to embrace an evangelical sexual ethic. The same expectation applies to heterosexual staff, although this raises fewer concerns with campus administrators. This position often puts many religious student groups, including evangelicals, in tension with campus administrators and LGBTQIA groups.

A better way forward: It is unlikely that religious sexual ethics will change substantially, particularly among certain religious populations (although many traditions speak with less uniformity than before, particularly among the younger generations). LGBTQIA opposition to these groups is similarly unlikely to abate. In this context, universities and colleges have the opportunity to prepare students with incompatible worldviews to work together for the common good in spite of their differences. As described previously in this section, this requires specific types of venues and aspirations that must be created and supported by the campus. It may take the form of carefully moderated conversations about each group's perception of the other, and it may take the form of common action around a shared social concern. It will require educators to dig deeply into their commitment to diversity and inclusion as they help both communities speak graciously, listen deeply, and relate respectfully.

Conclusion

Evangelical students are often some of the largest religious populations on campus with the most engaged students (in terms of weekly activities). They have a religious commitment to find ways to serve the campus. They often come with well-trained campus ministers who invest in the leadership development and cross-cultural competency of students. They can mobilize volunteers and community support. They could be wonderful partners, if you let them.

Additional Resources

- Chi Alpha Campus Ministries, www.chialpha.com
- Cru (previously Campus Crusade for Christ), www.cru.org
- Fellowship of Christian Athletes, www.fca.org
- InterVarsity Christian Fellowship, www.intervarsity.org
- Navigators, www.navigators.org

Mormon Students

The Church of Jesus Christ of Latter-day Saints is often referred to as the Mormon Church or the Church of Latter-day Saints. However, the preferred usage is the full name or, if a shorter name is needed, the Church or the Church of Jesus Christ. The label *Mormon* comes from the members' belief in the Book of Mormon as a sacred book of scripture. Although there is a slight preference to call members of the Church "Latter-day Saints," the term *Mormon* is also acceptable and widely used.

The Church of Jesus Christ of Latter-day Saints is commonly grouped with other churches belonging to the American Restoration Movement that emerged in the United States during the Second Great Awakening (from 1790 to 1840). Officially organized on April 6, 1830, in upstate New York, members consider the Church to be the restoration of the original church founded by Jesus Christ. Because it was established in the United States and has headquarters in Salt Lake City, Utah, many view the Church as an American institution. In 2016, Church membership exceeded 15 million in 188 nations and territories (Holland, 2016). About 6.5 million members resided in the United States and 8.5 million outside the United States. According to the National Council of Churches (2010), the Church of Jesus Christ of Latter-day Saints is the second-fastest-growing church and the fourth-largest Christian denomination in the United States.

The Nature of God and Potential of Humankind

Latter-day Saints believe that Jesus is their savior. They believe in the Bible and adhere to the 10 Commandments and Jesus's teachings to love God and neighbor. Although Mormons revere Joseph Smith (who lived from 1805 to 1844) as a prophet and president of the Church, they do not worship him. The Church's first article of faith declares, "We believe in God, the Eternal Father, and in His Son, Jesus Christ, and in the Holy Ghost" ("Articles of Faith," n.d.). Nevertheless, many mainstream Christians view Mormons as non-Christian, likely because of doctrines and texts unique to Latter-day Saints theology. For example, Mormons believe that historical evolutions in

Christian theology regarding the nature of God depart from the true nature of God, they have theologically distinct views on the nature and superiority of Jesus Christ, and they believe that as children of God they may ultimately become like Him. Despite these differences, Latter-day Saints may take issue with the assertion that they are not Christians or that the Church is nothing more than a cult. These views, or the way they are expressed, may be obstacles to greater interfaith engagement.

Religious Practices

Like other Christians, Mormons celebrate Easter and Christmas, but they do not generally observe the full liturgical calendar. The Sabbath is observed on Sunday. The focal point of public Sabbath worship services is the Sacrament meeting in which the sacrament (Eucharist) is administered in the form of bread and water. This sacrament is understood as primarily symbolic (not literal, like with some other Christian communities). Although not strictly enforced, the Church practices closed communion, meaning that only baptized members of the Church are invited to partake. Activities such as work, shopping, dining out, entertainment, sports and recreation are avoided on Sundays. Some Mormon students, for example, choose not to do schoolwork on the Sabbath as an expression of devotion.

A lay ministry governs the Church locally with most members serving in some capacity within their geographically defined ward (congregation) overseen by a bishop (pastor). Women officiate in a variety of leadership, instructional, and service roles, although they do not hold certain priesthood offices (e.g., bishop). Latter-day Saints college students are involved in lay ministry and may spend several hours a week in service activities. Because of the nature of this lay ministry, the expectation in the church is that every Latter-day Saint will be given some responsibility, known as a *calling*, to serve the members in their area.

Education

Mormons place significant value on secular and religious education alike. The Church operates several institutions of higher education: Brigham Young University (BYU) in Provo, Utah; BYU–Idaho in Rexburg; BYU–Hawaii in Laie; and LDS Business College in Salt Lake City, Utah. These institutions integrate religious education into their course offerings and degree requirements.

At other postsecondary institutions, the Church promotes religious education through its Institutes of Religion. Institutes are typically housed in buildings adjacent to college campuses, although some institutions offer on-campus space for these meetings (e.g., in an existing multifaith space), which can be an effective way to welcome Mormon students into the campus community. Students are encouraged to enroll in religious education courses each term and work toward graduation, which requires successful completion of several courses (e.g., New Testament, Old Testament, Teachings and Doctrine of the Book of Mormon, Eternal Family). Facilities that house institutes also frequently host worship services on Sundays and other religious and social activities throughout the week.

Chapters of the Latter-day Saints Student Association are present on many college campuses and may participate in interfaith efforts with other campus ministries. Familiarity with these organizations and their representatives allow student affairs professionals to direct Latter-day Saints students to these resources. By making contact with an institute director, institutional representatives may cultivate relationships with the Mormon community on campus.

Family and Lifestyle

The Church teaches that the family is central to the Creator's plan for the eternal destiny of His children. Related teachings include the eternal nature and purpose of gender, the importance of marriage and child bearing, and the sanctity of life and sexual relations. Although chapels or meeting houses are used primarily for regular Sunday worship services and social gatherings, temples are dedicated as holy houses of God, where Latter-day Saints who have proven faithful participate in sacred rites and ceremonies. These ceremonies include marriages, or *sealings*, that are considered valid for eternity. Reception of temple rites includes wearing sacred clothing called *temple garments* that are covered by modest dress.

Many Latter-day Saints students see their religious values differently from non–Latter-day Saints students and thus, often have a unique experience of campus climate and culture. For example, campus cultures that tacitly or explicitly showcase LGBTQ lifestyles; unisex restrooms, locker rooms, or residence halls; career prioritization; abortion; normalization of premarital sex; and revealing attire can contribute to Latter-day Saints students feeling like outsiders or pressured to compromise their beliefs.

Campus culture is conveyed through not only cocurricular activities and social engagement but also class assignments; for example, certain assignments that contain explicit sexual material may make some Latter-day Saints students uncomfortable. Additionally, authority figures can play a role in legitimizing or delegitimizing religious identities. For example, a Latter-day Saints performing arts student reported being told by her professors that she had ruined her career by getting married while still in school. Because students are dependent on professors for letters of recommendation, Mormon students may feel pressure to be silent about their religious beliefs to succeed academically and professionally.

Mormonism is frequently associated with polygamy or *plural marriage*, although the Church abandoned the practice more than 100 years ago. Modern polygamists may identify themselves as Mormon, but they are not permitted to join the Church unless they repudiate the practice. Although the Church shares a common history and some beliefs with those whom the media calls Mormon Fundamentalists, they are not associated with the Church.

Mormons are known for healthy living and long life. The Latter-day Saints teachings most frequently associated with health are canonized in the Doctrine and Covenants and are referred to as the *Word of Wisdom*:

> Among the provisions of the health code: no alcoholic drinks, no smoking or chewing of tobacco, and no "hot drinks"—believed to refer specifically to tea and coffee (some Mormons interpret this to include any caffeinated beverage, although this is not the official position of the Church). "Wholesome herbs," along with fruits and grains, are specifically recommended. Meat is to be used "sparingly." The Church also interprets the misuse of drugs—illegal, legal, prescription or controlled—as a violation of the health code. (Church of Jesus Christ of Latter-day Saints, 2018, para. 2)

These values conflict with social life at most college campuses, which may pose a challenge for some Latter-day Saints students. One student expressed a desire to socialize with peers and faculty but felt uncomfortable attending events where she was the only sober person present. Efforts to provide nonalcoholic beverages or alternatives to coffee and tea in social settings are noticed and appreciated by these students. Campus activities actively conceived as alternatives to drinking cultures on campus are also welcome opportunities for Latter-day Saints students.

Proselytizing

In 2016 more than 70,000 Latter-day Saints served as full-time missionaries. Most of these missionaries are 18 to 25 years old, who work in pairs with a companion of the same gender. Young women serve for 18 months and young men for 24 months. They serve at their own expense and often postpone or take leave from their postsecondary education to serve. Having focused on proselytizing as full-time missionaries, however, they may have trouble making the transition to an ecumenical setting when they return to their studies. Although Latter-day Saints students want to serve side by side with others not of their faith, they tend to have relatively little experience with cooperative interfaith engagement. Thus, gentle coaching and mentoring (e.g., encouraging a student to speak from one's own experience rather than in generalities) can help Latter-day Saints students be productive contributors to interfaith efforts on campus.

Advice

Latter-day Saints students often desire objectivity and fairness. They want to be valued members of a diverse educational community that respects and defends the beliefs of all its members. The Pew Research Center (2012) suggested that Mormons may perceive disapproval of their religious beliefs and practices from others. Educators can help by cultivating an environment of mutual understanding and respect.

Additional Resources

- Congregation locator, www.lds.org/maps/meetinghouses
- Institute of Religion locator, www.icl.lds.org
- Official Church website, www.lds.org

References

Alt, S. E. (2016, February 16). *We need to stop saying that there are 33,000 denominations.* Retrieved from http://www.ncregister.com/blog/scottericalt/we-need-to-stop-saying-that-there-are-33000-protestant-denominations

Articles of faith of the Church of Jesus Christ of the Latter-day Saints. (n.d.). Retrieved from https://www.lds.org/scriptures/pgp/a-of-f/1?lang=eng&country=fr

Balmer, R. (2016). *Evangelicalism in America.* Waco, TX: Baylor University Press.

Bebbington, D. W. (1989). *Evangelicalism in Modern Britain: A history from the 1730s to the 1980s.* London, UK: Unwin Hyman.

Christian Legal Society v. Martinez. (2011). 561 U.S. 661.

Church of Jesus Christ of Latter-day Saints. (2018). *Health practices.* Retrieved from http://www.mormonnewsroom.org/article/health-practices

Cox., D., & Jones, R. P. (2015). *How race and religion shape millennial attitudes on sexuality and reproductive health.* Retrieved from http://www.prri.org/research/survey-how-race-and-religion-shape-millenial-attitudes-on-sexuality-and-reproductive-health/

Del Rosario, M. (2014, January 28). *Seven key differences between Catholic and Protestant doctrine.* Retrieved from http://www.dts.edu/hendrickscenter/blog/7-key-differences-between-protestant-and-catholic-doctrine-del-rosario-mikel/

Eagan, K., Stolzenberg, E. B., Bates, A. K., Aragon, M. C., Suchard, M. R., & Rios-Aguilar, C. (2015). The American freshman: National norms fall 2015. Retrieved from http://www.heri.ucla.edu/monographs/TheAmericanFreshman2015.pdf

Galligan-Stierle, M. (2009). Millennials and ministry on college campuses. *New Theology Review, 22*(1), 5–15.

Gallup, G. H. (2002). *The most segregated hour.* Retrieved from http://www.gallup.com/poll/6367/most-segregated-hour.aspx

Glaude, E. (2014). *African American religion: A very short introduction.* New York, NY: Oxford University Press.

Hannum, K. (2016, January, 8). Nonprofit prophets: How women are leading the church. *U.S. Catholic, 81*(1). Retrieved from http://www.uscatholic.org/rticles/201601/nonprofit-prophets-30516

Hill, W. (2016). *Washed and waiting: Reflections on Christian faithfulness and homosexuality.* Grand Rapids, MI: Zondervan.

Holland, J. R. (2016, November). Emissaries to the church. *Ensign, 46*(11), 61–67.

Inazu, J. (2016). *Confident pluralism.* Chicago, IL: University of Chicago.

InterVarsity Christian Fellowship. (2016). *InterVarsity supports religious freedom.* Retrieved from https://intervarsity.org/news/intervarsity-supports-religious-freedom

InterVarsity Christian Fellowship. (2018). *A code of ethics for Christian witness.* Retrieved from http://evangelism.intervarsity.org/how/calling/code-ethics-christian-witness

Jacobsen, R. H. and Jacobsen, D. (2012). *No longer invisible: Religion in university education.* New York, NY: Oxford University Press.

King, M. L., Jr. (2010). *Stride towards freedom: The Montgomery story.* Boston, MA: Beacon Press. (Original work published in 1958.)

Lipka, M. (2014). *Young U.S. Catholics overwhelmingly accepting of homosexuality.* Retrieved from http://www.pewresearch.org/fact-tank/2014/10/16/young-u-s-catholics-overwhelmingly-accepting-of-homosexuality/

Marin, A. (2009). *Love is an orientation.* Downers Grove, IL: InterVarsity Press.

Martínez, J. (2015). *Among Catholics, fewer Latinos than Whites seek changes to the church.* Retrieved from http://www.pewresearch.org/fact-tank/2015/09/21/latino-catholics-white-catholics-changes-to-church/

Mayhew, M. J., Rockenbach, A. N., Correia, B. P., Crandall, R. E., Lo, M. A., & Associates. (2016). *Emerging interfaith trends: What college students are saying about religion in 2016.* Chicago, IL: Interfaith Youth Core.

Murphy, C. (2015). *Most U.S. Christian groups grow more accepting of homosexuality.* Retrieved from http://www.pewresearch.org/fact-tank/2015/12/18/most-u-s-christian-groups-grow-more-accepting-of-homosexuality/

Naselli, D. N., & Hansen, C. (Eds.). (2011). *The spectrum of evangelicalism.* Grand Rapids, MI: Zondervan.

National Council of Churches. (2010). *Catholics, Mormons, Assemblies of God growing; Mainline churches report a continuing decline.* Retrieved from http://www.ncccusa.org/news/100204yearbook2010.html

Newport, F. (2005). Who are the evangelicals? Retrieved from http://www.gallup .com/poll/17041/who-evangelicals.aspx

Noll, M. (2000). *American evangelical Christianity: An introduction.* Hoboken, NJ: Wiley-Blackwell.

Open and affirming in the UCC. (n.d.). Retrieved from http://www.ucc.org/lgbt_ona

Pew Research Center. (2011). *Christian traditions.* Retrieved from http://www .pewforum.org/2011/12/19/global-christianity-traditions/

Pew Research Center. (2012). *Mormons in America—Certain in their beliefs, uncertain of their place in society.* Retrieved from http://www.pewforum.org/2012/01/12/ mormons-in-america-executive-summary

Pew Research Center. (2015a). *Religious composition of U.S. adults.* Washington, DC Retrieved from http://assets.pewresearch.org/wp-content/uploads/sites/11/ 2015/05/Religious-Composition-of-U.S.-Adults.pdf

Pew Research Center. (2015b). *Religious landscape study.* Retrieved from http:// www.pewforum.org/religious-landscape-study/religious-tradition/catholic/ generational-cohort/younger-millennial

Resolution on homosexuals and the law. (1969). Retrieved from http://uccfiles.com/ pdf/1969-RESOLUTION-ON-HOMOSEXUALS-AND-THE-LAW.pdf

Shaw, E. (2015). *Same-sex attraction and the church.* Downers Grove, IL: InterVarsity Press.

Stances of faiths on LGBTQ issues: Evangelical Lutheran Church in America. (2015). Retrieved from http://www.hrc.org/resources/stances-of-faiths-on-lgbt- issues-evangelical-lutheran-church-in-america

Title IX, 20 USCA. Sec. 168 (1972).

U.S. Catholics open to non-traditional families. (2015). Retrieved from http://www .pewforum.org/2015/09/02/u-s-catholics-open-to-non-traditional-families/

16

UNDERSTANDING MUSLIM
STUDENTS ON CAMPUS

Altaf Husain

The Muslim student population on college campuses is growing for two reasons: the overall Muslim population in the United States is growing, and the United States continues to be a destination of choice for international students (Ali & Bagheri, 2009; Dey, 2012). Depending on the size of the Muslim student community on universities' campuses, administrations tackle issues related to accommodating the religious needs of those students as they arise. However, the growing population of Muslims college students is incredibly diverse, and educators in higher education are often unaware of the variety of needs of Muslim students. This chapter seeks to close that gap in two major sections: a brief overview of Muslim beliefs and worldview and foundational knowledge about Muslims with a particular focus on aspects affecting college students. Concrete advice for educators to support Muslims students on campus is provided throughout.

The Muslim community represents 23% of the global population, about 1.6 billion people (Pew Research Center, 2010). Although the U.S. Muslim population is much smaller at just 0.9% of the total U.S. population (Pew Research Center, 2014), the Interfaith Diversity Experiences and Attitudes Longitudinal Survey found that Muslim students made up a larger percentage of entering first-year students in fall 2015 at 1.9% (Mayhew et al., 2016). Learning to support these members of the second-largest religious community in the world is an essential ability for higher education professionals.

Muslim Beliefs and Basic Definitions

Muslim identity has multiple interwoven dimensions because of the comprehensive nature of Islam (Husain & Ross-Sheriff, 2011). Any human being, anywhere on earth, could essentially choose to be a Muslim as the identity is not tied to any particular geographical space. Muslims also vary by virtue of their knowledge and level of adherence or practice of the faith, their race, ethnicity, socioeconomic status, and level of education. The only common characteristic of the members of the *ummah* (the worldwide community of Muslims) is that they self-identify as Muslims. Yet the tremendous intrafaith diversity adds complexity to the Muslim identity (Pew Research Center, 2007). A Muslim college student in the United States could be of Black or African, Asian, Arab, Middle Eastern, European, or, increasingly, Hispanic origin. Along with the racial and ethnic dimensions of the students' identity, students may have a different immigration status. The influx of immigrants to America in the 1960s and 1970s (including many international Muslim students) resulted in an increase in native-born and second- and third-generation Muslim youths.

Essential Beliefs and Worldview

Adherents of the Islamic faith hold a central belief in monotheism. *Allah*, the Arabic word for God, is unseen, has no partners, and is omniscient and omnipotent (Ali, Liu, & Humedian, 2004). In the Islamic worldview, human beings are unique from other creatures because they are endowed with five senses, the capacity to experience feelings and emotions, the faculty of reason, and the will to choose their faith (Hodge, 2005). Because there is no compulsion to believe, one must do so voluntarily and intentionally. For many Muslims, life is considered a journey, with paradise as the aspirational destination of the afterlife.

Allah makes himself known to human beings through 99 characteristics and attributes. Among them are the Merciful, the Beneficent, the Loving, the Just, the Living, and the Creator (Burrell, 1989). The central holy text in Islam, the Qur'an, was revealed to the Prophet Muhammad, peace be upon him (a phrase Muslims typically recite after stating the Prophet's name as a form of reverence), between 610 and 632 CE. Among the prophets and revealed texts acknowledged by name in the Qur'an are Musa (Moses), who received the Torah; Esa (Jesus), who received the Old Testament; and Muhammad, to whom the Qur'an was revealed. After understanding the Islamic worldview, a person takes an oath or *shahada* (bears witness) by verbally testifying to the oneness of Allah and simultaneously acknowledging the role of Muhammad, peace be upon him, as a prophet sent by Allah. Thereafter every Muslim is obligated to take part in *salah* (praying), *zakah* (giving alms), *siyam* (fasting), and the *hajj* (pilgrimage).

A Muslim's worldview is shaped by six articles of faith, namely, belief in One God; Angels of God, such as the archangel Jibreel or Gabriel; Books of

God, Torah, Injil (Old Testament), and Qur'an; prophets of God (Abraham, Moses, Jesus, and Muhammad, among others); Day of Judgment; and Predestination. Two dominant sects in Islam are Sunni and Shiite Muslims. Among the major differences is that Shiite Muslims add a seventh article of belief, referred to as *wilayat/imamat*, to ensure the primacy of the family of the Prophet Muhammad. Therefore, the Shia tradition maintains that religious leadership in the ummah must be relegated only to the direct descendants of the Prophet Muhammad.

The Sunni and Shia division occurred nearly 1,400 years ago. It coincides with the death of the Prophet Muhammad and disputes the appropriate successor to lead all Muslims. Although this division is the source of political conflict around the world, even today in the United States, the Sunni and Shia communities coexist, and their children bring a spirit of coexistence to campus. Most Muslim students raised in the United States have been socialized to be aware of and respectful of the differences; however, students from countries where there is public discord between the two sects may find it difficult to share spaces of worship or to allow membership of one or the other sect in a chapter of the Muslim Student Association (MSA). Campus leaders who promote respect for intrafaith diversity can be very helpful in these situations.

Sources of Guidance

Muslims refer to two main sources for guidance, the Qur'an and the *sunnah*, which constitute the recorded teachings of the Prophet Muhammad. The sunnah covers everything from conduct in one's daily life to family and community life, and the teachings also prescribe specific manners in which obligatory duties are to be fulfilled. Included in the larger body of the sunnah is the *hadith*, which is the formal collection of the Prophet's particular sayings and quotations. Where the Qur'an provides principles, familiarity with the sunnah is often related to the level of religious socialization a young person received prior to entering college. On campus, MSAs are a primary source of support and community for Muslim students. One aspect of regular programming among MSA chapters is the organization of a study circle or *halaqa* to facilitate spiritual learning and discussions rooted in either chapters or verses from the Qur'an or hadith (Mubarak, 2007). These study circles allow students opportunities to attend or lead discussions ranging from everyday Muslim life to more specialized topics such as marriage, social justice, interfaith collaboration, and trending social issues. Through active interactions with these divine sources, students come to terms with the impact of the faith teachings in daily life but, as discussed later, these discussions could also trigger potential spiritual challenges.

Muslims on Campus

Muslim college students often navigate changing aspects of their lives, including the emergence of their religious self. The availability of safe spaces to navigate the impact of these changes is critical to ensure success in the academic, spiritual, and social dimensions of their lives. The following section focuses on many of the most pressing issues Muslim students face.

Impact of the Current Sociopolitical Climate

For many Muslim college students, the heightened interest in Islam in the twenty-first century adds a dimension of having to serve as a de facto ambassador or explainer of Islamic teachings (Peek, 2003). Muslim college students, often with absolutely no connection to events unfolding on the world stage, are asked to explain the prevalence of terrorist attacks and violent extremism carried out by individuals and groups claiming membership in the ummah (Nasir & Al-Amin, 2006).

For the generation that grew up after September 11, 2001, society was characterized by increased scrutiny and suspicion of Muslims. Muslim students often take one of two paths on campus: engagement or retreat. Either pathway likely involves a well-founded fear of anti-Muslim violence on campus or fear of being singled out by classmates or, worse yet, professors asking them to help everyone make sense of their people. Students who choose to engage proactively likely have developed certain coping mechanisms to navigate the campus environment without deleterious consequences on their academic performance or social experience. They may have had a solid support system in their family and community and therefore are able to engage faculty and classmates in dialogue with some stress but minimal adverse impact (Nasir & Al-Amin, 2006; Tyrer & Ahmad, 2006). On the other hand, some students have been subjected to intense bigotry and bullying throughout their early years. Because of minimal support, they may have become conditioned to retreat to the back of the classroom hoping to avoid any interactions, or worse, they may have experienced adverse impacts on their self-esteem.

Knowing the particular challenges Muslim students face, student affairs practitioners could ensure that opportunities are provided during orientation week for residence life staff and volunteer student coordinators to check in with all students. These staff and volunteers could look out for (a) verbalization of fears and anxieties from Muslim students during group discussions about the campus climate, (b) visceral discomfort and body language of Muslim students who choose not to express their views on topics like politics or sexual orientation, and (c) unusual numbers of absences from activities where such discussions are taking place. The objective is not to single out these students publicly but to compare notes among the staff and volunteers to ensure that support is provided for a student exhibiting these challenges.

More proactive engagement to support Muslim students in this challenging climate is also welcome. Attendance at Friday prayer services are obligatory for men, and a fair number of female students also attend these services on campus. Arranging for a higher education professional to make a brief announcement of support for the Muslim community at the end of the Friday prayer service or at a general body meeting of the MSA sends a strong, positive signal on two levels: the university takes seriously the psychosocial well-being of Muslim students and that seriousness is intentional, planned, proactive, and not an afterthought (e.g., when educators scramble to contact Muslim students in the aftermath of a national or international crisis involving Muslims).

Classroom experiences described here, in addition to other new experiences such as coming into contact with a broader, more diverse Muslim community on campus or experiencing the negative mass media portrayal of Muslims, may have a strong impact on Muslim students. Educators can help Muslim students identify the best support system needed to navigate these challenges, such as an academic adviser, faculty member, religious life professional, or the counseling and wellness center. If the crisis is rooted in faith and the theological tradition, the student may benefit from talking to the Islamic chaplain or a religious scholar in the local community. If the crisis is rooted in embarrassment (not knowing one's faith or resentment toward parents), the student may not need a Muslim to speak with and could be referred to the university counseling services. Finally, a theological crisis could be triggered because of self-hatred emanating from a realization that people are distorting the teachings of Islam to justify acts of terrorism and violent extremism. The crisis can trigger questions ranging from, "How often do I have to keep condemning terrorism when those terrorists have nothing to do with Islam?" to "What good is it to practice Islam if doing so could endanger my career and even my life?" There must be space to process those questions either among peers, with the campus chaplain, or with a trained helping professional (Mubarak, 2007).

Daily Accommodations and Practice Needs

Muslim college students will likely need accommodations to fulfill the obligation to perform daily prayers and to have access to halal food (Tyrer & Ahmad, 2006). Depending on the history and prevalence of the Muslim student population on a campus, these accommodations may already exist or may need to be added. If one is unsure, it is best to check with a Muslim chaplain or the MSA leadership; if neither of those entities exist, then the local community *masjid* or Islamic center are good alternatives.

Five Daily Prayers

The five daily prayers occur at appointed times, but there is flexibility to perform the prayers within a time block that can range from as short as 90 minutes to as long as several hours (Husain & Ross-Sheriff, 2011). Prior to performing the prayer, the student must complete a ritual cleansing known as the *wudhu*, using water. This can be a source of potential distress for students because some of the motions of the *wudhu* appear to be an attempt to take a shower while fully clothed. It involves washing one's hands and arms up to the elbow; washing one's face including cleansing the nostrils; wiping one's hair and ears with damp hands; and, depending on the particular school of thought, either wiping one's socks (feet up to the ankles) with damp hands or actually washing one's feet up to the ankles. A handful of universities have invested in the construction of footbaths, but for the most part, students must find solutions to manage this practice on their own, complete with the full-blown anxiety of having a student unfamiliar with this ritual walk in on the wudhu session in progress. Reactions from those students have ranged from "Are you trying to take a shower in the sink?" to "Washing your feet in the sink is unhygienic."

Some Muslim students have reported not praying at all on campus until they return to their apartments or residence halls to avoid these challenges. Because prayers must be completed at their appointed times, such intentional delays lead to feelings of guilt for not meeting the prayer requirements and even potential fights with parents who may not fully understand the circumstances that make their college-age children choose to delay their prayers. Thankfully, over the past several decades, alumni have developed and shared practical tips to surviving the wudhu with minimal embarrassment. Therefore, it is important to connect new Muslim students (especially international students) with the Muslim chaplain or the MSA leadership early in their campus experience so they can learn how others have learned ways to be comfortable in completing the prerequisite to prayer.

Students may complete the daily prayers individually or in congregation. A computer application is available that helps determine prayer times and real-time prayer direction. Other than facing in the direction of the Kabah (a holy site that is physically located in Makkah, Saudi Arabia), there are no other major requirements to offering the prayers. The area where the student stands should provide adequate privacy, given the positions of bowing and prostrating on the ground; be quiet enough to allow contemplation and reflection on the Qur'anic verses being recited; have minimal pedestrian traffic so the praying person is not distracted or becomes a source of distraction to others; and be clean of any visible impurities. If a designated multifaith chapel or prayer area on campus does not exist, students can be creative, and stories abound of those who have prayed in unused classrooms, under bleachers at football games, stairwells, hallways, and library aisles, to name a few. Administrators who have discovered students praying in these circumstances are often distressed, and Muslim students welcome support in finding more accommodating spaces on campus for praying.

Halal Food
Broadly speaking, Islamic teachings stipulate consuming food that is *tayyib* (nourishing in regard to ingredients) and halal (prepared according to express guidelines). In the context of food, tayyib would be closely associated with the current growth in the popularity of organic, locally sourced, grain-fed and free-range, and pesticide-free ingredients, although not all Muslims strictly adhere to this. Halal food is cooked without the use of alcohol; halal meat excludes pork and must be slaughtered according to strict guidelines. Similar to kosher requirements, there should be no interaction with nonpermitted ingredients during preparation (e.g., the use of the same pan to prepare a pork dish and then a chicken dish).

On campuses where the requests for halal food are new, student affairs professionals can learn more from the MSA leadership, the local Muslim community, a Muslim chaplain at another university, or the students making the request (Mubarak, 2007; Tyrer & Ahmad, 2006). Depending on the number of students making the requests for halal food, it may be more helpful for those students to be exempted from a required university meal plan. Ultimately, outreach activities by university staff to Muslim students during the summer prior to the start of the semester can help with understanding and if possible accommodate halal food requests.

Parent–Child Relationships

Muslim college students are not immune to the same stresses and strains affecting their peers in regard to relationships with their parents (Tyrer & Ahmad, 2006). The modern Muslim family is at once nuclear and extended, affected by separation and divorce, and diverse in the cultural and religious expectations of their children. For students who live at home and commute to campus, there may be more acute stresses because they see their parents on a daily basis, and they may be reminded about the need to maintain a high cumulative grade point average or to pursue a major in line with parental expectations (Dey, 2012; Tyrer & Ahmad, 2006). There may also be additional responsibilities such as assisting parents with activities of daily living such as meal preparation or other chores, thus causing students to miss some extracurricular activities. When students flag because of stress, depression, or poor academic performance, academic advisers and student affairs professionals should make some effort to appropriately explore this aspect of students' environment.

Students who live on campus may have similar stressors, and the level of stress could actually be greater than for students who live at home. Students may experience feelings of guilt for not being at home to help their family or when parents remind the student of the great sacrifices they are making to send their children to college. If students cannot return home because of distance or cost, especially around national and religious holidays, feelings of homesickness, loneliness, guilt, and resentment can be heightened. Reactions to these pressures may affect academic performance or other behaviors.

Too often, there is a perception that religiously inclined students either have healthy relationships with their parents or that their coping mechanisms such as prayer and meditation are sufficient to offset stressors from this domain of their lives. As student affairs professionals, it is helpful to consider ways to support Muslim students in developing healthy relationships with their parents (Mubarak, 2007).

Holidays and Holy Days

There are two major holidays in Islam but there are also various holy days. According to the prophetic tradition, the two major holidays are the *eid al fitr* and the *eid al adha* (the word *eid* means festival and may also be used as shorthand to refer to an upcoming holiday). Eid al fitr occurs at the end of the holy month of Ramadan which is the ninth month of the lunar calendar and is designated as the month of fasting (Ali & Bagheri, 2009). The eid al adha holiday coincides with the culmination of hajj or the pilgrimage to Makkah in Saudi Arabia. For both major holidays, the celebration consists of a congregational prayer during the morning followed by time spent enjoying food and the company of family and loved ones.

Accommodations specific to these two major holidays include rescheduling examinations or due dates for major presentations to allow the students to travel home or to participate in locally organized congregational prayer and festivities. The dates of these two holidays can be found through online sources such as www.moonsighting.com. Ensuring that faculty and academic advisers alike are aware of these dates can ease the burden on the students to have to explain the holidays to their instructors to seek an accommodation.

Some students may also celebrate other holidays. The first day of the month of Muharram is special as it marks the beginning of a new calendar year. For Shia students, the month of Muharram is also significant because of the various religious leaders who died or were assassinated during this month. Not unlike Christmas, some Muslims observe the date of the birth of the prophet Muhammad as a religious holiday known as Milad un Nabi.

As emphasized throughout this chapter, educators will be perceived as much more authentic if they work either with the local Muslim community, the MSA chapter, or the Islamic chaplain to determine the dates for these religious holidays and holy days. Ali and Bagheri (2009) recommend adding these dates to the university academic calendar. Student affairs professionals could also help by facilitating a meeting prior to Ramadan between the MSA and campus dining services to explore options to best accommodate the students' needs (Nasir & Al-Amin, 2006). If students request an accommodation to enable their peak academic performance while fasting during Ramadan, student affairs professionals should communicate to faculty members their full support. For students enrolled in campus meal plans, accommodations for the predawn meal associated with Ramadan, could include offering them a sandwich to go the evening before. The MSA chapter often coordinates a campus-wide effort to provide the postsunset meal or *iftar*. Various accommodations have been made with campus dining services for the evening meal as well. Some campuses have offered food to go, or if the students have arranged for their own meals from local restaurants, then the dining services offers bottled water, beverages, and dessert to students who are fasting and not using their campus meal plans during that month.

The observance of the fast is intended to help Muslims develop heightened God consciousness through abstaining from the typical activities of daily living such as eating, drinking, engaging in idle talk, and sexual intimacy with their spouse while simultaneously engaging in increased recitation of the Qur'an and in nightly congregational prayers at the masjid. For students who are away from their families for the first time, or for international students who are without their families, the observance of Ramadan can trigger intense feelings of homesickness. MSA chapters have helped these students by involving them in congregational activities. Some chapters have offered parents the opportunity to have Ramadan care packages delivered to those students on campus, a practice that student affairs professionals could consider supporting.

Impact of Campus Culture

Although the most obvious concern of parents is how well their children can handle and indeed thrive in the classroom, Muslim students, like most young adults, are just as likely to be concerned about thriving outside the classroom. Opportunities for downtime and socializing are also critical to the success of Muslim students just like any other students of their age group because the challenges of adjusting to campus life can be a source of stress.

Certain aspects of campus culture, such as the consumption of alcohol, experimenting with drug use, dating, and exploring one's sexuality, pose serious religious and cultural dilemmas for Muslim students. The religious prohibition of the consumption of any intoxicants or of premarital relationships combined with the intense social pressure to decompress after exams with classmates of diverse backgrounds presents dilemmas. Some students may choose either to go off campus or self-isolate to avoid all conflicts; others choose to participate in parties or other social gatherings then subsequently face intense personal guilt or shaming from other Muslim students. Still others will become fully adept at navigating the social terrain and enjoying themselves while observing relevant religious teachings. Being sensitive to such challenges, student affairs professionals could ensure that funding is available for Muslim students to organize their own social gatherings. Keeping sports facilities accessible for late-night games of volleyball, basketball, racquetball, or soccer also provides an especially helpful alternative.

Perhaps the greatest challenge some students face is the difficulty in even admitting their personal struggles with some of these aspects of campus culture. Providing resources such as counselors and helping Muslim students understand and navigate their personal and social discomforts is exceptionally helpful.

Muslim Women on Campus

In her ethnographic study of Muslim women on campus, Mir (2014) explores more generally what the college experience is like for Muslim women and in particular for the participants of her study. Although Muslim women may be denied access to education in some parts of the world, they are present on U.S. college campuses. Mir (2014) challenges anyone attempting to find just one description of a Muslim female college student, stating they are "sometimes emphatically different and sometimes indistinguishable from their majority American peers" (p. 6). In reality, the most emphatic difference is their outward appearance, that is, if the student wears the *hijab* (headscarf) or *jilbab* (the outermost garment, a full-length cloak or coat), and the overarching themes guiding selection of dress are modesty, respect, and dignity. Wearing the hijab is entirely the choice of the young woman, although family and social pressures can also be a motivating factor. Ali (2005) noted a young college student who did not wear the hijab until she arrived on campus because, she said, "I lived in a co-ed dorm and it was really the first time I had to deal with unwanted attention from guys" (p. 518).

Because the hijab is so distinguishable, it exposes Muslim women to potential verbal and even physical assaults from individuals who are motivated either by outright hatred of Islam or just ignorance. Student affairs practitioners should do what they can to protect Muslim women from these types of assault, which could include educating non-Muslims about clothing choices of Muslim women. Some women wear the hijab voluntarily, and some Muslim women do not wear a headscarf yet fully identify as a Muslim in word and practice.

Another distinction for Muslim women is related to student's understanding of common modes of greeting, such as a handshake or a hug. Some Muslim women may prefer to greet men with their right hand placed on their heart in lieu of a handshake. Educators should be aware that not shaking hands, standing more than an arm's length away in conversation, or not maintaining direct eye contact are all behaviors that some women believe exhibit appropriate modesty in interactions with members of the opposite gender and are by no means a sign of disrespect. It is especially relevant to ask permission from Muslim students before assuming physical contact will be welcome.

Conclusion

Muslim students appreciate knowing that the educators on campus are there to ensure that the students have a meaningful and supported college experience. The following recommendations should be a helpful summary in serving Muslim students:

1. Be authentic. Establish a working relationship with various segments of the Muslim student community and attend their activities when possible to develop rapport and trust.
2. Maintain neutrality. Given the diverse theological and practice differences among Muslim students, it is advisable for the staff to not advocate particular positions when a potential intrafaith conflict arises among the students.
3. Provide resources. Most important, actively provide and communicate existing resources and accommodations to Muslim students, particularly when they are new to campus.
4. Identify community leaders. Regular interactions with the Muslim student body will help identify either formal or informal leaders; local religious leaders can be a huge support as well.

5. Stay current. Although it is impossible to keep up with all relevant news, maintain awareness of local and national news to understand the larger dynamics affecting Muslim students.

Additional Resources

1. Council on American Islamic Relations, www.cair.com
2. Islamic Food and Nutrition Council of America, www.ifanca.org
3. Islamic Networks Group, www.ing.org
4. Islamophobia Research and Documentation Project, www.crg.berkeley ⁻.edu/content/islamophobia
5. Muslim Students Association of the United States and Canada, www .msanational.org

References

Ali, S. (2005). Why here, why now? Young Muslim women wearing hijab. *Muslim World, 95*, 515–530.

Ali, S. R., & Bagheri, E. (2009). Practical suggestions to accommodate the needs of Muslim students on campus. *New Directions for Student Services*, 125, 47–54.

Ali, S. R., Liu, W. M., & Humedian, M. (2004). Islam 101: Understanding the religion and therapy implications. *Professional Psychology: Research and Practice, 35*, 635–642.

Burrell, D. B. (1989). Ghazali and Aquinas on the names of God. *Literature and Theology, 3*, 173–180.

Dey, F. (2012). *Islam on campus: Identity development of Muslim-American college students*. (Doctoral dissertation). Retrieved from ProQuest Dissertations and Theses database. (UMI No. 3569431.)

Hodge, D. (2005). Social work and the House of Islam: Orienting practitioners to the beliefs and values of Muslims in the United States. *Social Work, 50*, 162–173.

Husain, A., & Ross-Sheriff, F. (2011). Cultural competence with Muslim Americans. In D. Lum (Ed.), *Culturally competent practice: A framework for understanding diverse groups and justice issues* (4th ed., pp. 358–389). Belmont, CA: Brooks/ Cole.

Mayhew, M. J., Rockenbach, A. N., Correia, B. P., Crandall, R. E., Lo, M. A., & Associates. (2016). *Emerging interfaith trends: What college students are saying about religion in 2016*. Chicago, IL: Interfaith Youth Core.

Mir, S. (2014). *Muslim American women on campus: Undergraduate social life and identity*. Chapel Hill, NC: University of North Carolina Press.

Mubarak, H. (2007). *How Muslim students negotiate their religious identity and practices in an undergraduate setting*. Retrieved from http://religion.ssrc.org/reforum/ Mubarak.pdf/

Nasir, N. I. S., & Al-Amin, J. (2006). Creating identity-safe spaces on college campuses for Muslim students. *Change, 38*(2), 22–27.

Peek, L. A. (2003). Reactions and response: Muslim students' experiences on New York City campuses post 9/11. *Journal of Muslim Minority Affairs, 23,* 271–283.

Pew Research Center. (2007). *Muslim Americans: Middle class and mostly mainstream.* Retrieved from http://pewresearch.org/assets/pdf/muslim-americans.pdf

Pew Research Center. (2010). *The global religious landscape.* Retrieved from http://www.pewforum.org/2012/12/18/global-religious-landscape-exec/

Pew Research Center. (2014). *Religious landscape study.* Retrieved from http://www.pewforum.org/about-the-religious-landscape-study/

Tyrer, D., and Ahmad, F. (2006). *Muslim women and higher education: Identities, experiences and prospects—a summary report.* Liverpool, England: Liverpool John Moores University and European Social Fund.

17

UNDERSTANDING JEWISH STUDENTS ON CAMPUS

Sheila Katz and Josh Feigelson

What's the one thing that more American Jews do than anything else? Observe major Jewish holidays? No. Visit Israel? No. Speak Hebrew? No. They go to college. In the 1920s an astonishing 42% of American Jewish college-age youths went to college (Moore, 1981). By the 1960s that rate had climbed to 80% (Greenberg, 1968), and today, scholars estimate that 85% to 90% of American Jews attend college or a university (Cousens, 2007). More than any other thing in American Jewish life, American Jews go to college. This chapter is designed to help student affairs educators understand the needs of Jewish students to serve them better.

Let's start with some common myths about being Jewish.

- "Jews are not a minority." Although many Jews have achieved the socioeconomic status of the upper or upper-middle class, Jews are still a religious and ethnic minority in every country outside Israel. There are between 5 and 7 million Jews in the United States, which is about 2% of the population. Although some Jews may enjoy aspects of privilege, it is important to remember that Jews are still a tiny minority population that has historically been oppressed.
- "All Jews feel the same way about Israel." This is incorrect. Jews have a variety of nuanced relationships with Israel, including many who don't have a relationship at all.
- "All Jews are White." Not true. Jews come from a wide range of racial backgrounds.
- "You can only be Jewish if you go to services and observe all holidays." Jewishness is not always conditional on religious activity. Students participate in their Jewish identity in a wide range of ways.

- "Jews have horns." No they don't. Period. And yes, there are still Jewish students who get asked this question on college campuses.

Understanding Jewishness

One of the most important things to know about Jewish students is that being Jewish is not the same thing as practicing Judaism. Judaism is a religion; Jewishness is an identity. Jews have developed many wide-ranging expressions of Jewishness, from varying levels of religious observance to studying the wisdom of the Jewish textual tradition to doing social justice work or Zionist activism to baking traditional foods to creating Jewish music and art. Jewish students have boundless ways of engaging with their Jewishness, all of them real and meaningful to them.

It is also important to adopt an intersectional approach to understanding Jewishness: A student's Jewishness is almost universally one strand in the braided challah bread that makes up their identity. Jews come from all types of ethnic, racial, and socioeconomic backgrounds. Well over half of Jewish students on campus today come from families in which only one of their parents is Jewish, meaning they likely also have family members from additional faiths (Cohen & Cohen, 2015).

For the purposes of this overview, we are going to focus on the religious expressions of Jewishness you are likely to encounter in your work on a college campus. Orthodox, Conservative, Reform, and Reconstructionist, described later in the chapter, refer to organized denominational movements in Judaism. (Visit www.myjewishlearning.com/article/the-jewish-denominations for more information.)

Some students who identify as Orthodox Jews perform ritual activities as required by traditional Jewish law. They observe Jewish food laws (keeping kosher), Jewish holidays (Shabbat and others), praying three times per day, and Jewish laws about sexual activity (not having sex before marriage and not cohabiting with or touching members of the opposite sex). Of course, like all emerging adults, many Orthodox-identified students will go through their own struggles about how they relate to these laws and practices while they are in college.

Some students identify as Conservative, Reform, or Reconstructionist Jews and engage in ritual activities in a variety of ways. They may go to religious services frequently or not at all, they might host a Friday evening Shabbat dinner, they might keep kosher by not mixing meat and milk but not practice some of the stricter observances of kosher laws like having separate utensils for dairy and meat products, and they likely conform to views and practices of sexuality that are more prevalent in the general culture. Some may have attended Jewish day schools, K through 8 or even high school, but overall these non-Orthodox Jews, the largest segment of the Jewish student population, show up in college with a much wider range of backgrounds and ways of expressing their Jewishness.

Regardless of their religious backgrounds, close to a quarter of Jews on campus prefer not to be labeled religiously and identify as "Just Jewish" (Hillel International, 2016, p. 6). Sixty-two percent of millennials say being Jewish is mainly a matter of ancestry and culture, whereas only 15% say it is mainly a matter of religion (Pew Research Center, 2013).

Ways to Help Religious Jewish Students

There are several ways student affairs educators can support Jewish students. Several of these refer to Jewish holidays, discussed later in the chapter.

- Don't assume that all students are comfortable touching individuals of different gender identities. Make sure icebreakers and residential life activities factor in the needs of religious students.
- Provide kosher options in the dining halls, which allows students who keep kosher to be integrated into campus life rather than separated at mealtime. (See the "Food and Dietary Laws" section later in the chapter for more details.)
- Check the holiday list prior to scheduling major campus events, exams, and speakers.
- Support students who need to take off from class to observe holidays.
- Make sure your university has an option to provide keys that are not electronic for students who observe Shabbat (see the "Non-working Holidays" section for more details).

Identity and Intersectionality

As stated earlier, Jewishness isn't just Judaism. Jewishness escapes as well as encompasses many of the typical markers we use to understand identity today; there is a religious dimension, an ethnic dimension (including a language dimension), a peoplehood dimension, and with the establishment of the modern state of Israel in 1948, a national dimension. Gender also plays a role for some Jews in their Jewish identities; they will identify as Jewish men, Jewish women, Jewish queers, Jewish transgender, and so on. Jewishness has long been an intersectional combination of many dimensions, and today, not all these dimensions will be relevant to any individual Jew.

Things to Consider

The following facts illustrate the intersectional dimensions of Jewishness. (Visit www.myjewishlearning.com/article/sephardic-ashkenazic-mizrahi-jews -jewish-ethnic-diversity/ to learn more about the diversity in the Jewish community.)

- Ten to 20% of American Jews today identify as Jews of color ("Counting Jews of Color in the United States," 2018). Although many people in America may have an image of Jews as White, Jews have many racial and ethnic identities. Some Jews do identify as White, many do not. Of the 20% of American Jews who self-identify as people of color, the two largest percentages are Black Jews and Sephardic Jews (one of the three distinct ethnic groups in the global Jewish community).

- Fifteen percent of American Jews today come from Russian-speaking families (Sarna, 2013). They or their parents left the former Soviet Union during the period of mass emigration in the late 1980s and 1990s. They are first-generation immigrants.

- Seventy-two percent of non-Orthodox Jews come from interfaith families (Cohen & Cohen, 2015). Although most Orthodox Jews come from families with two Jewish parents, the vast majority of non-Orthodox Jews, which is the vast majority of Jews on college campuses today, come from families where one of their parents is not Jewish. That means they may have grown up observing multiple religious traditions and inhabiting multiple cultures. Virtually all Jews today have relatives who practice or identify with other faiths.

Holidays and the Academic Year

The Jewish calendar is filled with several holidays. Apart from Shabbat, which happens every week, the dates of these holidays change from year to year because Judaism follows a lunar calendar. Because the lunar calendar is 354 days per year, the dates of the holidays fall back by 11 days every year. Additionally, the Jewish calendar adds a leap month every few years to keep the holidays in the same season, so although the precise date varies from year to year, the season does not.

Table 17.1 is a description of the major holidays. Please note that students vary in how they observe the holidays. Our aim here is to give a general introduction to the holidays and note what some traditional observances might include.

Non-Working Holidays

The term *non-working holidays* refer to days that are like Shabbat, in that work is prohibited and ritually observant students generally do not write, use electronics, travel, and so on. These prohibitions are not in place for holidays that are not non-working. Each Jewish holiday starts at sunset and continues through sunset the next day. Academic accommodations should be expected for these days, although not all Jews practice them the same. Some will attend class, others will not.

Ways to Accommodate Religious Students

Student affairs educators can play an important role in supporting Jewish students by adhering to the following suggestions.

- Distribute a list of major holidays from all faiths, including Judaism, so professors, offices, and organizations are discouraged from planning events and tests on those days.
- Institutionalize ways to request a religious absence from class by completing a form with the dean's office (or another campus professional). This process validates this absence as an excused absence.
- Work with religious groups to include religious foods in the dining hall for holidays to show you value religious diversity and inclusion. For example, offer matzah on Passover or apple-themed foods on Rosh Hashanah.
- Consider attending or hosting a Shabbat dinner or High Holiday services. These experiences tend to be open to all. Jewish students seeing faculty and administrators taking an active interest in who they are as Jews can build trust and a feeling of safety on campus.

Food and Dietary Laws

Traditional Jewish law requires Jews to abide by several dietary laws, which are collectively known as *kashrut,* or keeping kosher. Some people keep kosher because they believe God instructs us not to eat certain foods. Others keep kosher because there are laws about how to slaughter animals in the most humane way possible. Many keep kosher for a combination of these reasons or simply as a cultural practice.

As with virtually everything else in this chapter, individual Jews vary widely in their practice. Some are very strict in their adherence to kosher rules; for others, it is not an important part of their lives. The easiest way to know if a food is kosher is to look for kosher certification on food you are

TABLE 17.1

Descriptions of Major Jewish Holidays

Jewish Holiday	Number of Days	Description	Themes
Every Friday to Saturday Night			
Shabbat	One day, non-working	The Jewish Day of Rest: Per traditional Jewish law, Shabbat is a day for rest. Ritually observant students will not write, use electronics (including key cards), ride in a motorized vehicle, cook, or engage in many other activities defined as *worklike* for the full duration of Shabbat. Shabbat is traditionally marked by a festive dinner on Friday night. Religious services are held on Friday evening, Saturday morning, and Saturday afternoon.	Rest Unplugging Relaxation Intentionality
September/October			
Rosh Hashanah	Two days, non-working	The Jewish New Year: Rosh Hashanah marks the beginning of a 10-day period of introspection, including seeking forgiveness. It is marked by long synagogue services that include the ritual blowing of the *shofar* (ram's horn) as well as festive meals that feature apples and honey signifying a sweet new year.	New beginnings Reflection Self-improvement
Yom Kippur	One day, non-working	The Day of Atonement: The holiest day on the Jewish calendar, traditionally marked by fasting from sundown to just after sundown the next day. Features long synagogue services. Many students will aim to attend services rather than go to class.	Forgiveness
Sukkot	Seven days, first two days are non-working	Fall Harvest Festival: This harvest holiday is marked by eating meals in an outdoor hut called a *sukkah*. Ritually observant Jews treat eating in the sukkah as a requirement, so having a sukkah near dining facilities is an important thing to consider.	Home Wandering Temporariness Permanence

(Continues)

TABLE 17.1 (Continued)

Jewish Holiday	Number of Days	Description	Themes
Shemini Atzeret and Simchat Torah	Two days, non-working	During this holiday Jews complete the annual ritual cycle of reading the Torah. It is marked by dancing and songs. Simchat Torah celebration often involves alcohol.	Endings Beginnings Joy of study
November/December			
Hannukah	Eight days, work is permitted	Festival of Lights: Hannukah commemorates the victory of Jewish rebels over their Assyrian occupiers in ancient Israel. It is marked by lighting a special candelabra called a *hannukiah* or *menorah*. Eating oily foods such as potato pancakes and jelly donuts are customary.	Taking a stand Light in the darkness Minority cultures within majority cultures
January/February			
Tu BiShvat	One day, work is permitted	New Year for the Trees: In more liberal circles it has become a day to focus on Jewish environmental activism. Customs include eating fruit from the land of Israel including dates, figs, and almonds.	Rebirth Environment
February/March			
Purim	One day, work is permitted	Festival of Esther: Purim commemorates the survival of the Jews of ancient Persia. It is marked by a ritual communal reading of the Book of Esther in the evening, as well as giving gifts of food to friends and the poor during the day and having a festive meal. Often referred to by students as the Jewish Halloween (although it has nothing to do with Halloween) because people are encouraged to dress in costume for the reading of the Book of Esther. Some communities have the custom of drinking alcohol on Purim.	Taking a stand Role reversal Women's empowerment

Jewish Holiday	Number of Days	Description	Themes
March/April			
Passover	Eight days, first two days and last two days are non-working	Festival of Freedom: Passover commemorates the Exodus of Jewish slaves from Egypt more than 3,000 years ago (see the biblical book of Exodus). Passover is widely observed by most Jews. The first two nights feature the Seder, a special meal at which the story of the Exodus is recounted and discussed. In recent decades, Seders have moved to other nights or even before or after Passover. During Passover, the Torah prohibits eating or owning leavened products such as bread, cereal, pasta, and grain alcohol, and instead using matzah, a crackerlike bread.	Freedom Responsibility Thanksgiving Resisting oppression
May/June			
Shavuot	Two day, non-working	Festival of Torah: Shavuot commemorates presenting the Torah to the Jewish people. It is customary to stay up late on the first night of Shavuot to study Jewish texts.	Learning Study
July/August			
Tisha B'Av	One day, non-working	National Day of Mourning: A 25-hour fast day commemorating the many calamitous and sad events in Jewish history	Mourning

buying. There are many kosher-certification agencies (see www.crcweb.org/ agency_list.php and https://oukosher.org/the-kosher-primer/).

Kosher Basics

Jewish people keep kosher in the following ways:

- Eat only kosher meat. To qualify as kosher, meat has to
  - come from an animal that does not have sharp teeth (this excludes animals like pigs),
  - come from an animal that has a split hoof (this excludes animals like horses),
  - be perfectly healthy, and
  - be slaughtered according to traditional Jewish practice.
- Do not eat mixtures of dairy and meat (e.g., a cheeseburger, a turkey wrap with cheese, etc.)
- Do not eat shellfish
- Keep separate utensils for dairy and meat products including cooking, serving, and eating utensils. In most industrial kosher operations (including on college campuses), dairy and meat kitchens are separate. For more traditional students, keeping kosher food entirely separate is very important.
- Eat only kosher-certified foods or foods made from kosher-certified products in a kosher kitchen

Kosher on Campus

Over the past several decades, universities with substantial numbers of Jewish students have developed kosher dining options in dining halls. This is an incredibly important gesture to welcome many Jewish students. Take the following guidelines into account.

- Do not assume that just because Jewish students have not expressed a need for kosher food that the need does not exist. If your university does not offer kosher dining, you might work with your dining service to find out if Jewish students would take advantage of a kosher dining option if the option existed.
- For many Muslim students, kosher meat also satisfies the requirements of halal dietary laws. Because other students may be interested in kosher food for other reasons there will likely be a population of kosher dining users in addition to Jewish students.

- Some universities have placed kosher dining in a Hillel building, which has pluses and minuses. It can help Jews build internal community, but it can also be exclusive for many. We recommend that the optimal situation is for the university to offer kosher dining in a university dining hall to make Jewish students feel as fully integrated into the university community as possible.

Anti-Semitism

Sadly, Jewish history is filled with stories of hatred and persecution inflicted on individual Jews and Jewish communities all over the world. Jews have been victims of physical attacks, social and economic marginalization, enslavement, and genocide. Although we would hope that the twenty-first century would bring about a more tolerant world in which Jews could be accepted and embraced, anti-Semitism continues to be a powerful force that affects Jews around the world, including in the United States and college campuses.

On campus today, half of Jewish students say they have witnessed or experienced anti-Semitism (Mulhere, 2015). Although these episodes can be public, such as a swastika painted on a Jewish fraternity house or hate speech directed at Jews, more frequently students report anti-Semitism takes subtler forms. Often anti-Semitism is linked with Israeli politics (see the next section on Israel).

Questions to Ask

To assess whether Jewish students on your campus are experiencing anti-Semitism, reflect on the following:

- When engaging in conversations or thinking about Jewish students on campus, try replacing *Jewish* with another minority label such as African American; Muslim; or lesbian, gay, bisexual, transgender, or queer (LGBTQ). Would you respond the same way?
- Are Jewish students being shut out of conversations or leadership positions on campus simply because they are Jews?
- Are Jewish students assumed to hold particular political views? Regardless of their political views, is that a legitimate reason to exclude them from participation in campus life?

Israel and Boycott, Divestment, and Sanctions

The subject of Israel is one of the hottest issues on campus today. Jewish students have a wide range of feelings, ideas, political commitments, and levels of activism when it comes to Israel. Some students know a lot about Israel, some know little. Some were born there, or they may have relatives and friends who live there, and some may not have any connections in Israel. Some are highly engaged in Jewish ritual and community life and some are not. Like everything else in this chapter, you should not assume anything about a Jewish student's relationship with Israel.

How Do Jewish Students Relate to Israel?

Some students may feel passionately about Israel because they understand it to be the historic homeland of the Jewish people, a place central to the narrative of the Torah, Jewish liturgy, Jewish literature, and Jewish life for 3,000 years. Some may feel strongly because the State of Israel, founded in 1948, grants immediate citizenship to any Jew, and therefore serves as a refuge for Jews fleeing persecution, perhaps for their own family or potentially for themselves. Some may feel strongly because they see the State of Israel as a representative of Jews around the world and therefore of themselves. They may identify with Israeli athletes in the Olympics, Israeli discoveries in technology, or Israeli cultural achievements. They may also hold Israel to a high moral standard, perhaps especially regarding its treatment of non-Jewish citizens and residents under its jurisdiction. Some may feel strongly because Israel has multiple dimensions as a land, a longing, and a dream for the Jewish people.

Some students might feel strongly for a combination of these reasons or for entirely other reasons. Or they might not feel strongly at all. Do not make assumptions regarding how much students know or care about Israel. When appropriate, ask students why Israel does or does not matter to them and how.

Birthright Israel

One way that hundreds of thousands of Jewish students have interacted with Israel over the past two decades is as participants on Birthright Israel trips. Birthright Israel is a joint project of the Israeli government and the American Jewish community that takes students to Israel for the first time for a 10-day trip with their peers. The focus of this trip is more on students' identities as members of the Jewish people and less on education about Israel. Birthright Israel is a significant opportunity for Jewish students on campus. Organizations like Chabad and Hillel are likely to run these trips.

Study Abroad

Israel is a global leader in higher education, boasting leading institutions in the arts, sciences, and humanities. Many universities have established study abroad programs with Israeli universities, and each year thousands of students, Jewish and non-Jewish, participate in these programs.

Boycott, Divestment, and Sanctions Campaign

In recent years, the Boycott, Divestment, and Sanctions campaign (BDS) has become highly active on an increasing number of campuses. Arising from opposition to Israel as a Jewish state and a belief that Israel's policies and practices oppress the Palestinian people, the BDS campaign tries to pressure universities to cut ties with Israel in a variety of ways, including economic boycotts, divestment of university holdings from companies that do business in Israel, and even academic boycotts of Israeli universities and professors. The campaigns can take various forms, including student government resolutions and full student body referendums. The campaigns are largely symbolic—no university has ever divested from Israel, a decision most often determined by the Board of Trustees—with the goal of spreading an anti-Israel narrative to as many students as possible. Although some might agree with the BDS campaign's founding principles, as a movement BDS is highly complex and not at all monolithic; many involved in the movement have explicit ties to overt anti-Semitism.

When BDS campaigns come to a campus, many Jewish students will feel a great deal of stress and pressure, especially when the campaigns involve attempts to shut down events featuring Israeli speakers or highly public campaigns over student government. Jewish students are likely to confront multiple competing narratives about Israel, and student activists may not do a good or fair job of distinguishing between Israeli and Jewish identity, assuming, for instance, that all Jewish students feel the same way about Israel.

In many cases, BDS campaigns have led to incidents of anti-Semitism. Jewish students have been denied participation in student groups and student governments based on their real or perceived political views. Pro-BDS groups have increasingly adopted a position of nonnormalization, in which even cosponsoring a non–Israel-focused event with a Jewish organization is deemed to be participating in the continued occupation of the Palestinian people. This kind of position is viewed by many Jewish students and organizations as not only counterproductive but also antithetical to university life.

Ways to Support Jewish Students When It Comes to Israel

For student affairs educators seeking to support Jewish students, the following actions can be effective:

- Help them articulate what they are feeling. Jewish students may be caught in a difficult pull of competing loyalties. Ask them to tell you about it and simply listen.
- Help them find knowledge. Many students realize they are not equipped with enough knowledge of history to participate in campus debates about Israel. Help them find courses on Israeli history. If your campus has a Hillel, find out if it has a Jewish Agency for Israel Fellow, who is a specialized Israel educator, and consider referring them. Call your colleagues at Hillel for sources of information.
- Look out for anti-Semitism. Are Jewish students being held to a different standard than other students? Is the language of protest spilling over into anti-Semitic words and actions? If so, consult your university's relevant policies on hate speech and help build an environment of greater respect and understanding.
- Create informal ways for dialogue. Many Israeli and Palestinian advocacy groups have policies against formally working with each other. Universities can play an important role in bringing together small groups of students for dialogue.

Jewish Institutions on Campus Jewish Studies Programs

Many campuses feature academic programs in Jewish studies that offer courses in a wide range of areas including Jewish history, the Jewish Bible, rabbinic literature, Jewish films, the Holocaust, and contemporary Israel. Faculty in these programs can be enormous resources for Jewish students on campus. Many Jewish studies courses are taken by students from another faith, helping more students on campus understand and empathize with the Jewish people while also learning from the wisdom of Jewish teachings in ways that are relevant for them. For more information on Jewish Studies programs, consult your university's website or the Association for Jewish Studies.

Hillel International

Hillel International is the largest Jewish campus- and community-based organization in the world serving the college-age population. Working with hundreds of thousands of students globally to help Jewish students make an enduring commitment to Jewish life, learning, and Israel, Hillel is a pluralistic organization that serves students at more than 550 colleges, universities, and communities in North America and in 15 countries.

Chabad

Chabad Jewish student centers are found on over 210 campuses nationwide. Chabad seeks to be a home away from home for Jewish students and also provides a wealth of spiritual and social programs for students. Chabad houses tend to be more traditional with religious practices that align more closely with the Conservative or Orthodox denominations. However, Chabad and Hillel can differ from campus to campus, so it is beneficial to get to know each community on its own.

Conclusion

The following are some summary thoughts on supporting Jewish students on campus:

- Include professionals from Jewish organizations on campus in campus training sessions. Hillel and Chabad professionals often are first responders to the issues students are facing; equipping them leads to better student support.
- Allow students to miss class for religious holidays.
- Do not schedule major campuswide programming or reunions on religious holidays.
- Offer kosher food in dining halls throughout campuses.
- Respond to anti-Semitism when it happens, and let students know that campus is not a place for any kind of hate, including hate toward religious groups.
- Make sure Jewish professionals and groups are included in programming regarding justice, faith, and diversity on campus.
- Participate in Jewish events on campus to build relationships with Jewish staff and students.

Additional Resources

- Anti-Defamation League, www.adl.org
- Chabad-Lubavitch Movement, www.chabad.org
- Hillel International, www.hillel.org
- Jewish Agency for Israel, www.jewishagency.org
- Jewish Council on Public Affairs, www.jewishpublicaffairs.org
- Jewish Federation of North America, www.jewishfederations.org
- My Jewish Learning, www.myjewishlearning.org

References

Cohen, M. & Cohen, M. (2015). *Millennial children of intermarriage: Touchpoints and trajectories of Jewish engagement.* Retrieved from https://www.brandeis.edu/cmjs/pdfs/intermarriage/MillennialChildrenIntermarriage1.pdf

Counting Jews of color in the United States: The changing nature of Jewish identity. (2018). Retrieved from http://www.bechollashon.org/population/north_america/na_color.php

Cousens, B. (2007). *Hillel's journey: Distinctively Jewish, universally human.* Washington, DC: Hillel.

Greenberg, I. (1968). Jewish survival and the college campus. *Judaism: A Quarterly of Jewish Life and Thought, 17,* 259–281.

Hillel International. (2016). *Measuring excellence: Summary of student outcomes findings.* Retrieved from https://www.rosovconsulting.com/wp-content/uploads/2016/12/Hillel-Measuring-Excellence-Student-Outcomes-Survey.pdf

Moore, D. D. (1981). *B'nai Brith and the challenge of ethnic leadership.* Albany, NY: SUNY Press.

Mulhere, K. (2015, February, 24). Campus anti-Semitism. *Inside Higher Ed,* Retrieved from https://www.insidehighered.com/news/2015/02/24/bias-reported-survey-jewish-college-students

Pew Research Center. (2013). *A portrait of Jewish Americans.* Retrieved from http://www.pewforum.org/2013/10/01/jewish-american-beliefs-attitudes-culture-survey/

Sarna, J. (2013). *Toward a comprehensive policy planning for Russian-speaking Jews in North America.* Retrieved from http://ejewishphilanthropy.com/wordpress/wp-content/uploads/2013/08/Toward_a_Comprehensive_Policy_Planning_for_Russian-Speaking_Jews_in_North_America.pdf

18

UNDERSTANDING SECULAR STUDENTS ON CAMPUS

Lyz Liddell and Nick Stancato

Americans who do not identify with organized religion are one of the largest, fastest-growing, and least-understood groups in our nation. The percentage of nonreligious individuals is even higher among younger generations, which means that higher education professionals' ability to support their students must include at least a basic understanding of this population. In this chapter, we present some of the different subgroups in the larger nonreligious demographic, discuss various intersectional identities and other factors that may influence students' engagement with their own identity, and identify trends in the typical experience for nonreligious students. Finally, we offer ways institutions and educators can provide better support for nonreligious students on campus.

Demographic Trends

The number of students who do not identify with any organized religion has grown tremendously in recent decades. According to the 2014 Pew Religious Landscape Survey (Wormald, 2015), nearly 23% of Americans are religiously unaffiliated, up from just 16% in 2007. Among Americans ages 18 to 29, an astounding 36% are religiously unaffiliated, with numbers leaning even higher among younger millennials. Other surveys report similar findings.

There is less research available on the nonreligious than for nearly any other worldview-identity group in the United States. This makes it difficult to learn about a rapidly growing, complex, diverse group of students. Further, many major surveys historically have tended to group all of the "nones" (individuals who indicate they are not affiliated with a religious tradition) into one mass category, obscuring significant differences and subgroups.

However, many distinctions in this group are worth considering. It is not the case that this entire demographic group is nontheistic in addition to nonreligious; some 40% claim they don't believe in a god, and 55% still maintain varying degrees of belief in a deity. More than two-thirds of this group neither prays nor attends religious services yet one-third does. Only a subset self-identifies with labels such as atheist (6%) or agnostic (7%). (The identity label question among the nonreligious and nontheists is contentious and is discussed later in this chapter.)

Major Groupings of the Nonreligious

Despite the complexity, several groupings can be helpful in understanding the nonreligious demographic. Although less formal than a national research poll, our experiences show that these groupings indicate shared experiences or perspectives that may be helpful in relating to nonreligious students on campus.

Self-Identification

Perhaps the most obvious way to place individuals in this demographic is by the label or identity they choose for themselves. Among those indicating "none," the larger group can be broken down into three major categories: intentionally secular (those who hold a salient nontheistic identity), spiritual but not religious (those who do not hold a religious affiliation but maintain a spiritual identity), and those for whom religious identity simply isn't salient. Although these categories are unlikely to appear in a Pew survey, they are helpful when considering approaches toward a given student.

In the first two of these categories, we can draw some additional distinctions. The *intentionally secular* is a complex group and typically includes individuals identifying as atheist, agnostic, Humanist, free thinking, secular, and even some satirical terms such as *pastafarian* (a lighthearted or satirical view of religion). It should be noted, that when used in this context, the term *secular* indicates a nonreligious, nontheistic worldview, rather than a preference for a society with separation of church and state. The degree of importance individuals place on their preferred worldview identity label varies, with some individuals freely using different labels in different contexts while others adamantly maintain a specific label and the nuances that go with it. For example, it may be fundamentally important to an individual identifying as agnostic that the question of a god's existence cannot be answered, and applying a determinative label such as atheist is depriving them of an aspect of their worldview identity. Other students may use the term *atheist* in casual conversation but prefer the term *humanist* in groups more familiar with secular terminology. As with other identity categories, student preference matters, and educators can learn a great deal about a student's self-identification by simply asking for and respecting the preferred terminology.

There are also helpful delineations in the *spiritual but not religious* group. Some individuals in this group use the term *spiritual* to refer to a soul, spirit, energy, or similar concept that transcends the natural and physical world. Others use the same term to refer to feelings of awe and wonder about life and the universe without any implication of supernatural or metaphysical occurrences; this latter group can be described as naturalist, indicating a belief system centered on the natural as opposed to the supernatural world. Understanding this distinction can be helpful when working with individuals in this identity group, as naturalistic people may be turned off by language referring to a metaphysical soul or practices they may regard as superstitious, whereas a more transcendent individual may find such language affirming and supportive.

Religious Background

Another way to understand nonreligious individuals is to consider their religious background and understand whether they have arrived at a nonreligious identity by way of leaving a religious worldview or whether they were raised independent of religion. The answer to this question can have a significant impact on a nonreligious person's perspective and needs, although, as always, it is important to remember these are just examples and that each individual's experiences will vary.

In college many students move away from the religion they were raised in, far more so than during high school or later in life. There are several reasons for this. College is often the first time students are fully autonomous, without their parents, offering the opportunity to experiment and explore identities they might not have experienced at home. Further, young people are being exposed to a plethora of new ideas and cultures in college, providing opportunities to reconsider assumptions and consider new perspectives.

Leaving religion can be a peaceful, smooth transition. Some may find they are able to retain relationships with religious family members, friends, and colleagues despite differences in worldviews. The program Openly Secular can facilitate these transitions by providing tools and resources for secular and religious individuals. Some nonreligious individuals even remain members of their religious community, valuing the benefits of such a community even though they may not share the theology.

For others, leaving a religion can be a difficult, emotionally trying experience. Family members who retain a religious perspective may be a source of conflict for an openly nonreligious individual, withholding emotional, financial, or other forms of support. Departure from a religious community may mean the loss of friendships and community support, a network critical to finding employment, and sometimes even separation from a spouse or domestic partner and children.

For students, departure from religion can lead to additional challenges. Holiday breaks may involve dealing with religious family members who berate or belittle them for their worldview or navigating situations where they are pressured or outright forced to participate in religious activities they do not find meaningful or may even experience as offensive or hurtful. A student adopting a secular worldview while attending a religious institution may face pervasive opposition from that institution and may find it extremely difficult to obtain ideological support or even ideologically compatible counseling services, particularly when spiritual guidance is delegated to a religious chaplain. Even on public campuses, however, students can struggle to find support for their nonreligious identity (Goodman & Mueller, 2009).

The religion an individual is leaving may also have a deep impact on that transition. A former student at the University of California–Irvine, Heina Dadabhoy was raised in a Muslim family whose observation of the tradition involved deep familial and community commitments. Those leaving a tradition with such commitments may have less flexibility and freedom to be open about their secular identity or a reduced ability to abstain from religious practices around their family (H. Dadabhoy, personal communication, August 30, 2016). Former Muslims in particular also may find themselves contending with the twin bigotries of hatred of Muslims and hostility toward atheists.

One way individuals may cope with potential conflict over a departure from religion is by withholding their secular identity. Responses to Secular Student Alliance surveys have provided some insight into this experience. For example, students attending college using a religious scholarship may have to hide their secular identity lest they lose the funding to continue their education, which was the case for one secular student at Portland State University, who remained anonymous throughout her interactions with the Secular Student Alliance. At religious institutions, secular individuals may fear—rightfully or not—that their worldview may result in their being ostracized or expelled, and they hide their worldview to avoid such repercussions. For several years, leaders of the secular student group at Baylor University operated entirely anonymously and underground out of fear of retaliatory expulsion by the university.

Although choosing not to disclose a secular identity may preclude some conflicts, it can create a stressful situation when people feel they are not able to freely express their identity or be true to who they are. They may still suffer some of the same familial pressures such as attending religious services or participating in prayers. They may also be subjected to attitudes dismissive or hostile to their worldview. For example, atheists are often portrayed as a threatening out-group in many conservative evangelical traditions.

An individual who was raised without religion likely has fewer of these challenges to navigate and may even deny the existence of those challenges when others report them. Individuals raised without religion may have a less salient secular identity than those who have moved away from religion, if the question of religion simply hasn't been important in their upbringing. Others may come from households with an intentionally secular worldview and as as a result may have a strong secular worldview.

Culture Versus Theology

Many religious traditions carry cultural elements that one can adhere to separate from the theological beliefs. Because U.S. culture is heavy with Christian influences, many Americans participate in activities or traditions that originated in religion regardless of the original theological intent. One of the most obvious examples is Christmas, which has been so thoroughly embedded in American culture that one might argue there are two separate versions of the same holiday: the religious observation of Jesus's birth, and the secular celebration with Santa and snowmen. Many nonreligious individuals observe such traditions as a by-product of their upbringing in a given culture.

For some, however, the cultural traditions of religious groups are particularly salient despite a nontheistic worldview. The most common example of this is a group generally referred to as "secular Jews" or "humanistic Jews," who are from a culturally Jewish background and have stepped back from the religious theology while maintaining a strong identity with the Jewish culture. Organizations like the Society for Humanistic Judaism provide support for local congregations and individuals holding this particular identity, and participants often still observe Jewish holidays and traditions.

This combination of identities leads to complicated interactions with some of the more common nonreligious groups. Northwestern University alumna Miri Mogilevsky found herself alienated in college as a secular Jew because secular student activism and dialogue at her institution focused on arguing against Christianity and debating Christians. Not coming from a Christian background, she found the conversations largely irrelevant and "was more interested in doing what many secular Jews focus on doing, which is building community, creating traditions, and developing secular ethics" (M. Mogilevsky, personal communication, August 30, 2016). The focus of secular student groups differs from one educational institution to another, and may differ from year to year at a single institution. As demonstrated by Miri's example, the intersection of the focus of the group and an individual's religious and cultural beliefs can be complex.

Nonreligious Versus Antireligious

It is a common assumption and stereotype that nonreligious individuals (and particularly atheists) are antireligious. The reasons for this assumption are complex, and an analysis of the many myths about nonreligious individuals is beyond the scope of this book. For the purposes of this chapter, it suffices to raise awareness of the stereotype.

Nonreligious individuals may in fact have the opinion that religion is harmful, particularly if they have witnessed or experienced conflict or harm in the name of religion and may engage in activism. But to attribute this opinion to all nonreligious individuals, or even a subset, would be an unfair application of a harmful stereotype that such individuals already endure. Furthermore, many secular and nonreligious individuals want to engage positively across lines of religious identity and find being in relationship with and learning from religious members of their community to be valuable and important.

Intersectional Identities

Higher education professionals are well aware that no identity exists in a vacuum. The intersections of an individual's worldview identity and other identities are as complex as any other intersection. However, a few specific identity interactions are noteworthy.

Research on the decline of religion among younger generations suggests that one of the leading reasons young people are leaving religion is the negative attitudes toward lesbian, gay, bisexual, transgender, and queer (LGBTQ) individuals of religious organizations (Cox, Navarro-Rivera, & Jones, 2014). Separate research points to a higher percentage of atheists among those who identify as LGBTQ than among the population as a whole, particularly among younger generations (Becker & Brazelton, 2013; Pew Research Center, 2013). However, support for secular individuals in organized LGBTQ activism is often lacking. For example, a prominent LGBTQ conference in 2016 included 21 programs related to specific religious traditions, but only 3 related to secular identities (Creating Change Conference, 2016). Author and activist Greta Christina (2008) reflects a common sentiment among LGBTQ atheists when she said that she feels more at home as "as a queer in the atheist community than . . . as an atheist in the queer community" (para. 6). Atheist student activist Rukia Brooks (2015) further proclaims that she has felt more comfortable as a trans woman in her school's Secular Student Alliance than the Gay Student Alliance.

The intersection of Black and secular identities can be similarly complex. According to Pew Research statistics, about 80% of Black Americans identify strongly as religious, particularly Christian (Pew Research Center, 2015). Given the historical role the church has played in the Black community, it is particularly challenging for African Americans to openly identify as atheist. African Americans identifying as secular risk being ostracized by loved ones and also being stigmatized as a traitor to the community. Mandisa Thomas, president of Black Nonbelievers, said people can be seen as rejecting their Blackness by being atheist (M. Thomas, personal communication, August 26, 2016).

By being aware of the complex identity intersections described in this section, student affairs practitioners can be better prepared to support students with those identities. When attempting to understand the campus climate for secular students, it is especially important to understand the experience of those who identify as LGBT or Black, in addition to being secular.

Effects of Environment on Secular Identity Salience

Prevailing cultural attitudes can have a significant impact on the importance of an individual's secular identity. In areas with higher proportions of nonreligious individuals, someone with a nonreligious identity can often feel like it's not a big deal or as though everyone thinks like he or she does. Nonreligious individuals in these environments may be more likely to identify as spiritual but not religious or simply as part of those indicating "none." They may seek to distance themselves from religious traditions they find distasteful, such as anti-LGBT sentiment, but otherwise see themselves as normal rather than needing to adopt a secular identity label to differentiate themselves from a theistic norm.

However, in environments where religion is more common or publicly visible, often in more conservative, rural, or southern parts of the country, a nonreligious identity becomes more salient in contrast to the surrounding religiosity. Research predicting commonality of secular groups supports this observation, noting that a higher percentage of evangelical Protestants in a county can predict a higher presence of organized nonbelievers as well (García & Blankholm, 2016). One interpretation of these findings is that higher social pressure to be religious may cause nonreligious individuals to more intentionally form a community in response. Ostracism of secular individuals in these types of communities can also be common and vitriolic: Lamar University student Amber Barnhill was ostracized, bullied, threatened, and even lost her job for her defense of nonreligious identities (A. Barnhill, personal communication, September 30, 2016).

Obviously, different environments can affect nonreligious students. The student's home environment could have an influence on the student's self-identification, as described previously in this chapter. Also, because of the relative religiosity of a campus climate, students who may not have a particularly observable secular identity at home may find themselves more strongly cleaving to an identity at an institution where religiosity is pervasive.

To illustrate, take the case of the nonreligious student at a religious institution. The student may have chosen the institution for its academic programs or for financial factors (parental support, scholarships, etc.) regardless of its affiliation. It is also common for students to begin college at a religious institution that matches their worldview only to move away from that religious identity during their college experience. Students in this situation may feel pressure to hide their secular identity. If open about their worldview, they may struggle to find support among their peers or from the institution because of their differences in belief.

Some religiously affiliated institutions do not allow nonreligious students to formally organize. For example, the University of Notre Dame and Baylor University have both repeatedly denied recognition for secular student groups (Grasgreen, 2012), and some religious institutions threaten nonreligious students with expulsion (Zavadski, 2015). Notably, many religiously affiliated institutions allow secular students to attend and form intentional communities at the institution, and in varying ways they support secular student identity development. Institutions such as California Lutheran University and Colgate University are strong examples (Mehta, 2011; Supiano, 2011).

Stereotypes and Challenges

It is likely not a bold statement to say that America is a nation that privileges Christianity and its followers. Less visible but perhaps even more pervasive is an underlying privilege of those who hold any god belief; that is, the assumption that everyone has some kind of theistic belief even if the details vary from individual to individual. This favoring of theism can be seen in countless ways, from saying bless you when someone sneezes to prayers at commencements and sporting events to the fact that we generally recognize the validity of allowing individuals flexibility for religious observances but balk at offering the same for an unspecified personal reason.

This *theonormativism*, like any societal privilege, can have unintended negative consequences for the nonreligious. Foremost among these concerns is the erasure of secular identities in the public sphere, depriving nonreligious individuals of societal affirmation of their worldview. A heavy normalization of theism also contributes to a perception that nontheism is wrong, aberrant, or deviant, reinforcing stereotypes and discrimination faced by the nonreligious.

Nonreligious individuals are subject to a wide variety of stereotypes about their worldview, most of them negative. During an activity about stereotypes at an Interfaith Youth Core leadership institute, a brainstorming session resulted in the following words associated with the term *atheism*: *jaded, cynical, godless, reactionary, angry, crazy, protest, narrow, fear, confused, antireligion,* and *know-it-all* (alongside some more supportive terms including *brilliant, awareness of mortality, sure, rationalist,* and *confidence*). In comparison, in the same exercise, *agnosticism* produced the terms *indecisive, noncommittal, searching, open, confused, unsure,* and *spiritual,* whereas *humanism* resulted in *affirming, utilitarianism, morals, ethical, compassionate, organized,* and *peaceful*. Other common stereotypes are that nonreligious people lack a moral compass, hate religion or religious people, or are suffering some trauma that resulted in their lack of belief. Students in particular are often assumed to be going through a phase because of their young age.

The nonreligious also face various stigma and discriminatory behaviors based on their worldview, including social ostracism, coercion, slander, general social disapproval, and being "outed" against their will by others (Hammer, Cragun, Hwang, & Smith, 2012, p. 12). Some of these forms of coercion are unique to a nonreligious perspective, such as being forced to swear religious oaths for public office or jury duty, being subjected to prayer or chaplain visits in hospitals, and being expected to participate in religious prayers or services. These factors can contribute to stress and stress-related health concerns just like any other persistent discrimination.

Difficulties on Campus

Nonreligious students on campus may find themselves an odd fit with respect to campus services and programming. Although many institutions endeavor to accommodate a variety of worldviews, the nonreligious often slip through the cracks or do not feel welcome in existing programs. Part of this is a consequence of a kind of language barrier because the words typically used to discuss worldview identities are drawn from a theonormative position. Words and phrases like *interfaith* and *spiritual life* are not necessarily terms that appeal to a nonreligious student. A campus may have nondenominational chaplain services, but regardless of the willingness of the chaplain to serve nonreligious students, nonreligious students often do not feel a religiously affiliated chaplain can meet their worldview-related needs. However, there is an exception: A small number of institutions in the United States have Humanist chaplains among their programmatic offerings. Perhaps the most visible of them is Greg Epstein, the Humanist chaplain at Harvard University, whose long-standing, successful program has served as a model for other Humanist chaplaincies.

A related challenge for nonreligious students on campus involves the question of organizing student groups. There are several hundred organized student groups at college campuses throughout the United States, but in many cases these groups struggle to find support and belonging on campus. Even at institutions without a religious affiliation, student governments or administrators have blocked groups affiliated with the Secular Student Alliance from forming. This reaction is more common at religious campuses (Winston, 2011), although, as noted earlier, some religious campuses are highly supportive of secular student groups. Once recognized, such groups may struggle to find the appropriate classification. Is an organization dedicated to nonreligious students a religious organization, or is it something else? When categorized with other religious groups, the organization may miss out on potential members as nonreligious students skip over the entire section of religious organizations, whereas a classification separate from religious groups can exclude such organizations from worldview-related opportunities, such as participation in interfaith programs.

Students with an intentionally secular identity have an advocate at the national level in the Secular Student Alliance, an educational nonprofit specializing in organizing and supporting secular students (learn more at www .secularstudents.org). This organization is a resource for students, educators, institutional staff, and administrators, and is a valuable source of information and advocacy related to secular students.

Recommendations for Educators

Regardless of your own worldview identity or your position on campus, there are several things you can to do make your campus a more supportive environment for nonreligious students, faculty, and staff. Some are simple matters of language and inclusivity, and others are more substantial projects that may require resources and administrative support to implement.

Language can be a major factor in setting the tone of an environment for any marginalized group, and the nonreligious are no different. Simply remembering to include *nonreligious* when listing identity groups, or adapting phrases such as *people of all faiths* to *people of all faiths and no faith* (However, beware of implications of variations on this constructions, such as the well-intentioned but disparaging phrase *people of all value systems and no value systems*). In his inaugural address, President Barack Obama (2009) described America as "a nation of Christians and Muslims, Jews and Hindus, and non-believers" (para. 21), the first presidential acknowledgment of secular individuals on record. The secular community cheered and cried; it was a momentous sign that its members were welcome as part of the fabric of the country.

Beyond language, you may endeavor to advocate specifically on behalf of the nonreligious members of your institution. Many nonreligious people have found that speaking up on their own behalf results in harassment, bullying, or ostracism, and allies can be few and far between. Advocacy is particularly important if you have a religious identity. Religious allies are powerful voices for the nonreligious, just as men are necessary advocates for women's rights, White people have a role in conversations about race, and straight cisgender folks stand up for their LGBTQ brethren. Examples of this kind of advocacy might include asking how nonreligious students might participate in interfaith programming; ensuring that options for nonreligious students are included in campus identity surveys; and including nonreligious perspectives in materials such as campus brochures, orientation materials, and student and staff training materials.

Whether simply including the nonreligious in your language or advocating for nonreligious inclusion on relevant issues, you will help overcome a larger societal factor: the invisibility of the nonreligious. Atheism has long been seen as a societal taboo, a subject inappropriate for polite company. One of us attended an interfaith gathering in which a participant struggled to even utter the word atheist, much less use it as someone's preferred identity label. Speaking up and including the nonreligious in your conversations helps reduce the invisibility of this demographic, combat stigma and marginalization, and normalize nonreligious identities.

Another way you are uniquely positioned to provide support for nonreligious students is by staying alert for instances of harassment, bullying, or threats on your campus and taking such threats seriously when they arise. Most campuses would take swift action after reports of a Black student union's flyers being defaced and destroyed or threats against a Hillel group; however, reports of these types of behaviors against nonreligious students are often dismissed, trivialized, buried under red tape, or similarly mishandled, according to student responses to Secular Student Alliance surveys. Flyer vandalism is so common that the Secular Student Alliance has a section on its website specifically dedicated to handling it and includes ways to respond if the administration chooses to ignore the problem. Having a staff or faculty member corroborate the incident can go a long way to these issues being taken seriously and addressed by your institution.

Professionals who have the power to do so should consider creating spaces on campus that are intentionally welcoming and accessible to secular students. One way to do this is to find spaces on your campus intended for use by all students but may have names that deter nonreligious students, such as a spiritual life center. Simply renaming these spaces can go a long way toward sending a message of inclusivity, using terms like *meaning-making*, *worldview*, and *life stance*, among others. Alternatively, you might create spaces specific to nonreligious students, such as reflection centers, reading rooms stocked with resources on secular worldviews, or similar spaces. If your campus doesn't already have a student organization for secular students, consider starting or encouraging one.

Another option is to consider is programming that intentionally appeals to nonreligious students. Although nonreligious students don't share one single observance the way religious students might, there are many opportunities to create events that are likely to resonate with nonreligious students and perhaps also religious students, such as a winter solstice celebration, Darwin Day (February 12), Carl Sagan Day (November 9), and many others (see www.secularseasons.org). If your campus hosts National Day of Prayer activities, consider also providing activities for the concurrent National Day of Reason, or combine the two into an interfaith Day of Service.

A particular area where nonreligious students' needs often go unmet is in crisis or trauma. In the wake of personal difficulty, natural disasters, or campus-shattering events (e.g., student suicides or campus violence), religious students have a wealth of supportive activities to choose from: candlelight services, prayer vigils, spiritual counseling, and the like. Public ceremonies, particularly for mourning, are also heavily laden with religious language, ritual, and references. Nonreligious students in these situations often struggle to find support consistent with their worldview and can find religious appeals stressful and adding to their distress rather than helping to resolve it. There is a tremendous opportunity here for the education of mental health professionals and campus response efforts, but at the very least, creating safe, supportive spaces for nonreligious students to respond to and reflect on these situations is a much-needed first step.

Additional Resources

The following are campus-based secular organizations:

- Secular Student Alliance and its Secular Safe Zone project, secularstudents.org, www.secularsafezone.org
- Openly Secular, focuses on supporting the nonreligious while maintaining social relationships with friends and family, www.openlysecular .org

The following are national nonprofit organizations:

- American Atheists, www.atheists.org
- American Humanist Association, www.americanhumanist.org
- Center for Inquiry, www.centerforinquiry.net

The following are some specific support networks:

- Black Nonbelievers, www.blacknonbelievers.wordpress.com
- Ex-Muslims of North America, www.exmna.org
- Hispanic-American Freethinkers, www.hafree.org/en
- Society for Humanistic Judaism, www.shj.org

References

Becker, B. K., & Brazelton, B. (2013, March). *Creating safe spaces at the intersection: atheist/non-religious LGBTQ students.* Sponsored session presented at the American College Personnel Association 2013 Annual Convention, Las Vegas, NV.

Brooks, R. (2015, June 10). It was through the Secular Student Alliance that I found a voice [Web log post]. Retrieved from http://the-orbit.net/greta/2015/06/10/it-was-through-the-secular-student-alliance-that-i-found-a-voice-guest-post-by-rukia-brooks-for-ssa-week/

Christina, G. (2008, December 16). Being an atheist in the queer community [Web log post]. Retrieved from http://the-orbit.net/greta/2008/12/15/being-an-atheist-in-the-queer-community

Creating Change Conference: Advancing LGBTQ Liberation. (2016). Retrieved from https://www.creatingchange.org/wp-content/uploads/2016/01/cc16_program _1_4_16.pdf

Cox, D., Navarro-Rivera, J., & Jones, R. P. (2014, February 26). *A shifting landscape: A decade of change in American attitudes about same-sex marriage and LGBT issues.* Retrieved from http://www.prri.org/research/2014-lgbt-survey/

García, A., & Blankholm, J. (2016). The social context of organized nonbelief: County-level predictors of nonbeliever organizations in the United States. *Journal for the Scientific Study of Religion, 55*(1), 70–90. doi:10.1111/jssr.12250

Goodman, K. M., & Mueller, J. A. (2009). Invisible, marginalized, and stigmatized: Understanding and addressing the needs of atheist students. *New Directions for Student Services,* 125, 55–63. doi:10.1002/ss.308

Grasgreen, A. (2012, March 19). Atheist, on a religious campus. *Inside Higher Ed.* Retrieved from https://www.insidehighered.com/news/2012/03/19/atheist-secular-students-becoming-established-religious-campuses

Hammer, J. H., Cragun, R. T., Hwang, K., & Smith, J. M. (2012). Forms, frequency, and correlates of perceived anti-atheist discrimination. *Secularism and Nonreligion,* 1, 43–67. Retrieved from https://secularismandnonreligion.org/articles/abstract/10.5334/snr.ad/

Mehta, H. (2011, December 1). *New campus atheist group at Colgate.* Retrieved from http://www.patheos.com/blogs/friendlyatheist/2011/12/01/new-campus-atheist-group-at-colgate/

Obama, B. H. (2009). President Barack Obama's inaugural address. Retrieved from https://www.whitehouse.gov/blog/2009/01/21/president-barack-obamas-inaugural-address

Pew Research Center. (2013). *A survey of LGBT Americans.* Retrieved from http://www.pewsocialtrends.org/2013/06/13/a-survey-of-lgbt-americans/7/

Pew Research Center. (2015). *Religious landscape study.* Retrieved from http://www.pewforum.org/religious-landscape-study/racial-and-ethnic-composition/black/

Supiano, B. (2011, February 27). A group for secular students finds its way on a Christian campus. *Chronicle of Higher Education.* Retrieved from https://www.chronicle.com/article/A-Group-for-Secular-Students/126518

Winston, K. (2011, November 4). At religious campuses, atheist groups operate underground. *USA Today.* Retrieved from http://usatoday30.usatoday.com/news/religion/story/2011-11-04/atheist-college-campus/51073822/1

Wormald, B. (2015). *Religious landscape study.* Retrieved from http://www.pewforum.org/religious-landscape-study/age-distribution/

Zavadski, K. (2015, March 31). Lose your faith, get expelled at BYU. *Daily Beast.* Retrieved from https://www.thedailybeast.com/lose-your-faith-get-expelled-at-byu

19

UNDERSTANDING BUDDHIST, SIKH, AND HINDU STUDENTS ON CAMPUS

Upali Sraman, Rahuldeep Singh Gill, and Varun Soni

Although they are represented in smaller populations at colleges and universities, Buddhist, Sikh, and Hindu students are active and often quite visible on U.S. campuses. In this chapter, members of these communities speak about the particular experiences of Buddhist (by Upali Sraman), Sikh (by Rahuldeep Singh Gill), and Hindu (by Varun Soni) students. It is important to note that although scholars situate these traditions in the broader concept of religion, Eastern religions can often look quite different from Western traditions. Concepts and practices do not always adhere to culturally Western assumptions about religion. Professionals should take particular care not to make assumptions about what it means to be religious, particularly in regard to traditions whose beliefs and practices can be quite diverse.

Buddhist Students

Buddhism on American college campuses can have many forms. Although Buddhism has historical roots in Asian countries and cultures, a growing number of North American converts have adopted Buddhist practices and identities, complicating the picture of what it means to be a Buddhist today. Buddhists represent about 7% of the world's population (Pew Research Center, 2010). As far as Buddhists in the United States, the Pew Research Center (2014) states that Buddhists account for 0.7% of the national population. However, significant concerns with Pew's methodology have been raised, and it is likely that the actual percentage of Buddhists in America is between 1.0% and 1.3% (Pew Research Center, 2015). According to the Interfaith Diversity Experiences and Attitudes Longitudinal Survey, self-described Buddhists were 1.6% of the entering first-year class in fall 2015 (Mayhew et al., 2016).

The following is an overview of diversity in the Buddhist tradition, including common ethical beliefs and practices, to guide educators as they seek to support Buddhist students on campuses across the country.

Diversity of Buddhist Traditions

Like most religious traditions, Buddhism is internally diverse; which is reflected in the countries where Buddhists live across the globe, in what they consider to be their principal scriptural texts; and in their cultural, ritualistic, and spiritual or contemplative practices. In North America too, Buddhist immigrants from these different countries tend to retain their distinct identity and practices, often intent on authentically passing down their religious, cultural, and linguistic heritage to children growing up in North America.

Educators need to be cognizant of this diversity to avoid making assumptions about particular practices. Because of the tremendous popularity of His Holiness the Dalai Lama, many are more familiar with Tibetan Buddhism than the other Buddhist traditions. However, what is generally referred to as Tibetan Buddhism (or Vajrayāna) has many subdenominations that are typically practiced in the Himalayan regions of Tibet, Bhutan, Mongolia, India, Nepal, and China. Although it is not essential to understand these distinctions, it is important to be aware that Vajrayāna is distinct from Mahāyāna (more prominent in China, Japan, South Korea, Laos, Vietnam, Hong Kong, Singapore, Malaysia, and Taiwan) and Theravāda (prominent in Sri Lanka, Thailand, Myanmar, Cambodia, Bangladesh, and India).

All these traditions accept the authority of the Shakyamuni Gautama as the historical Buddha (tentatively dated c. 563 or c. 480 BCE; scholars do not have a unanimously accepted date), whose teachings laid the foundation for Buddhism in North India. It must be emphasized that the Buddha is not an equivalent of God. All traditions of Buddhism accept many buddhas who existed in the past. The teachings of the Buddha are referred to as the *dharma*, a multivalent term sometimes translated as the *truth* or *law*. The community of Buddhist followers is referred to as *sangha*. In each of these traditions, the concept of the Buddha, his teachings (the *dharma*), and the contemplative practices have undergone significant development over 2,500 years of transmission and practice.

This internal diversity can be attributed to the mutual influences of interpretations of Buddhism and the cultures that practice the tradition. The diversity of Buddhist traditions demonstrates the many ways people engage with Buddhist texts and ideas for individual and collective moral transformation. The distinctive differences among the traditions are palpable in day-to-day life (Gyatso & Chodron, 2014; Strong, 2015).

Ethical Principles

Despite the differences among Buddhist traditions, there are common ethical values that all Buddhists are encouraged to follow. Very simply stated, Buddhists are encouraged to avoid or refrain from morally harmful conduct, to develop wholesome habits and attitudes, and to purify and cultivate the mind. The devotional and contemplative practices in Buddhism are oriented toward cultivating a better understanding of oneself and one's activities. The very basic standard of ethical values in all Buddhist traditions is subsumed in the five precepts (*pañcasīla*) of refraining from harming living beings, refraining from taking what is not given, refraining from engaging in sexual misconduct, refraining from speaking falsehoods (including distortion of truth, harsh speech, inappropriate gossip), and refraining from consuming alcohol. Although these practices are to be avoided, Buddhist followers are encouraged to develop positive and wholesome qualities of benevolence, compassion, wisdom, and so forth (Hanh, 1998; Gyatso & Chodron, 2014).

In some Mahāyāna traditions, followers aspiring to become *bodhisattvas* (compassionate beings dedicated to serving the world) also take additional vows. Past buddhas and bodhisattvas are regarded as exemplars for serving the world with great compassion and wisdom. These religious figures also demonstrate that every person is capable of achieving ethical perfection and awakening, transcending egoistic limitations, and serving others altruistically by coming to realize that everything in the universe is interconnected and interdependent. Therefore, all beings have an ethical responsibility to safeguard each other by developing good qualities and actively caring for others in whatever ways possible. In particular, the practice of generosity through giving gifts, comforting others, or providing physical support is very prominent in all Buddhist traditions.

Buddhism is also known for having strong values of equality. The earliest recorded Buddhist texts denounce discrimination of people based on such traits as their family of birth, gender, color, race, region, and so on. Therefore, every person, in fact every sentient being, is regarded with dignity and respect, as one would regard oneself. All these values have inspired Buddhist social and environmental activists in modern times.

Observance

Buddhist monks and nuns have prescribed codes and rules of conduct according to their distinctive monastic denominations. There are no such strict religious injunctions for lay people regarding their dress and food. Although vegetarianism is generally preferred by many Buddhists, not all Buddhists are vegetarian. Buddhist shrines or places of worship typically contain images of the Buddha and his disciples. Māhayāna and Tibetan temples may also have images of various bodhisattvas and protector deities. Monastic members are regarded as respected figures in their community and are greeted with special terms of respect, typically translated as *venerable* in English.

The scriptural canon in Buddhism is as diverse as the Buddhist traditions themselves and is available in various languages such as Pāli, Sanskrit, Chinese, and Tibetan. Buddhists in different countries also have versions of these texts in their vernacular languages and use these texts for worship and liturgical practices. The Theravāda liturgical text is known as Paritta, or Book of Protection, and is composed of selected discourses or sutras of the Buddha. Mahāyāna liturgies contain eulogies and aspirations of the bodhisattvas. "The Heart of the Wisdom Sūtra" (*Prajñāpāramitā-hrdaya sūtra*) is also very popular among all forms of Mahāyāna and Vajrayāna Buddhism. All the Buddhist traditions have developed extensive contemplative techniques for developing compassion and wisdom; Theravāda followers are widely known for *vipassanā* (insight meditation), Mahāyānists following Zen (or Chan in Chinese) for *zazen*, and Vajrayāna or Tibetan Buddhists for *dzogchen* and various tantric visualization practices.

Buddhist students on college campuses may require access to a space that can be used as a shrine for regular ceremonies or for particular practices, including chanting, meditation, and other forms of worship. Some students prefer to keep shrines in their residences, which requires a clean and quiet space (separate from a kitchen or bathroom). Student affairs professionals should engage with Buddhist students to be sure they have the necessary space and resources to practice their tradition in the campus community. To prevent reducing this rich and incredibly diverse religion into any single practice, it is important to talk with all Buddhist students rather than implementing change based on any single student's interpretation of Buddhism.

Religious Festivals and Ceremonies

Each of the Buddhist traditions has its own distinct religious festivals. Generally, however, days of the full moon are regarded as more sacred, and each of these days has some connection to significant events in the life of the Buddha. The most significant of them is the Vesak Full Moon, which typically falls in May or June, marking the birth, enlightenment, and death (Parinirvāna) of the Buddha (Saka Dawa in Tibetan Buddhism). However, the exact date differs based on the calendars various Buddhists use. This festival marks an occasion to recollect the Buddha's life story and contemplate his teachings to enhance one's ethical life. In addition to sermons and speeches by monks and participants, cultural and artistic performances based on an event from Buddha's life are also common.

The Ullambana or Hungry Ghost Festival celebrates the joy of liberating beings from inferior realms and is a major ceremony in all the Mahāyāna traditions. In addition to this major festival, smaller ceremonies of ancestor worship are also prominent in all forms of Buddhism. Based on their cultural and geographical closeness to other religions, Buddhists also may participate in non-Buddhist festivals and ceremonies. For example, South Asian Buddhists may participate in Diwali (Festival of Lights) celebrations, although they are commonly understood as a Hindu holiday; Japanese Buddhists may celebrate holidays that are typically understood as Shinto, Confucian, or Taoist in origin.

These are important cultural experiences that international students may miss in United States. Students on U.S. campuses may wish to celebrate these ceremonies in the campus community or with local Buddhist temples or other communities. Student affairs professionals should help students seek connections with the local Buddhist community whenever it seems to be a good fit for a student.

Buddhism in the North American Context

In North America it is generally assumed that Buddhism exists in two primary modes: first, as a practice among the Asian immigrant population, and second, as a practice among non-Asian Americans (Prebish, 1979; Seager, 2012). However, this picture is incomplete as it discounts the experience of second-generation children who are strongly Buddhist, strongly Asian and American, but are not immigrants. Asian immigrants, in particular, are often intent on retaining and transmitting their cultural heritage to their children born here. Asian American college students may feel caught between two cultures: American in public and Asian at home. Because of these pressures, some of the ritualistic practices may be a cause of embarrassment for some, depending on the reactions of their non-Buddhist peers. At the same time, many young people take great pride in their cultural heritage. Educational institutions have the opportunity to support students as they celebrate their distinct cultural and religious identities free from embarrassment or ridicule.

Non-Asian Buddhists, by contrast, are often primarily interested in the Buddhist meditative practices such as mindfulness. The increasing popularity of mindfulness as a remedy for various psychological and physical challenges draws people of different religious backgrounds to Buddhism, many of whom take up Buddhist identity by conversion. These meditative practices are adapted to suit the North American context; meditation centers, rather than Buddhist temples, have become more prominent in the United States. Mindfulness practices are conducted in secular spaces like schools, hospitals, and even in the headquarters of World Bank and Google. Traditional Buddhists do welcome the use of mindfulness for physical and psychological benefits, but in such secular adaptations, practitioners are expected to be sensitive to and respectful of the religious roots of the Buddhist practices.

There are no superior or inferior forms of Buddhism. Asian Buddhists, whether immigrants or American born, should not be fetishized, and individuals should refrain from telling others how Buddhists are supposed to be. Buddhist terms like *karma* or *Zen* should not be used inappropriately to refer to Buddhists in a manner that objectifies their Buddhism. Instead, in matters related to religious and cultural identity and practices, individuals in positions of power should admit their limited understanding of Buddhism with an open mind and an expression of curiosity to support the needs of the students.

Additional Resources

- Buddhist Churches of America, www. buddhistchurchesofamerica.org
- Buddhist Education and Information Network, www.buddhanet.net
- Daily Buddhism: Plain English Guide to Buddhism, www.daily buddhism.com
- *Journal of Global Buddhism*, www.globalbuddhism.org

Sikh Students

Sikh students are those who have some affiliation with Sikhi (also known as Sikhism), a 500-year-old monotheistic tradition from Punjab, a borderland of Pakistan and India. Sikhi professes obedience to 10 Gurus, religiopolitical guides who lived in succession between 1469 and 1708. Most Sikhs live their life in accordance with the teachings of these guides as enshrined in the Guru Granth Sahib, a 1,430-page anthology of divine revelations in poetry form, some written by authors who are premodern Hindu and Muslim poets from the subcontinent. Sikh houses of worship are called *gurdwaras*, and these form the base institutions for Sikh communities that have been established outside of Punjab (Mann, Numrich, & Williams, 2001). Although accurate numbers are difficult to acquire, there are probably currently between 250,000 and 750,000 Sikhs in the United States (Pew Research Center, 2012).

Foundational Knowledge

This diverse population may include graduate students from India working in labs at research-intensive institutions, commuters from agricultural towns at California State universities, children of non-Asian converts to Sikhism, or practitioners of hybrid religiosities from interfaith families. Most students in this category are likely to be ethnic South Asians whose parents or grandparents emigrated from Punjab. At some colleges there may be no Sikhs, one, or a few. Large public institutions might have a robust Sikh Students Association, a Bhangra (Punjabi cultural dance) team, and strong Sikh participation in South Asian student clubs.

Because the early Sikh movement rejected the religious practices of its South Asian context, Sikhs are often less concerned about dietary restrictions and prayer accommodations than practitioners of other faiths. One major caveat to this general trend is that many Sikhs interpret adherence to a vegetarian diet as part of their faith. A more widely regarded Sikh practice calls for adherents to keep their hair unshorn and tidy in a *dastar* (turban that many Sikh men and some Sikh women wear) or under a *dupatta* (head scarf, which some Sikh women wear). This practice of uncut hair (*kesh*) is one of the five commands given by Guru Gobind Singh, which also includes carrying a wooden brush for the hair (*kangha*), wearing a metal bracelet (*kara*), wearing a particular undergarment (*kachera*), and carrying a small sword (*kirpan*). Each of these practices carries deep religious meaning for Sikhs who chose to follow them (Singh, 2014). However, many students who identify as Sikhs do not adhere to these practices.

Sikh holidays commemorate the life events of the Gurus and their families, the most important being the birth celebration of the first Guru, Baba Nanak, in November and elevation of the Sikh people to the Khalsa (sovereign community) in April (an event called Vaisakhi). Sikh celebrations often coincide with other South Asian festivals like Diwali, yet they take on a different socioreligious identity in the Sikh community.

Sikhs who follow the practice of turban tying have been the victims of hate crimes and violence across the United States. According to the Sikh Coalition (2016), a civil rights organization, Sikhs are a thousand times more likely to suffer hate crimes than the typical U.S. citizen, and at least nine Sikh Americans have been killed in hate violence since 2001. The turban is one of the strongest markers of Sikh identity, and for centuries, convincing others of an independent Sikh identity has created anxiety for many Sikhs. In communities of Sikhs, this can manifest as concern about maintaining the correct practice or facing the judgment of family, friends, and acquaintances. Sikh youths in the West spend considerable energy trying to differentiate what is essential to Sikh identity and what influences in their lives can be relegated to family norms or culture.

Common Cultural Values

Sikhs are members of a religious community that is a minority everywhere except for a few hundred square miles in northwest India. Sikhs stand out from the fold because of their hair and headwear practices. Practitioners who choose to forgo these practices face judgment and condemnation from others, whereas those who do adhere to these practices may be considered backward by more assimilated members of the community. Educators who are dealing with Sikh students in conflict or challenging situations should appreciate the considerable pressures that religious identity, practice commitments, and family obligations place on members of this population.

Family, Gender, and Sexuality

Perhaps the most pressing concerns emerge from the South Asian, specifically Punjabi, culture practiced in Sikh households. Students often see their Sikh faith as deeply egalitarian but experience conflict with strong constraints their families place on them to adhere to family norms, especially hierarchical relationships of elders over the young, men over women, and family over outsiders. Sikh women students may bear particularly grueling transitions in their personal development as they are trying to stake their own ground as independent, educated adults.

Women's issues related to the maintenance of hair do not receive the same attention that men's do, but the challenges are no less daunting. For example, women in the community are asked to be brave supporters of turbaned males' tribulations, whereas their own negotiations with religious practice go unnoticed. Women may face stigma on how they choose to groom themselves, and this may come from Sikhs as well as non-Sikhs (Kaur & Singh, 2014). Higher education practitioners can use active listening techniques and mirroring to empower Sikh women and men to understand the particular predicaments that complexities of gender identity place on individuals.

Sikh life places great emphasis on marriage and monogamy and idealizes the family unit. Although the norm of nuptials arranged completely by family is no longer as severe an expectation as it was for past generations, many traditional assumptions about marriage persist. Therefore, young Sikhs often bear expectations of establishing career credentials so they can launch monogamous heterosexual relationships with other Punjabi-Sikhs of comparable socioeconomic backgrounds. In Sikh practice, the very act of wedding two individuals parallels the soul's ascent to union with the divine.

Although young Sikh Americans are themselves generally very accepting of diverse sexual orientations, issues on sexuality are fraught with heightened anxieties around religious, cultural, and familial obligations. Higher education professionals should understand that minority religious practitioners like Sikhs might need extra support to work out issues related to their own sexuality, as well as those of people in their social networks. Open discourse about sexualities is not a public norm in Sikh society, where diverse sexual orientations can often be shunned, ridiculed, or ignored. Theologically, radical Sikh acceptance of diverse social status and promotion of gender equality are values that contemporary Sikhs leverage in movements toward acceptance of sexual identities.

Social Class

Punjabi Sikhs are largely a successful immigrant community in the United States, but this success has come with personal costs. Not all Sikhs enjoy the upper-middle-class life of their coreligionists, and some may face the added stigma of what it means to succeed in life. These play heavy roles in career choices as well as in decisions about a proper course of study, which academic advisers and other student life practitioners should be aware of when working with Sikh students.

Many Sikhs glorify hard work as one of the pillars of Sikh life, which can be magnified by the social pressures of success in immigrants. What that means in a neoliberal global society has not been parsed by the community. Students need time and space to understand their own callings while examining the source of specific demands on their time and future plans. Sincerity of intentions and ethical obligation to the common good are more theologically grounded principles, according to Sikh normative teachings, than pressures to work hard.

Race and Ethnicity

To be a Sikh in the West is not just to belong to a religious, or even cultural, category of people. It is also a highly racialized existence, marked by ethnic difference and religious obligations that out one as different from the mainstream. That is to say, for Sikh students negotiating their religious difference from the majority society, they are simultaneously experiencing issues of racial, ethnic, and cultural stigmatization. For example, observant Sikhs of South Asian heritage are visually different ethnically and also because of their turban and hair practices.

The pressures Sikh students face may lead to differing relationships with people of White, South Asian, or Middle Eastern descent. Surprising alliances or divisions can manifest themselves based on group identity. On some campuses, Sikh students have cosponsored antihate programming with Muslim student groups. On others, the solidarity of Sikhs with the cause of Palestinians has made Sikhs ignore the plight that Jewish students face with anti-Semitism.

Relationships with Hindu peers and superiors may be particularly fraught with challenges because of the complex history that Sikhs and Hindus have experienced as a religious community in India. From a Sikh perspective, the fear of domination of Sikh life by India's Hindu majority has shown up in Sikh history, perhaps never more traumatically than in the 1984 invasion of the holiest Sikh gurdwara by the albeit secular Indian army.

Discourse in the broader Sikh community can often challenge Hindu and Muslim others, stemming from traumas memorialized as part of South Asian heritage. Some Sikh students may have been told of ancestors' mistreatment at the hands of Muslim Pakistanis during the partition of the subcontinent in 1947. Others may be raised in environments where the Hindu majority in India is seen as a menacing other. More recently, extremist Hindu elements, buoyed by the resurgence of the Bharatiya Janta Party, a Hindu nationalist political party, have made life difficult for all religious minorities in India. In California a controversy about history textbooks pitted Hindu nationalists against Dalit, Muslim, and Sikh advocacy groups (Sian, 2013). However, it is worth noting that progressive Hindus lent support as allies to Sikhs during this challenge as well. Interfaith engagement can be a powerful tool to break these stereotypes on campuses. For example, when Sikhs are mistaken as being Middle Eastern and Muslim, one should consider the intent underlying that assumption. Using social media, a Sikh creative named Humble The Poet summarized the potential discriminatory thought behind this kind of mistake: "The problem isn't that you're mistaking me for someone of Islamic faith. . . . The problem is that you think there's something wrong with that" (@humblethepoet, 2015).

The greatest assets that Sikhs have in contributing to religious diversity lie in Sikh values and history. First, the value of community engagement and service (*seva*) in the Sikh tradition maps well onto models of interfaith engagement used at college and university campuses today. Second, the Guru Granth Sahib, or holy body of Sikh scripture revered as Guru, contains the writings of the Sikh Gurus, Hindu saints, and Muslim masters in a statement of interfaith harmony. Third, Sikh tradition is not an exclusivist faith: Sikhs do not believe they have the exclusive and ultimate truth, but rather that divine truth manifests itself in myriad ways. Ultimately for Sikhs, the highest expression of truth is in a life devoted to the common good and helping others.

Additional Resources

- Jakara Movement, www.jakara.org
- National Sikh Campaign, www.sikhcampaign.org
- Sikh Coalition, www.sikhcoalition.org
- Sikh Research Institute, www.sikhri.org

Hindu Students

Hinduism is the third largest religion in the world with more than 1 billion followers, but the vast majority of Hindus live in India, and the only majority Hindu nations in the world are India and Nepal (Pew Research Center, 2010). The Hindu population in the United States is about 2 million, making Hinduism the fourth largest religion in the country (Pew Research Center, 2014). The Interfaith Diversity Experiences and Attitudes Longitudinal Survey found that Hindu students represent 1.29% of the entering first-year class of fall 2015 (Mayhew et al., 2016). According to the Pew Research Center (2014), Hindus rank among the highest educated and highest income earning religious communities in the United States, but on college and university campuses Hindu American students bring with them a wide diversity of socioeconomic backgrounds, educational experiences, and political perspectives. For campuses that have large populations of international Indian students, Hinduism on campus becomes even more diverse and complex.

At its core, Hinduism is a pluralistic tradition, and most Hindus believe that all the world's great religions are equally valid paths to ultimate truth. In many ways, Hinduism is a disorganized and decentralized religion, as there are no common texts, rituals, languages, practices, pilgrimages, or deities that connect all Hindus. However, most Hindus believe in a theological framework that postulates that everyone has an individual soul that is a reflection of God, and that the goal of Hindu life is for the individual soul to become liberated from the cycle of rebirth and suffering to become one with God. Unlike the Abrahamic traditions, Hinduism is based on conceptions of reincarnation and cyclical time, and puts the feminine divine (God as mother as opposed to God as father) right at the heart of the religion (Flood, 1996).

Religious Accommodation

Many colleges and universities have formal policies focused on religious accommodation, especially in regard to excused student absences for the observation of holy days. Although there are many significant Hindu holy days in the liturgical year, there are no legal or theological requirements for observation that would necessitate an accommodation as part of a general university policy on the observation of holy days. Accordingly, it can be up to each individual professor's discretion whether to accommodate a Hindu student's request to miss class for religious observation. Student affairs professionals can help Hindu students find and attend services at the local temple or at other Hindu communities.

Even though Hindu students will probably not avail themselves of religious observation accommodation policies, many Hindu students do require accommodation with vegetarian food, just as Jewish and Muslim students are accommodated for kosher and halal food. Many Hindu students, and almost all Jain students, are vegetarian or vegan as a function of their religious and spiritual identities, beliefs, and practices. Therefore, campus dining halls should accommodate student requests for strictly vegetarian or substantive vegan cuisine. Students may also request vegetarian Indian regional cuisine for different events and ceremonies throughout the year as well. In such cases, a local Indian restaurant or Hindu temple may be able to help.

Holy Days

For Hindus, the most important holy day in the liturgical year is Diwali, the Festival of Lights that marks the beginning of the Hindu New Year and usually falls in October or November. Diwali is also a significant holy day for Jains, Sikhs, and Buddhists, so Diwali can be a creative opportunity for interfaith programming for South Asian students on campus.

At most colleges and universities, Diwali is celebrated as a a religious and cultural event, and many Diwali programs feature dance and music performances from different student groups. Often, students who are not Hindu will attend Diwali, making the event large and costly, especially if food is being served. As a way of supporting Hindu student life on campus, student affairs professionals have the opportunity to work closely with Hindu student leaders to make sure they have an appropriate venue and the necessary funding for their annual Diwali event.

Given that Diwali is the Festival of Lights and is traditionally celebrated by lighting candles, it is imperative that students have the opportunity to light candles, or tea lights, as part of their Diwali worship. This might involve fire codes and other public safety restrictions on campus, so student affairs professionals can anticipate this challenge and work with student leaders in advance to figure out a solution.

The other two holy days that Hindu students might celebrate on campus are Ganesha Chaturthi and Holi. Ganesha Chaturti usually falls in August or September and often coincides with the beginning of the academic year. The holy day involves the worship of Ganesha, a beloved Hindu deity known as the Remover of Obstacles and the Lord of Auspicious Beginnings. For Ganesha Chaturthi, students may need a multipurpose venue for worship where people can remove their shoes and where worshippers can light candles and burn incense (Huyler, 1999).

Holi is the Festival of Color and usually falls in February or March. Holi is celebrated, or played, by throwing colored powder on other celebrants. It can be a visually stunning spectacle and an enjoyable intercultural opportunity on campus. For Holi, Hindu student leaders would likely request an outdoor space, like a quad or a park, on campus.

Worship and Spiritual Exploration

On most college and university campuses, Hindu student organizations meet for weekly *aarti*, or congregational prayer. Some organizations may also do weekly *bhajans*, which is also a form of worship with communal singing and occasional dancing. Several colleges and universities have dedicated Hindu prayer spaces on campus, but in the absence of a dedicated space, educators can work closely with Hindu student leaders to reserve a space on campus that can be used on a weekly basis. Ideally, the venue would also include secure storage space so that students can store their *murtis*, or deity images or statutes, and other worship materials. For the purposes of worship, students should be allowed to light tea lights and burn incense in the venue.

Hinduism does not have a single sacred text but rather a series of sacred texts, including the Vedas, the Upanishads, the Brahmanas, and the Bhagavad Gita. Hindus from different traditions may categorize these texts differently, but they are generally all considered to be *shruti* (revealed texts, understood to be the divine word) as opposed to *smrti* (remembered texts, understood as written by humans). Other smrti texts include the Mahabarata, the Puranas, and the Ramayanas. All of these texts can provide students with a connection to Hindu history and tradition (Flood, 1996).

Some colleges and universities also offer their Hindu students pastoral care and spiritual counseling with Hindu chaplains on campus. There are a number of innovative ways that colleges and universities can support Hindu chaplains on campus, and Hindu chaplain positions in higher education range from volunteers to full-time university employees. In addition to providing pastoral care and spiritual counseling, Hindu chaplains also organize campus events, participate in campus interfaith services, facilitate scriptural study opportunities, and lead weekly aarti services.

Interfaith and Intercultural Engagement

At large universities with significant populations of Indian international students, there may be a plurality of Hindu perspectives, practices, traditions, philosophies, and approaches represented on campus. In these cases, student affairs professionals can work closely with Hindu student leaders to provide rich opportunities for intrafaith engagement so that students from all over the Hindu world can meet, learn, and grow with one another. Such campuses may also provide opportunities for a broad collaboration and engagement among Hindu student groups and the other South Asian groups on campus representing specific regions (India, Pakistan, Sri Lanka, etc.) or specific cultural traditions (Bollywood dance, Indian classical music, South Asian social justice, etc.).

Additionally, with the rise of interfaith student groups on U.S. college and university campuses, Hindu student organizations can now be in conversation with interfaith student leaders so they can participate in campus programs, events, and opportunities aimed at increasing religious literacy and learning across theological and cultural differences. Indeed, in so many ways and on so many campuses, Hindu student leaders are also interfaith leaders, and they proactively bring together students of different faiths around shared hopes, concerns, and aspirations.

Another unique opportunity for Hindu students on campus is to learn more about their heritage through academic courses on Hinduism and through cultural immersion and enrichment programs in India. For many Hindu students born and raised in the United States, their university experience may be their first opportunity to engage their faith tradition from a critical, historical, or scriptural perspective, and it might also be their first opportunity to study abroad in India or participate in a service-learning opportunity in South Asia. Accordingly, a university experience offers Hindu students the unique and unparalleled opportunity to study their own cultural heritage and religious identity from scholarly and spiritual perspectives and to think deeply about how their faith translates into personal and professional conduct and intentions. Given the richness of this opportunity, educators can think expansively about how they convene their colleagues, whether professors, study abroad coordinators, academic advisers, chaplains, mental health professionals, career counselors, or community leaders, to fully support their Hindu students in the extraordinary depth of exploration and experience and research and study that is available to them on campus.

Additional Resources

- Art of Living Foundation, www.artofliving.org
- Chinmaya Mission Worldwide, www.chinmayamission.com
- International Society for Krishna Consciousness, www.iskcon.org
- Vedanta Society, www.ivsweb.org

References

@humblethepoet. (2015, December 7). The problem isn't that you're mistaking me for someone of Islamic faith . . . the problem is that you think there's something wrong with that [Twitter post].

Flood, G. (1996). *An introduction to Hinduism.* Cambridge, England: Cambridge University Press.

Gyatso, B. T., & Chodron, B. T. (2014). *Buddhism: One teacher many traditions.* Boston, MA: Wisdom.

Hanh, T. N. (1998). *The heart of Buddha's teachings.* New York, NY: Broadway Books.

Huyler, S. (1999). *Meeting god: Elements of Hindu devotion.* New Haven, CT: Yale University Press.

Kaur, M., & Singh, N. G. K. (2014). *Her name is Kaur: Sikh American women write about love, courage, and faith.* Phoenix, AZ: She Writes Press.

Mann, G. S., Numrich, P., & Williams, R. B. (2001). *Buddhists, Hindus, and Sikhs in America.* New York, NY: Oxford University Press.

Mayhew, M. J., Rockenbach, A. N., Correia, B. P., Crandall, R. E., Lo, M. A., & Associates. (2016). *Emerging interfaith trends: What college students are saying about religion in 2016.* Chicago, IL: Interfaith Youth Core.

Pew Research Center. (2010). *The global religious landscape.* Retrieved from http://www.pewforum.org/2012/12/18/global-religious-landscape-exec/

Pew Research Center. (2012). *How many U.S. Sikhs?* Retrieved from http://www.pewresearch.org/2012/08/06/ask-the-expert-how-many-us-sikhs/

Pew Research Center. (2014). *Religious landscape study.* Retrieved from http://www.pewforum.org/about-the-religious-landscape-study/

Pew Research Center. (2015). *America's changing religious landscape.* Retrieved from http://www.pewforum.org/2015/05/12/americas-changing-religious-landscape/

Prebish, C. (1979). *American Buddhism.* North Scituate, MA: Duxbury Press.

Seager, R. H. (2012). *Buddhism in America.* New York, NY: Columbia University Press.

Sian, K. P. (2013). *Unsettling Sikh and Muslim conflict: Mistaken identities, forced conversions, and postcolonial formations.* Lanham, MD: Lexington Books.

Sikh Coalition. (2016). *Hate crimes: A quick information sheet for South Asians.* Retrieved from https://www.sikhcoalition.org/resources/hate-crimes-a-quick-information-sheet-for-south-asians-by-saalt

Singh, J. (2014). Sikhs as a racial and religious minority in the U.S. In P. Singh and L. E. Fenech (Eds.), *The Oxford handbook of Sikh studies* (pp. 524–533). Oxford, England: Oxford University Press.

Strong, J. S. (2015). *Buddhisms: An introduction*. London, England: Oneworld.

EDITORS AND CONTRIBUTORS

Editors

Kathleen M. Goodman is assistant professor of student affairs in higher education at Miami University. She earned her PhD at the University of Iowa in May 2011. Her dissertation focused on the relationship between diversity and learning. While at Iowa, she was a research assistant at the Center for Research on Undergraduate Education. Prior to that, she held an administrative position at the Association of American Colleges & Universities. Goodman's research and teaching interests include the impact of college experiences on student development; diversity and equity in higher education; spirituality, life purpose, and atheist college students; and incorporating critical perspectives into quantitative research.

Mary Ellen Giess has served numerous senior roles in her tenure at Interfaith Youth Core (IFYC), including stewarding one of IFYC's highest level programmatic partners in the White House through the President's Interfaith and Community Service Campus Challenge. Giess joined IFYC in 2008 after completing her master's at Harvard Divinity School. Giess earned her undergraduate degree at the University of North Carolina at Chapel Hill, where she subsequently launched her professional career in the Office of New Student and Carolina Parent programming. She has published articles for the *Washington Post, About Campus, Chronicle of Higher Education, Inside Higher Ed,* and the *Journal of College and Character.*

Eboo Patel is a leading voice in the movement for interfaith cooperation and is the founder and president of Interfaith Youth Core, a national nonprofit working to make interfaith cooperation a social norm. He is the author of *Acts of Faith* (Beacon Press, 2007), *Sacred Ground* (Beacon Press, 2012), and *Interfaith Leadership* (Beacon Press, 2016). Named by *US News & World Report* as one of America's Best Leaders of 2009, Patel served on President Barack Obama's inaugural Faith Council. He is a regular contributor to the public conversation on religion in America and a frequent speaker on the topic of religious pluralism. He holds a doctorate in the sociology of religion from Oxford University, where he studied on a Rhodes scholarship.

Contributors

James P. Barber is associate professor of education at the College of William & Mary. Barber is an expert in the areas of college student development, assessment of student learning, and integrative learning with degrees from the University of Michigan, Bowling Green State University, and Grand Valley State University.

Katie Brick worked in University Ministry at DePaul University from 2005 to 2016, serving as chaplain and director of the Office of Religious Diversity. She received a BA in history from Northwestern, an MBA from Northwestern, and an MDiv degree from Catholic Theological Union.

Benjamin P. Correia-Harker is director of assessment and research at Interfaith Youth Core, developing interfaith assessment services and resources and guiding research and findings dissemination related to Interfaith Youth Core's research initiatives. He holds a BA in religious studies from the College of Idaho, an MSEd in higher education and student affairs from Indiana University, and a PhD in higher education from Loyola University Chicago.

Christy Moran Craft is an associate professor of student affairs and college student development at Kansas State University. Craft holds a BS in psychology from Bradley University and a PhD from the University of Arizona in Tucson.

Mari Luna De La Rosa is assistant professor in the Department of Education at Azusa Pacific University. De La Rosa holds a BA from the University of California at Santa Barbara, an MPA from Arizona State University, and a PhD from Claremont Graduate University.

Ariel Ennis is the assistant director at the Of Many Institute for Multifaith Leadership at New York University. He is the author of *Teaching Religious Literacy: A Guide to Religious and Spiritual Diversity in Higher Education* (Routledge, 2017). Ennis is currently enrolled in an MBA program at New York University, where he received a BA in Jewish history and civilization.

Josh Feigelson is dean of students at the University of Chicago Divinity School. Formerly the founder and executive director of Ask Big Questions, a civic initiative developed by Hillel International seeking to change the world change the world through better conversation, Rabbi Feigelson holds a PhD from Northwestern University, ordination from Yeshivat Chovevei Torah Rabbinical School, and a BA from Yale University.

Rahuldeep Singh Gill is associate professor of religion at California Lutheran University, having earned his doctorate at the University of California at Santa Barbara. Gill's scholarly interests include the evolution of Sikh institutions over the tradition's history, and he also serves as California Lutheran's campus interfaith strategist.

Holly Holloway-Friesen is an assistant professor of higher education at Azusa Pacific University. Holloway-Friesen holds a BA in biology and literature from Claremont McKenna College, an MEd in college student affairs from Azusa Pacific University, and a PhD in higher education from Claremont Graduate University.

Altaf Husain serves as an associate professor in the Howard University School of Social Work. He received his PhD in social work from Howard University and his master of science in social administration from the Mandel School of Applied Social Sciences at Case Western Reserve University. He presently serves as vice president of the Islamic Society of North America and served as president of the national Muslim Students Association for two terms.

Greg Jao serves InterVarsity Christian Fellowship USA as senior assistant to the president, leading InterVarsity's response to situations where the ministry's presence is challenged by campus administrators. Jao holds a BA from the University of Chicago and a JD from Northwestern University School of Law.

Sheila Katz is the vice president for student engagement and leadership at Hillel International, working with more than 550 campuses and hundreds of thousands of Jewish students around the world. She has a BA in politics from Ithaca College, an MS in teaching from Pace University, and is a proud alumna of the Wexner Field Fellowship through the Wexner Foundation.

Megan Lane served as cocurricular partnerships manager at Interfaith Youth Core from 2012 until 2017, working with student affairs professionals and other campus staff to determine the best ways to support interfaith cooperation on their campuses. Lane holds master's degrees in religion and higher education administration.

Lyz Liddell is a widely respected freethought activist and organizer. Previously, Liddell served for many years as director of campus organizing for the national Secular Student Alliance, coordinating the campus organizing team to deliver the alliance's services and resources to affiliate groups and individual students.

Matthew J. Mayhew is the William Ray and Marie Adamson Flesher Professor of Educational Administration with a focus on higher education and student affairs at The Ohio State University. He received his BA from Wheaton College, his MA from Brandeis University, and his PhD from the University of Michigan.

Cassie Meyer works with faculty engaging interfaith in the classroom at Interfaith Youth Core. She holds an MA from the University of Chicago Divinity School and has taught at several universities and seminars. She regularly writes about interfaith and higher education and is a contributing editor to the *Journal of College and Character.*

John A. Monson is director of information services for seminaries and institutes of religion at the Church of Jesus Christ of Latter-day Saints. Monson earned a PhD in instructional systems technology from Indiana University and an MS in educational technology from Utah State University.

J. Cody Nielsen is the founder and executive director of Convergence on Campus and executive director of the Wesley Foundation, a Boston Cambridge ministry of higher education. Rev. Nielsen holds a master of divinity from Wesley Theological Seminary, an MA in mental health counseling from the University of Northern Iowa, and is completing a PhD in higher education administration at Iowa State University.

Alyssa N. Rockenbach is Alumni Association Distinguished Graduate Professor in the Department of Educational Leadership, Policy, and Human Development at North Carolina State University. She is an interdisciplinary scholar with an interest in religious and worldview diversity issues in higher education and received her BA in psychology from California State University, Long Beach, and her MA and PhD in education from the University of California, Los Angeles.

Eric Paul Rogers is a researcher for seminaries and institutes of religion at the Church of Jesus Christ of Latter-day Saints. He holds a PhD from

Brigham Young University and an MA from University of Texas at Austin. Rogers specializes in institutional research and is particularly interested in interfaith engagement and religious schism.

Tricia A. Seifert is head of the department of education and associate professor in the adult and higher education program at Montana State University. She also maintains an affiliate faculty appointment in the higher education program at the Ontario Institute for Studies in Education at the University of Toronto. Her current research examines how postsecondary institutions organize to support student success.

Jenny L. Small is an adjunct instructor in the School of Education at Boston College and an independent scholar. Small holds a PhD from the University of Michigan; an MA from Teachers College, Columbia University; and a BA from Brandeis University. Her research has focused on the spiritual lives of religiously diverse college students and how students use language to define their identities.

Jeremy T. Snipes is an assistant professor in the Department of Educational Leadership at Southern Illinois University–Edwardsville. Snipes has a BA from Baylor University and a PhD in higher education from Indiana University. His research focuses on how Black atheist students understand their identity in college.

Varun Soni is the vice provost of campus wellness and crisis intervention and dean of religious life at the University of Southern California. He is the first Hindu to serve as the chief religious or spiritual leader of an American university. Soni holds a BA from Tufts University; an MTS from Harvard Divinity School; an MA from the University of California–Santa Barbara; a JD from the University of California–Los Angeles; and a PhD from the University of Cape Town.

Upali Sraman is a Bangladeshi Buddhist monk and served as Tufts Buddhist Chaplaincy Intern from 2014 to 2015. Educated in Sri Lanka, he earned an MDiv from Harvard Divinity School, and his subjects of interest include South Asian religious studies and Buddhist studies. Ven. Sraman is currently pursuing a PhD at Emory University.

Nick Stancato is the chair of the Board of Directors for Convergence on Campus. He was formerly the program manager of the Secular Student Alliance. He graduated from The Ohio State University and is also a board member of the Ohio Chapter of Americans United for the Separation of Church and State.

Karla Suomala is a senior trainer and educator at the Institute for Curriculum Services, after serving 15 years as a religious studies professor at Luther College. She earned her PhD in Hebrew and cognate languages from Hebrew Union College–Jewish Institute of Religion in Cincinnati, where she focused on Jewish literature in the biblical, Greco-Roman, and early rabbinic periods.

Tarah Trueblood is the director of the Center for American and World Cultures at Miami University of Ohio. She earned a JD from the University of Nebraska, an MDiv and an MA from Graduate Theological Union, and a BS from the University of Kentucky. Trueblood previously served as director of the Interfaith Center at the University of North Florida and the executive director of the Wesley Foundation at the University of California–Berkeley.

Sherry K. Watt is professor in the higher education and student affairs program and the chief diversity office inaugural faculty fellow at the University of Iowa. Watt holds a PhD and an MS from North Carolina State University and a BA from the University of North Carolina at Greensboro. Her research focuses on identifying skills needed to engage in dialogues across controversial social difference.

Sentipensante Pedagogy

Educating for Wholeness, Social Justice and Liberation

Laura I. Rendón

Foreword by Mark Nepo

"Rendón has written a pedagogic masterpiece with immense potential to transform teaching and learning in the K–12 system. Her pedagogy gives voice to what teachers have been yearning for in their hearts and minds."—*Héctor Garza*; *President; National Council for Community and Education Partnerships; Washington, DC; and Monterrey, Mexico*

Laura Rendón offers a transformative vision of education that emphasizes the harmonic, complementary relationship between the *sentir* of intuition and the inner life and the *pensar* of intellectualism and the pursuit of scholarship; between teaching and learning; formal knowledge and wisdom; and between Western and non-Western ways of knowing. In the process she develops a pedagogy that encompasses wholeness, multiculturalism, and contemplative practice, that helps students transcend limiting views about themselves; fosters high expectations, and helps students to become social change agents.

22883 Quicksilver Drive
Sterling, VA 20166-2019   Subscribe to our e-mail alerts: www.Styluspub.com

Also available from Stylus

PETER MAGOLDA and KELSEY EBBEN GROSS

It's All About Jesus

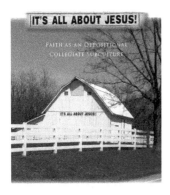

Faith as an Oppositional Collegiate Subculture

Peter M. Magolda and Kelsey Ebben Gross

Foreword by Andrew J. Seligoshn

"The authors fill a void in higher education which, while not being hostile, has been indifferent to the presence of faith-based student organizations; perhaps largely out of misunderstanding of the important role they can play in students' lives. Though focused on a specific student organization, the authors offer broader lessons about religion in higher education, cocurricular pedagogy, student culture, and student learning... *It's All About Jesus* not only immerses the reader in this unique collegiate subculture but also serves as an instructive ethnographic study for those considering or conducting qualitative research."—*Journal of College Student Development*

The authors hope this book spurs discussion on topics such as campus power and politics, how organizations interact with the secular world around them, and how members can improve their organizations. Additionally, this text urges secular readers in student affairs to consider the many benefits, as well as liabilities, of "parachurches" as co-curricular learning sites on campus. Lastly, this book will serve as a compelling case study for courses on qualitative research within religion studies, anthropology, sociology, and cultural studies fields.

(Continues on preceding page)